PERFECTLY PECULIAR!

RIPLEY ®
PUBLISHING

a Jim Pattison Company

PERFECTLY PECULIAR!

Ripley's
Believe It or Not!

PUBLISHING

Executive Vice President, Intellectual Property Norm Deska
Vice President, Archives and Exhibits Edward Meyer
Director, Publishing Operations Amanda Joiner

Editor Jessica Firpi
Junior Editor Jordie Orlando
Project Design Luis Fuentes, Penny Stamp
Cover Design Penny Stamp
Text Geoff Tibballs
Proofreader Rachel Paul
Indexer Johnna VanHoose Dinse
Production Coordinator Amy Webb

WARNING Some of the stunts and activities are undertaken by experts and should not be attempted by anyone without adequate training and supervision.

PUBLISHER'S NOTE While every effort has been made to verify the accuracy of the entries in this book, the Publisher cannot be held responsible for any errors contained in the work. They would be glad to receive any information from readers.

FRONT COVER IMAGE Larry Da Leopard—a tattoo artist who covered his body in over 1,000 leopard spots, claiming they have given him the ability to see in the dark and run fast.

Published by Ripley Publishing 2017

Ripley Publishing
7576 Kingspointe Parkway, Suite 188
Orlando, Florida 32819 USA

1 3 5 7 9 10 8 6 4 2

ISBN 978-1-60991-176-8 (USA) | ISBN 978-1-78475-721-2 (UK)

Library of Congress Control Number: 2016952652

Some of this material first appeared in
Ripley's Believe It or Not! Reality Shock!

Manufactured in China in December 2016
First Printing

Random House Books
20 Vauxhall Bridge Road
London SW1V 2SA

Random House Books is part of the Penguin Random House group of companies whose addresses can be found at global.penguinrandomhouse.com.

Ripley Entertainment Inc. has asserted the right to be identified as the author of this Work in accordance with the Copyright, Designs and Patents Act 1988.

First published in Great Britain in 2017 by Random House Books

www.penguin.co.uk

A CIP catalogue record for this book is available from the British Library.

For more information regarding permission, contact:
VP Intellectual Property
Ripley Entertainment Inc.
7576 Kingspointe Parkway, Suite 188
Orlando, Florida 32819 USA
publishing@ripleys.com
www.ripleys.com/books

CONTENTS

Ripley's World 6

Weird but True! 14

Wild Things 64

Peculiar Bodies 112

Unusual Novelties 154

Feats to Beat 194

Artistic License 228

Acquired Taste 270

Odd Enterprises 300

Index 354

Acknowledgments 376

The Talented
Robert Ripley

Once in a blue moon, someone appears with true star quality. You know the kind of person—a door opens, they walk in and the whole room turns to look and wonder. Marilyn Monroe had that rare, proper X-factor; Nelson Mandela, too; and Jack Kennedy... and so did Robert Ripley.

Never anything but dapper in sharp suits and spats, Ripley was the guy to know, from 1918 when he started work at *The New York Globe*, penning his daily Believe It or Not! cartoon that reported on the world's wildest weird-ities, until the day he died in 1949 after a lifetime spent in pursuit of strange stories.

The big star in a giant solar system, Ripley had a multitude of dazzling achievements spinning around him. There were the museums—Odditoriums—that he built to house the bizarre artifacts he collected, a pioneering TV and radio career that saw him reporting from a shark tank and from behind Niagara Falls, and his worldwide exploration, which took him to Papua New Guinea, ice-bound Russia and central China—locations that, at the time, most people had barely even heard of. No wonder Americans couldn't get enough of him. At one time, he was said to be more popular than the President!

Today, the Ripley's empire has gone galactic—with 31 Odditoriums, three aquariums, a warehouse stacked with thousands of exhibits, 30,000 photos and 100,000 cartoons, and a huge fan base that extends right around the world.

Hawaii was one of Ripley's favorite destinations, and he would make five trips to the islands in his lifetime. On his last trip, in 1948, he rode a traditional outrigger canoe in the surf with some locals, something he had enjoyed on his first journey to the islands in 1922. These canoes have been raced in islands in the Pacific for centuries.

In 1940, the *Nehi News* gave Robert Ripley's broadcasting aptitude the splash it deserved. In the same year, *Radio Guide* said Ripley's radio show was "consistently the most interesting and thrilling program on the air." Robert Ripley's unbelievable broadcasting achievements included being the first person to broadcast around the world simultaneously, and as featured in this *Nehi News* front cover, in 1940 he presented the world's first underwater radio broadcast—from the bottom of a shark-filled tank in Florida's Marineland. Ripley's continues its association with the aquatic world today with its three world-class aquariums, the largest of which opened in Toronto, Canada, in 2013.

WARM DAYS AHEAD MORE BUSINESS GREATER PROFITS

STUDY MANUAL MONEY

NEHI NEWS

Volume 2, No. 2

MARCH, 1940

RADIO PROGRAM HITS N POPULARITY PE

After a series of spectacular broadcasts, which moved at a fast clip, ROYAL CROWN station coast-to-coast radio program featuring "Believe-It-Or-Not" Bob Ripley has hit a new peak. Following the opener in New York February 16th, Ripley and the cast sojourned where two outstanding programs were broadcast. The listening audience has steadily inc the program is now rated one of the top half-hour shows on the air.

Stimulated by scores of favorable program reviews, which include the prized Variety Daily columns, and innumerable letters and gratifying expressions from ROYAL CROWN the cast is determined to march the program to an even greater height.

The St. Augustine, Florida, "Marine Studio" was heralded a broadcast triumph by m columnists, and proved an exciting ventur Ripley and the listeners. The daring pre won a number of hearty program endorsen many letters stated that ROYAL was putting thrill into radio listenin

In pictorial form we review t lights of the program broadcast from land—located near St. Augustine, Fl

TOO LATE NOW! Bob Ripley dons the diver's suit ... willingly but not enthusiastically.

TO SHARK-INFESTED WATERS! Down in the deep he goes to tell the world how it feels to meet a man-eating shark face to face.

A HUNGRY PORPOISE FED BY HAND! Lurching forward at great speed, the mammal feeds from human hands.

WE'RE ON THE AIR! Action and thrills are sent through these radio engineers to over a million listening radio fans.

CBS

At home, Ripley mixed with the literati and glitterati of the U.S. In Port Moresby, in Papua New Guinea, it was more a case of headhunters (left), and in Fiji, it was a human cannibal (right), both in 1932.

At the peak of his popularity, Ripley received 170,000 letters a week—more than Santa Claus—and fans across the U.S. mobbed him for autographs.

LOOK WHAT WE'VE BEEN UP TO!

Here at Ripley's we pride ourselves that everything in this book is definitely true—no picture is doctored, no story exaggerated, and nothing is ever invented.

Such standards don't make life easy. Ripley's researchers, correspondents, writers and editors spend all year hunting for the special ingredients that make up each one of our books—trawling through files, combing social media, following up leads that could end up at home or abroad. The trail might wind up in a story bigger and bolder than any before . . . but if there's no proof of truth, it's not in!

We've collected thousands of stories for this new book and have met some amazing people along the way—some of our favorites are featured here.

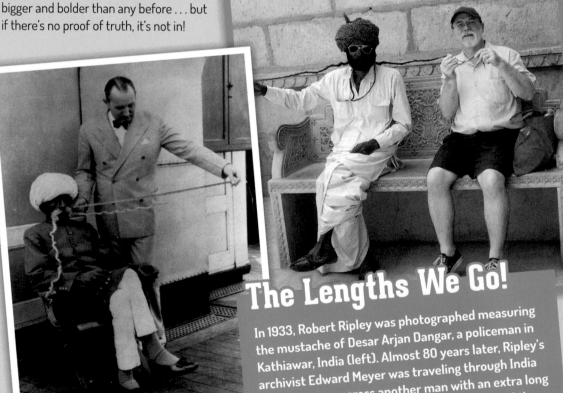

The Lengths We Go!

In 1933, Robert Ripley was photographed measuring the mustache of Desar Arjan Dangar, a policeman in Kathiawar, India (left). Almost 80 years later, Ripley's archivist Edward Meyer was traveling through India when he came across another man with an extra long mustache. He turned out to be the grandson of the original long-mustached gentleman—and both of them had a mustache over 8½ ft (2.6 m) long!

Well Done!

Master carvers Ray Villafane and Andy Bergholtz carved a 1000-lb (454-kg) pumpkin into a giant gremlin. See pages 286-291.

1,000 lbs

Art Good Enough To Eat!

Artist Carl Warner transforms food into stunning works of art. Our London museum held an exhibition of his work, including this delicious winter scene made from pastries.

RIPLEY'S WENT SHOPPING!

Ripley's bought this etching of Paul McCartney on a VW Beetle hood . . .

In 2014, Ripley's took possession of a giant, smelly hairball that had been removed from the stomach of a tiger! Check out the full story on page 84.

. . . and we acquired a portrait of Marilyn Monroe made from packing tape.

Tiger Hairball!

Jump on Board!

School Odditorium

With Ripley's Believe It or Not! books being firm favorites in their classroom, ingenious fourth graders at Kelly Mill Elementary School in Forsyth County, Georgia, made their very own Ripley's Odditorium at their school. Packed with weird and wonderful exhibits handmade by the students, it attracted 1,500 visitors!

This papier-mache model shows the unbelievably long hair of Asha Mandela, featured in Ripley's *Strikingly True*.

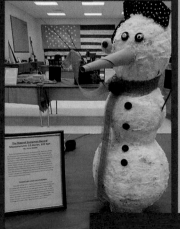

A giant snowman (left) and a tall king penguin (standing beside its creator, Matthew Arundale) were two of the larger exhibits.

Ripley Tattoo

Christopher Sudduth from Phoenix, Arizona, loves Ripley's so much he has a tattoo of Robert Ripley holding a shrunken head on his arm.

The original photo on which Christopher based his tattoo.

Magic Mail

Ripley's ran a Ready, Set, Mail contest in 2013 to find the weirdest piece of mail that could be sent to our Florida HQ, with just one rule—no envelope, box or wrapping of any kind could be used, and the address and postage had to be stuck directly to the item. Here are some of the items we received, including Michele Cassidy's winning entry—an entire McDonald's meal glued to a paper plate, with the address on the underside!

WINNER!

Weird but True!

Underwater Wonderland

To capture this magical underwater scene, Russian amateur photographer Yuri Ovchinnikov stuck his head through a hole in the frozen Tianuksa River and took pictures of what he saw.

The idea came to him after his son accidentally put his foot through the ice and discovered the winter wonderland beneath the surface. The natural light creates a range of colors as air pockets up to 2 ft (60 cm) deep extend down to transparent ice columns and crystalline shapes. Beneath the air pockets, water still flows.

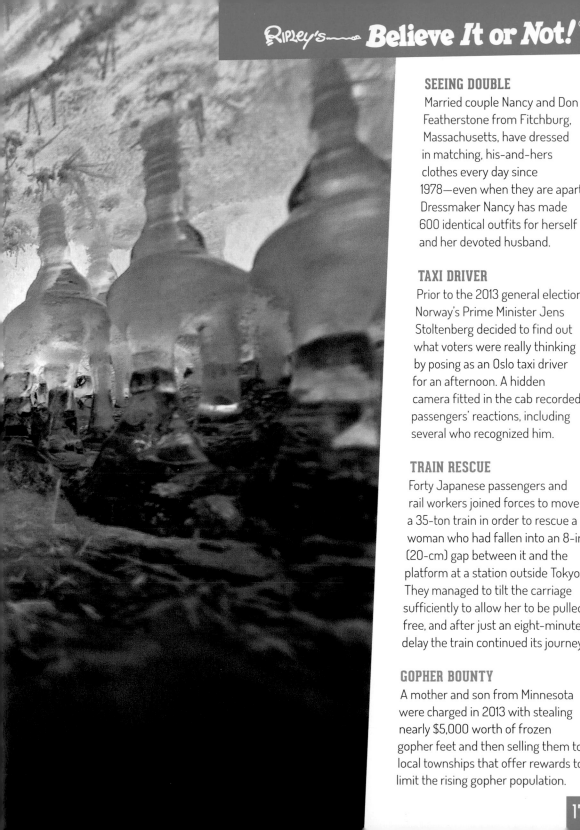

SEEING DOUBLE

Married couple Nancy and Don Featherstone from Fitchburg, Massachusetts, have dressed in matching, his-and-hers clothes every day since 1978—even when they are apart. Dressmaker Nancy has made 600 identical outfits for herself and her devoted husband.

TAXI DRIVER

Prior to the 2013 general election, Norway's Prime Minister Jens Stoltenberg decided to find out what voters were really thinking by posing as an Oslo taxi driver for an afternoon. A hidden camera fitted in the cab recorded passengers' reactions, including several who recognized him.

TRAIN RESCUE

Forty Japanese passengers and rail workers joined forces to move a 35-ton train in order to rescue a woman who had fallen into an 8-in (20-cm) gap between it and the platform at a station outside Tokyo. They managed to tilt the carriage sufficiently to allow her to be pulled free, and after just an eight-minute delay the train continued its journey.

GOPHER BOUNTY

A mother and son from Minnesota were charged in 2013 with stealing nearly $5,000 worth of frozen gopher feet and then selling them to local townships that offer rewards to limit the rising gopher population.

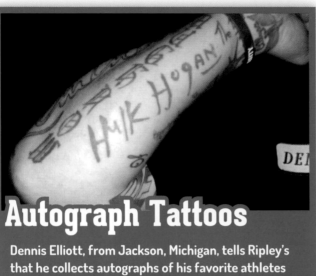

Autograph Tattoos

Dennis Elliott, from Jackson, Michigan, tells Ripley's that he collects autographs of his favorite athletes and celebrities—and then goes straight to a tattoo parlor to have the exact autograph inked on his skin. More than 40 stars, including Mike Tyson, Coolio, Magic Johnson, Dennis Rodman and Hulk Hogan, have already indirectly signed his body.

JET-POWERED COFFIN

Inventor Robert Maddox from Medford, Oregon, has designed a jet-powered coffin inspired by *The Munsters* that does 0 to 60 mph (0 to 96 km/h) in just nine seconds. Based on Grandpa Munster's Dragula, the Maddoxjet Coffin Car has a cockpit for the driver to sit behind a wooden coffin with a steel tubing undercarriage. It took Robert a month to build at a cost of $1,300.

MEN IN SKIRTS

When railway bosses in Stockholm, Sweden, refused to allow male train drivers to wear shorts to work in the hot summer weather, the drivers got around the ban by wearing skirts instead!

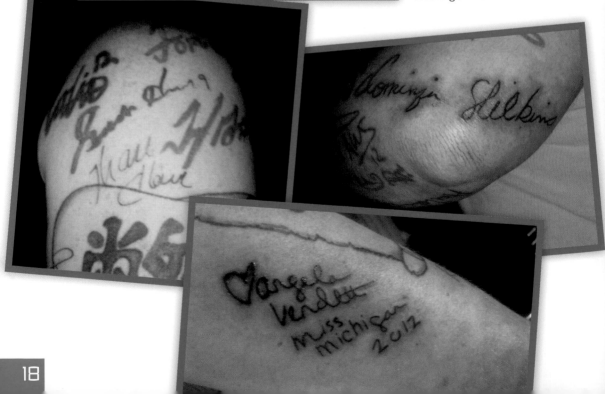

CHEAP WEDDING

When Georgina Porteous and Sid Innes got married near Inverness, Scotland, in 2013, their wedding day cost them just £1 ($1.50)—the price Georgina paid for the vintage wedding gown that she bought on a website where people can swap unwanted items. The bride handcrafted the rings herself from deer antlers, the 70 guests brought their own food to the reception and everything else was either donated or sourced for free.

SAME NAME

Two weeks after moving into a house in Barnsley, England, in 2012, 40-year-old former soldier Richard Midgley found three 1937 gas masks in an old box in the attic, including one with his name on it!

MAILED OUT OF A JAIL

Turkish prisoner Yasar Bayrak went on the run after he successfully mailed himself out of a jail in Willich, Germany, in 2008 in a giant FedEx box used for dirty laundry.

EMERGENCY LANDING

A single-engine airplane landed safely on a street in San Jose, California, in the middle of rush-hour traffic. Noticing a malfunction shortly after taking off from nearby Reid Hillview Airport, the pilot was forced to make an emergency landing and managed to avoid all the traffic on the busy road before slowing to a halt in a right-turn lane.

BOTTLE MESSAGE

Diving in Michigan's St. Clair River, Dave Leander spotted a bottle sticking out from under a thick layer of silt, and when he looked inside he found a message written by two young women 97 years earlier, in 1915.

Superhero Name Change

To highlight his love of superheroes and sci-fi, Daniel Knox-Hewson (left) changed his name to **Emperor Spiderman Gandalf Wolverine Skywalker Optimus Prime Goku Sonic Xavier Ryu Cloud Superman HeMan Batman Thrash**. His friend, Kelvin Borbidge (right), became **Baron Venom Balrog Sabretooth Vader Megatron Vegeta Robotnik Magneto Bison Sephiroth Lex Luthor Skeletor Joker Grind**.

Ride That Gator!

California was once home to a spectacular tourist attraction where visitors could stroke, feed and even sit on fully grown 300-lb (136-kg) alligators.

The California Alligator Farm was opened in Los Angeles in 1907 by "Alligator Joe" Campbell and his partner Frances Earnest, and for just 25 cents, up to 130,000 people a year watched jaw-dropping reptile talent shows and live displays. The alligators even learned to climb ladders and dance the waltz.

The alligators ranged in size from just a few inches long to up to 13 ft (4 m) and were kept apart, according to size, to stop the biggest of them from eating the smallest. Visitors to the farm, however, were encouraged to wander and even swim among them.

Despite their fearsome reputation, the alligators were very gentle, and the only recorded casualty on the farm was a guide who lost an arm while doing a demonstration with his head in an alligator's mouth. Luckily, visitors helped pull him free and he escaped with his head intact!

Campbell, a former ostrich rider, acquired his alligators by mimicking their calls in the wild. They would then rise to the surface of swamps and rivers, where they could be caught and taken to the farm.

Following a decline in visitor numbers, the farm closed in 1984, ending with a five-day cowboy-style rodeo to catch all the alligators, which were then flown to a private reserve.

The California Alligator Farm

The California Alligator Farm

SEE THE TRAINED ALLIGATORS

1000 ON EXHIBITION

OPEN EVERY DAY

Our Only SALESROOM is at the Farm

We make a specialty of Alligator Bags Ornamented with Genuine Alligator Heads and Claws

One of the most novel and interesting sights in the world. Most stupendous aggregation of Alligators ever exhibited.

OPPOSITE LINCOLN PARK
LOS ANGELES, -:- CALIFORNIA
Lincoln Park Cars Stop at the Door CAPITOL 2400

Alligator Goods at Wholesale Prices

Ames Bros Company

A snapshot of the past—a 1920s brochure for the California Alligator Farm, home to over 1,000 reptiles.

From time to time, floods caused the water levels of the farm's lakes and swamps to rise alarmingly, allowing the alligators to escape. The reptiles would turn up in nearby public ponds, or in the gardens and swimming pools of neighboring houses!

The farm advertised the largest gator in captivity, claiming it was around 500 years old—an exaggeration given the average lifespan for an American alligator is about 60 years. The farm also provided trained reptiles for Hollywood films, including *Tarzan* and Disney's *The Happiest Millionaire*.

The alligators were not only kept as a tourist attraction. The farm also produced alligator skin handbags, belts and purses—some decorated with genuine alligator heads and claws—which were all sold in the gift shop.

SOUVENIR from the CALIFORNIA ALLIGATOR FARM, LOS ANGELES, CAL.

"Drop In."

M

PLACE A STAMP HERE

675:—"Chicken Dinner" at the Alligator Farm, Los Angeles, Calif.

145817

Scene at the California Alligator Farm
Los Angeles, Cal.

The star of the show was Billy, who was caught in 1906 in a swamp near New Orleans. Surprisingly docile, Billy would allow his handlers to put a saddle or reins on him to give children a ride. He would astonish tourists with his tricks, which included sliding down chutes and taking part in underwater battles with famous alligator wrestler George Link. Billy appeared in many films between the 1920s and 1960s, chosen for his reliable reaction to food—as soon as meat was dangled nearby he would open his mouth, ready for the perfect shot.

FISH SMUGGLER

A Vietnamese man tried to smuggle seven live tropical fish into New Zealand by hiding them in plastic bags in his pants pockets—but his plan floundered when Auckland Airport officials noticed water dripping from his bulging clothes.

LOST KING

A skeleton found beneath a city-center parking lot in Leicester, England, in 2012 was proved by DNA testing to be that of King Richard III of England who was killed at the nearby Battle of Bosworth in 1485. After the battle, his body was missing for more than 500 years.

QUADRILLION DEBT

Chris Reynolds of Delaware County, Pennsylvania, became one of the biggest debtors in the world for a minute when his e-mailed monthly balance statement from PayPal mistakenly told him he had a negative balance of more than $92 quadrillion! His debt was short-lived, however, as his balance showed the expected zero when he logged into his PayPal account.

TIME TRAVELER

Ed Grigor from Endicott, New York, lost a gold watch engraved with his name in 1959—but 53 years later it was found over 2,000 mi (3,200 km) away in Las Vegas, Nevada, and returned to him.

HITLER'S TOILET

Adolf Hitler's toilet has been in Greg Kohfeldt's autoshop in Florence, New Jersey, since 1952. The toilet was installed by the shop's previous owner and came from the Nazi dictator's favorite yacht, the *Aviso Grille*.

ROBOT ATTENDANT

Alex Cressman and Laura Wong had a 10-lb (4.5-kg) bomb-disposal robot serve as ring bearer at their wedding in Annapolis, Maryland. The bride, a mechanical engineer, helped design the Dragon Runner robot, which was controlled during the ceremony and reception by one of her friends wearing a special backpack.

Squirrel Knot

In June 2013, six young squirrels were found in Regina, Saskatchewan, knotted together by their tails so that they could move in only one direction as a large furry mass. They were carefully untangled at an animal clinic and all released back into the wild with their tails intact.

Franz Reichelt was an Austrian-born French tailor who invented a revolutionary parachute suit in the early 20th century.

The Flying Tailor

The invention and popularization of airplanes and flight at this time had caused safety concerns about falling from a great height, and this led to a number of people trying to invent an effective parachute. One such man was Franz Reichelt, who designed a parachute suit to be worn like a coat, so that the wearer could blend in with the general public while wearing the safety device.

Franz refined his "flying coat," and after numerous failed tests with dummies, he decided that the reason his invention did not work was because of the short drop distances. He decided to test his suit by jumping from the Eiffel Tower in Paris, France—then the tallest man-made structure in the world—and on February 4, 1912, Franz stood on the first platform of the Eiffel Tower, some 200 ft (60 m) off the ground, wearing his parachute suit. With his attempt captured on film, he jumped, fell, and hit the frozen ground without the parachute deploying, causing a dent in the French pavement and, sadly, his own death.

WEIRD BUT TRUE!

PEN PALS

After exchanging approximately 3,000 letters over a period of a staggering 74 years, pen pals Norma Frati of Portland, Texas, and Audrey Sims of Perth, Australia, finally met for the first time in 2013 when 83-year-old Audrey flew to the U.S.A. The women had been pen pals since Norma was 13 years old and Audrey was only nine.

PAPER DOLLS

Amnah Al Fard from the United Arab Emirates spent two years making 1,145 three-dimensional, miniature paper dolls. Each doll took about three hours to make, and she used a total of 2,500 ft (762 m) of paper and 10 lb (4.5 kg) of glue.

YELLOW PAGES

Plasterer Jimmy Newton from Devon, England, took up some flooring in a house and found a yellowing newspaper cutting containing a picture of himself on a soccer team in 1985, 28 years earlier.

Book Chain

Seattle Public Library in Washington State kicked off its Summer Reading Program for 2013 by toppling 2,131 discarded and donated books in a domino-like chain.

26

EAR EXHIBIT

U.S. artist Joe Sola created six oil paintings that were so tiny that his exhibition was held inside the gallery owner's ear! As even a single paintbrush bristle was too large, he used a 0.12-mm acupuncture needle along with a microscope to see what he was painting. Each painting was composed of tiny granules of pigment, mounted on small white backgrounds and placed in the ear canal of Los Angeles gallery owner Tif Sigfrids for public viewing.

BLACK TURF

West Salem High School, Oregon, plays its home football matches on black turf—the school saved nearly $150,000 because it did not have to have the synthetic turf dyed green.

LAUNDRY BLAZE

Nicola Boulton and her daughter Claire escaped a fire at their house in Leicester, England, after recently tumble-dried tea towels spontaneously combusted.

STRANGE DEATHS

Just after sunset on days between September and November each year, hundreds of birds from over 40 different species die after crashing into buildings and trees at Jatinga, a village in Assam, India. Disoriented by the monsoon fog, the birds are attracted to the village lights and fly blindly toward them, hitting walls and trees en route. To promote tourism, the local authorities have created an annual Jatinga Festival around the mysterious "bird suicides."

CORPSE COMPANION

Eighteen months after his death in December 2010, Charles Zigler of Jackson, Michigan, was still sitting in his favorite armchair, watching TV. His housemate, Linda Chase, kept his mummified body, washing it and dressing it every day, and talked to it while watching NASCAR races.

DIVE DAY

Despite vomiting and suffering bruises on his legs, 25-year-old Dennis Bettin, a student at the German Sport University in Cologne, made 714 dives from a 10-ft-high (3-m) board over the course of 24 hours in June 2013, equivalent to a dive every two minutes.

Photo On Moon

When U.S. astronaut Charles Duke landed on the Moon as part of the Apollo 16 mission, he left a family photo on the lunar surface hoping that intelligent alien life forms might discover it. Before placing the picture showing himself, his wife and two sons in a plastic folder, he wrote on the back, "This is the family of Astronaut Duke from Planet Earth. Landed on the Moon, April 1972."

Village of Dolls

There are more life-size straw dolls than humans in the remote village of Nagoro, Japan.

There are only 51 people in the village but 150 dolls, each one representing a resident who has moved away or died. Created by local woman Mizuki Ayona, the dolls, dressed in rags and old clothes, appear all over the village—on fences, at the bus stop and one in the abandoned school following the death of its last student.

STINKY TOWN

A pile of goat manure spontaneously caught fire at a farm in Windsor, Vermont, spreading a stink throughout the town and up to 5 mi (8 km) away.

CHIMNEY GEESE

People in Victorian Britain who could not afford chimney sweeps dropped live geese down their chimneys instead.

STING OPERATION

An attempted armed carjacking in Craighall, South Africa, was foiled when the suspects were chased down the street by an angry swarm of bees.

TERMITE TERROR

An elderly lady in southern China lost over $10,000 of her savings after termites chewed through the bills. The termites actually nibbled more than $60,000 worth of cash that she had kept in a drawer, but luckily the bank managed to verify many of the damaged bills.

BONKERS FOR CONKERS

A company that runs parking lots in Manchester and Leeds, U.K., introduced a temporary scheme in the fall of 2013 whereby motorists could pay for parking time with conkers—the fruit of the horse chestnut tree. Each conker was worth 20p (32 cents) apiece.

COW COSTUME

An 18-year-old man was accused of stealing 26 gal (98 l) of milk worth $92 from a Walmart store in North Stafford, Virginia—while dressed as a cow. He made his escape on all fours and proceeded to hand out the stolen milk to passersby.

DELAYED TWINS

Maria Jones-Elliott from Glenmore, Ireland, gave birth to twin girls 87 days apart. Baby Amy was born three months prematurely, but then the contractions stopped. The mother stayed in the hospital for nearly three months until the other twin, Katie, was born.

Technicolor Cheesecake

Customer Angelina Carroll was knocked out by the tie-dye cheesecake she was served at the Summerville, South Carolina, branch of U.S. pizza chain Mellow Mushroom. The colorful sweet treat was chocolate and vanilla flavored with a drizzle of strawberry syrup.

WEIRD BUT TRUE!

LAST REQUEST

When football fan Scott Entsminger died at his Ohio home in 2013, he had one last request for his favorite team. His obituary read: "He respectfully requests six Cleveland Browns pallbearers so the Browns can let him down one last time." The Browns' last championship title came way back in 1964, and fans recently branded their stadium the "factory of sadness" after a series of disappointing results.

PACKED HIMSELF IN A SUITCASE

Mexican prisoner Juan Ramirez Tijerina tried to escape jail in Chetumal by packing himself into his girlfriend's suitcase. Guards spotted Maria del Mar Arjona looking nervous after visiting him when she left the prison pulling a bulky case. When they opened it, they found 19-year-old Ramirez, who was serving a 20-year sentence for illegal weapons possession, curled up inside.

TODDLER MAYOR

Bobby Tufts was reelected mayor of Dorset, Minnesota, in August 2013—even though he was not yet old enough to attend preschool! He was first chosen to be mayor of the small town (population about 25) in 2012 at age three, and his pro-ice-cream campaign proved such a vote-winner that he was elected again 12 months later.

GARDEN TREASURE

A 6-in-thick (15-cm) carved granite garden step at Bronwen Hickmott's home in Devon, England, turned out to be a Buddhist temple moonstone—an elaborately carved decorative stone artifact—that's at least a thousand years old. It was one of only seven of its type in the world and sold for over £550,000 ($875,000) at an auction!

CAR BURIAL

After her death in 1998, 84-year-old Rose Martin was lowered by crane into a grave at Tiverton, Rhode Island, inside her beloved 1962 Chevrolet Corvair. The grave was lined with concrete, and some car parts were removed to make room for Rose's coffin. Despite taking up four burial plots, 6 in (15 cm) still had to be sawed off the car so it would fit into the grave.

RARE COIN

A rare 1913 Liberty Head nickel, which had first been discovered in a car wreck before being mistakenly branded a fake and left abandoned in a closet for decades, sold at an auction in Chicago, Illinois, for more than $3.1 million in 2013.

RARE FIND

Martin Kober from Buffalo, New York, found a $300 million painting by Michelangelo behind his couch.

Nie held a 131-ft-long (40-m) rubber hose to his right nostril and kept his left nostril and left ear covered to prevent pressure leaks.

Nasal Power

In Chengdu, China, Nie Yongbing took just 21 minutes to inflate four tires with his nose—while two adults stood on each tire. His doctor once told him that blowing up balloons with his nose would improve his health, but balloons did not prove challenging enough so he graduated to tires.

Skateboarding Mouse

Shane Willmott has taught his pet mice to skateboard by building them a miniature skate park in the backyard of his home in Queensland, Australia, where they ride mouse-sized boards down vertical ramps and even through a ring of fire. Shane, who has also taught his mice to surf, said, "They love it. Mice are built to surf and skate because their center of gravity is so low. When they do fall off, they want to get straight back on board."

SKIN SLICE
Torz Reynolds from London, England, spent 1½ hours using a sharp scalpel to slice the tattooed name of her ex-boyfriend, Stuart May, from her body. She then mailed the severed piece of inked skin to him.

SENT HOME
The mummified body of Australian Aboriginal Tambo Tambo was sent home for burial in 1993 after lying in a funeral home in Cleveland, Ohio, for 109 years.

NAKED PRANK
A naked man had to be rescued from a washing machine while playing a game of hide-and-seek at his home in the town of Mooroopna in Victoria, Australia. He hid inside the top-loader so he could surprise his partner but became stuck—and it took police officers 20 minutes to free him using olive oil as a lubricant.

MULTIPLE TWINS
In 2013, Highcrest Middle School at Wilmette, Illinois, had 24 sets of twins in a single grade.

SLEEP DRIVER
Thought to be suffering from a type of sleepwalking disorder, a woman drove 185 mi (300 km) from Hamilton, New Zealand, to Tauranga while asleep at the wheel. She drove for five hours—and even sent text messages from her cell phone along the way. She was eventually found slumped over the wheel in the driveway of her former home.

SNAIL MAIL
Scott McMurry of Vienna, Virginia, received a postcard from his mother in April 2012—55 years after she put it in the mail.

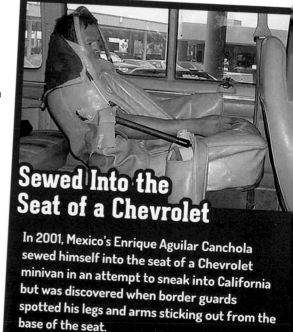

AERIAL ESCAPE

Dropped from an airplane at 14,000 ft (4,270 m), escape artist Anthony Martin from Sheboygan, Wisconsin, freed himself from shackles and a locked casket while plummeting toward the ground at 130 mph (209 km/h) before safely deploying his parachute. He had been handcuffed to a belt around his waist and chained to the inside of the wooden casket. A prison door lock for which no key existed was screwed into place to make the casket supposedly escape-proof, but, although the box rocked wildly from side to side on its rapid descent, Martin pushed his way to freedom at about 6,500 ft (1,980 m).

WEBBED WETSUIT

Inspired by BASE jumpers' wingsuits, French designer Guillaume Binard has invented a wetsuit with webbing between the legs and arms to enable divers to glide through the water like a manta ray.

BLANK SPACE

When the dictator of Zaire, Joseph Mobutu, was overthrown in 1997, his face was cut out of thousands of banknotes to save printing new ones.

Sewed Into the Seat of a Chevrolet

In 2001, Mexico's Enrique Aguilar Canchola sewed himself into the seat of a Chevrolet minivan in an attempt to sneak into California but was discovered when border guards spotted his legs and arms sticking out from the base of the seat.

Sumo Marathon

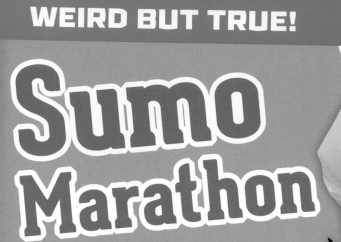

Around 150 competitors donned inflatable suits and ballooned into sumo wrestlers to wobble around Battersea Park in London, England, for the annual 3-mi (5-km) Sumo Run.

Billed by organizers as an event designed to put the fun back into fun runs, the runners jogged around the park trying not to fall over and pop themselves.

LIFE SAVERS

When 67-year-old Dorothy Fletcher, from Liverpool, England, suffered a heart attack on a flight to Florida, her life was saved because 15 of her fellow passengers happened to be cardiologists en route to a conference in Orlando. So when the stewardess asked for medical assistance, they all stood up, eager to help. They quickly fed drips into the patient's arms and used the in-flight medical kit to stabilize her condition. The plane was diverted to North Carolina, where Mrs. Fletcher received further treatment in intensive care before going on to make a full recovery. Her daughter Christine said, "My mum wouldn't be here today if it wasn't for those cardiologists on the plane, and we didn't even know their names."

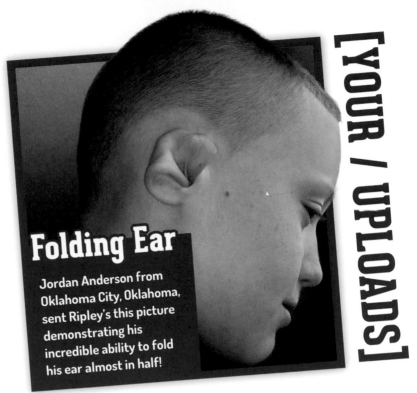

Folding Ear

Jordan Anderson from Oklahoma City, Oklahoma, sent Ripley's this picture demonstrating his incredible ability to fold his ear almost in half!

LONG CLUB

Golf professional Michael Furrh of Arlington, Texas, used a 14.2-ft-long (4.3-m) driver—almost four times the length of a normal club—to hit a ball 144 yd (131.7 m) through the air. He has previously hit a drive off a 6-ft-high (1.8-m) tee, while standing on a ladder.

SWEET BREATH

Nicole Jones from New York City is addicted to eating deodorant. She eats half a stick a day and goes through 15 a month. She says, "It is really soft. It feels like it melts in my mouth. It has its own unique taste."

FAMILIAR FACE

Sixty-four-year-old Henry Earl from Lexington, Kentucky, has been arrested more than 1,500 times over the course of his life—so often that his various police mug shots have been turned into an online video. Since his first arrest in 1970, he has spent nearly 6,000 days in jail—an average of more than one day in three behind bars.

SUSPICIOUS MIND

U.S. President Franklin D. Roosevelt would never travel on the 13th day of the month and would never host a White House dinner with 13 guests.

Skydive Knockout

Experienced skydiver James Lee from Gloucestershire, England, miraculously survived after being knocked unconscious by another jumper in a freak accident at 12,500 ft (3,800 m). After jumping from the plane over Wiltshire, 25-year-old Lee was hit on the back of the head by a fellow skydiver, the impact knocking him out. Seeing him in distress, two other parachutists bravely delayed activating their own cords and saved his life by diving towards him and pulling his cord to deploy his chute. Lee soon regained consciousness and floated down safely to the ground—but with no memory of the drama that had occurred.

QUARTERS BACK

Ordered to repay $500,000 in insurance money, a man from Harrisburg, Illinois, protested against the decision by paying off $150,000 of the amount in quarters. He had the 50-lb (23-kg) bags of coins—that's 160 bags weighing a total of almost four tons—delivered by truck.

RIDERS' SCREAMS

The Gold Striker roller coaster at the Great America theme park in Santa Clara, California, was shut down temporarily because riders were screaming too loudly. As the shrieks exceeded the decibel limit agreed with adjacent properties, Great America covered a portion of the track in a soundproof tunnel before reopening the ride.

LOVING COUPLE

High school sweethearts Les and Helen Brown of Long Beach, California, were born on the same day in 1918, were married for 75 years, and died just one day apart in July 2013.

GINGERBREAD MANSION

Residents of Bryan, Texas, built a full-sized gingerbread house that was big enough to accommodate a family of five. The house, which measured 60 x 42 ft (18 x 13 m), used 1,800 lb (816 kg) of butter, 7,200 eggs, 7,200 lb (3,266 kg) of flour, 2,925 lb (1,327 kg) of brown sugar and was decorated with 22,304 pieces of candy, bringing its calorie count to 36 million!

NOSE PAINTER

Born with cerebral palsy, paraplegic French Canadian artist Gille Legacy paints with his nose. Although he has no movement in his arms and legs, he has full use of his brain and by dipping his nose in paint—a technique he has been using since the age of eight—he has had his paintings exhibited throughout the U.S.A., Canada and France.

CEMETERY BED

Homeless Fábio Beraldo Rigol has slept in a cemetery in São Paulo, Brazil, for over 13 years. He sleeps in a six-chamber burial crypt next to the skeleton of his dead friend who is buried there.

FORMATION JUMP

In July 2013, 101 female skydivers jumped from airplanes to form a flower shape in midair over Kolomna, Russia.

UNION OF ONE

Herbert Jenkins of Detroit, Michigan, is the only member of the Assistant Supervisors of Street Maintenance and Construction Association labor union.

MEMORABLE DATE

Cheryl Bennett and Steven DeLong of Amesbury, Massachusetts, decided to get married on January 9, 2013, as it was the same date as the town's ZIP code—01913.

LUCKY TICKET

After accidentally throwing a scratch-off lottery ticket in the trash, Joseph and Joanne Zagami of North Attleborough, Massachusetts, retrieved it to find they had won $1 million.

HONESTY PAYS

The honesty of homeless man Billy Ray Harris of Kansas City, Missouri, who returned a diamond ring that had been accidentally dropped into his collection cup, was rewarded when he received almost $192,000 in donations from 6,000 people around the world after the ring's owner, Sarah Darling, set up an online fund-raising page for him.

[YOUR / UPLOADS]

Squat Circle

Uche Emelife from Nigeria sent Ripley's this picture of the greatest number of people—24—sitting down without actually using a seat.

37

MATH TEST

Canadians who win lotteries and prize draws must solve a simple math problem to collect their prizes because games of pure chance are illegal in Canada.

HEAVY PRICE

Robert McKevitt was fired for inappropriate use of company property after using an 8,000 lb (3,628 kg) forklift to free a chocolate bar that had got stuck in a vending machine at Milford, Iowa.

HID IN A PLANE'S OVERHEAD LOCKER

A man hid in a plane's overhead luggage compartment at Pearson Airport, Toronto, in 2012, but was discovered before the flight took off for Panama City.

PRIVATE CELLS

A jail in Fremont, California, allows prisoners to upgrade to better, private cells with cable TV at a cost of $155 a night—the same as a three-star hotel in the area.

MILLIONAIRE CLEANER

Yu Youzhen from Wuhan, China, is a property millionaire yet still works as a street cleaner for less than $10 a day. The 54-year-old mogul has been waking up at 3 a.m. six days a week since 1998 to sweep roads in order to set a good example to her children.

GPS DETOUR

Sixty-seven-year-old Sabine Moreau meant to drive only 38 mi (60 km) to meet a friend at her local railway station in Brussels, Belgium—but when her GPS told her to keep going, she ended up 900 mi (1,450 km) away in Croatia. In the course of her two-day detour, she crossed five international borders, but she was so distracted that it was only when she arrived in Zagreb that she realized she was actually no longer in Belgium.

FUNERAL SING-A-LONG

Robert Nogoy from Pampanga in the Philippines makes coffins equipped with karaoke machines to lighten up funerals.

Two Noses

Snuffles, a five-month-old Belgian shepherd dog at an animal rescue center in Glasgow, Scotland, was born with a rare congenital defect that makes it look like he has two noses. Instead of his nostrils being fused together, they are split down the middle, allowing him to move both halves of his nose independently!

Burning Man

This spectacular picture of a burning man was captured by Montreal-based photographer Benjamin Von Wong without using any special effects—but don't worry, it was all planned and nobody got hurt.

Eager to capture the unique imagery of fire, he posted a message on Facebook asking, "Who wants to be lit on fire?" Fellow photographer Jo Gorsky volunteered to be the stuntman and was set ablaze wearing special flameproof clothing and fire retardant gelatine on his skin. The greatest danger to his safety was the strong winds that suddenly sprung up, making the fire more difficult to control.

WRONG DOOR

Jiang Wu got so drunk following a night out in Qingdao, China, that he mistook a shipping container for his budget hotel and woke up to find himself sealed in for a two-week boat trip due to leave for the U.S.A. Luckily, he had his phone with him, but although he rang the police, there were thousands of containers and they had no idea which one he was in. Eventually, by hammering on the metal side, he was tracked down to a box stacked 60 ft (18 m) in the air.

BAD TIMING

A burglar who broke into a house in Palm Beach County, Florida, made the mistake of leaving his phone behind—and his identity was revealed when his mother rang just as police officers arrived at the crime scene.

BUSY JAILS

Although the U.S. has only 5 percent of the world's total population, it has 25 percent of the world's prison population—some 2,200,000 people behind bars.

LIFE SAVER

While Scott Janssen was participating in Alaska's 2012 Iditarod Dog Sled Race, one of his dogs collapsed and stopped breathing, but he was able to revive the dog with mouth-to-snout CPR.

SOLITARY EXISTENCE

For five years until his death in 2012, Englishman Brendon Grimshaw lived alone on a tropical island in the Seychelles. He had only his dogs and 120 giant tortoises for company.

WEIRD BUT TRUE!

$17,500 TIP
Aurora Kephart, a bartender at Conway's Restaurant and Lounge in Springfield, Oregon, is often tipped by a customer with tickets from the state lottery. In October 2013, one such ticket won her $17,500.

LEGALLY DEAD
After disappearing from his Arcadia, Ohio, home in 1986 and being officially declared dead eight years later, Donald Miller Jr. turned up alive in 2005, but he was told he could not have a driving license because he was still legally dead. A Hancock County judge rejected Miller's request to reverse the 1994 death ruling because he said there is a three-year limit for death notices to be repealed.

JESUS TILE
Pilgrims flocked to Phoenix Sky Harbor International Airport, Arizona, in June 2013 after a smudge resembling Jesus was found on a floor tile in Terminal 3.

BEAUTY MASK
Women who are worried about their appearance can now simply glue on an expressionless face, thanks to the Uniface mask devised by Zhuoying Li, a graduate from New York City's Parsons School for Design. Li created the mask—with large eyes, long lashes, a high nose bridge and narrow chin and cheeks—as a comment on modern society's unrealistic standards of beauty.

LUCKY CATCH
A Saskatchewan fisherman was reunited with the camera he had dropped into a lake several months earlier after it was retrieved from the water by a cormorant. Passerby Karen Gwillim from Saskatoon spotted the bird standing on a bridge with the camera around its neck. When the bird surprisingly allowed her to take the camera, she found that the card inside contained 239 recoverable photos, which she then posted on Facebook to locate the owner.

CHANCE DISCOVERY
In 2013, Peter Dodds from Derbyshire, England, bought an old biography of Winston Churchill from a local charity shop and found it contained a postcard sent in 1988 by his own brother in the U.S.A. to their mother.

Surf Skier
Chuck Patterson is a pioneer in the extreme sport of "surf skiing," surfing down waves on water skis! The veteran mountain skier from California converted to surfing and experimented with custom skis designed to cut into the water. Chuck has even conquered 40-ft (12-m) waves at the "Jaws" surf break in Maui, Hawaii, one of the world's largest—so big that a jet ski had to tow him into position to catch the wave.

Sidewall Surfing

The new craze among car-mad youths in Saudi Arabia is driving their cars at high speeds on just two wheels, and if that's not crazy enough, their friends come along for the ride—on the outside of the vehicle! Sidewall surfing, as the stunt is known, is the latest extreme motorsport to catch on in the country, where drifting—sliding cars sideways at high speeds—is also a popular underground activity.

Blood Popsicle

As temperatures in Australia hit 115°F (46°C) in January 2014, it became so hot that zookeepers gave Harari, a lion in Melbourne Zoo, a popsicle made from 8 gal (30 l) of frozen blood to help him keep cool. They also made frozen meat, fish and fruit into popsicles for Honey, a Syrian brown bear.

HID INSIDE THE LANDING GEAR OF A JUMBO JET

A 20-year-old Romanian man hid inside the landing gear of a jumbo jet on its 97-minute flight from Vienna, Austria, to London, England, in 2010 and survived despite enduring temperatures of –42°F (–41°C) and a severe lack of oxygen.

BLIND DEVOTION

Blind couple Claire Johnson and Mark Gaffey from Stoke-on-Trent, England, fell in love and got engaged after their seeing-eye dogs Venice and Rodd hit it off during training classes.

TREASURE HAUL

In 2013, treasure hunters Rick and Lisa Schmitt from Sanford, Florida, together with their grown-up children Hillary and Eric, found an estimated $300,000 worth of gold coins and chains from the wreckage of a fleet of 11 ships that sank in a 1715 hurricane while en route from Havana to Spain.

NO SWEAT!

Swedish engineers have invented the Sweat Machine, a device that converts human sweat into drinking water. It works by extracting perspiration, which is 99 percent water, from people's clothes and purifying it.

BICYCLE HEARSE

The Sunset Hills Cemetery and Funeral home in Eugene, Oregon, has a pedal-powered, three-wheeled bicycle hearse. The company even offers special bamboo caskets that look like bicycle baskets.

DISCOUNT DONUTS

A 48-year-old man was arrested in Pasco County, Florida, for impersonating a police officer in an attempt to get cheap donuts. The man regularly flashed a fake badge to workers at a Dunkin' Donuts stall and demanded a police discount before staff became suspicious and alerted the real cops.

Comic Strip

Combining his love of tattoos and comics, artist Patrick Yurick from San Diego, California, has had four blank panels tattooed on his forearm that he fills in daily to create an ever-changing comic strip. He had the tattoo inked on his left arm so that he could draw with his right hand. It takes him about 15 minutes to draw each strip onto his flesh.

FREEWAY PROPOSAL

More than 300 bikers blocked off part of the busy #10 Freeway in Los Angeles, California, so that Hector "Tank" Martinez could get down on one knee on the tarmac to propose to his beloved girlfriend Paige Hernandez.

STOWED AWAY IN A BUS WHEEL ARCH

A 21-year-old Tunisian man stowed away in the wheel arch of a bus for 30 hours in 2011, hanging on grimly as it traveled 500 mi (800 km) across Europe.

WEIRD BUT TRUE!

LOTTERY LUCK

Three members of the Oksnes family, from the tiny Austevoll Islands off Norway's west coast, have won the lottery in six years, picking up a combined jackpot of more than $4 million.

NAKED PROTEST

Hundreds of cyclists rode through the streets of Lima, Peru, in March 2013 without any clothes on in the city's eighth annual naked bike ride to protest over poor traffic safety.

DIG THIS!

Retired JCB driver Billy Jones from South Wales was carried to his funeral in the bucket of the mechanical digger that he drove for 40 years.

RARE PENNY

A rare 1792 experimental penny that was never put into circulation and is one of only 14 still in existence sold for $1.15 million at an auction in Schaumburg, Illinois, in 2012.

DOG TAGS

Kelly Grace of Brisbane, Australia, found the dog tags of U.S. soldier John W. Sackett near a former army base and returned them to his family after tracking them down online 70 years after he had lost them during World War II.

BRIDGE STOLEN

Thieves in western Turkey stole an entire metal bridge, measuring 82 ft (25 m) long and weighing 22 tons.

Banana Piano

A new kit called MaKey MaKey turns everyday objects into touchpads so that you can use bananas as piano keys. The MaKey MaKey uses a USB cable to connect its circuit board to your computer. If you upload a piano on a computer webpage and attach the ends of bananas to MaKey MaKey, the bananas become piano keys allowing you to play a tune! The device works with any material that can conduct at least a tiny bit of electricity, including modeling clay, ketchup, pencils, coins and even people.

High Chair

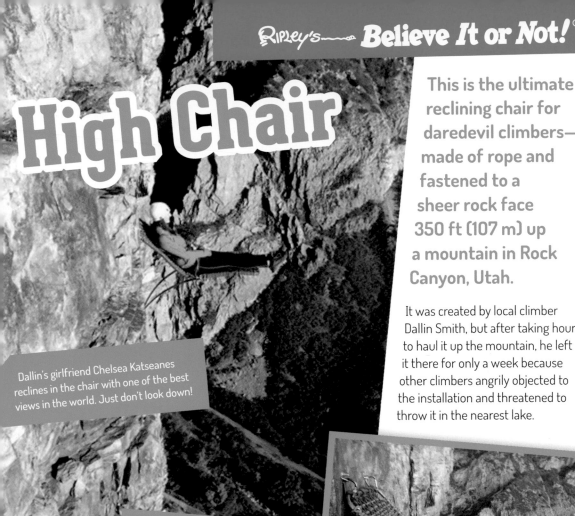

This is the ultimate reclining chair for daredevil climbers—made of rope and fastened to a sheer rock face 350 ft (107 m) up a mountain in Rock Canyon, Utah.

It was created by local climber Dallin Smith, but after taking hours to haul it up the mountain, he left it there for only a week because other climbers angrily objected to the installation and threatened to throw it in the nearest lake.

Dallin's girlfriend Chelsea Katseanes reclines in the chair with one of the best views in the world. Just don't look down!

The chair took Dallin several weeks to make, using two surplus climbing ropes woven around a metal frame and securely fastened to the rock face by two strong hooks.

EAR PRINT
A man was arrested for multiple burglaries in the French city of Lyon after leaving his ear print behind at 80 robberies. He would press his ear up to the front door to check that nobody was at home, but in doing so he left behind incriminating evidence.

COIN TOSS
A 2013 mayoral election in the Philippines was decided by the toss of a coin. Marvic Feraren and Boyet Py both received 3,236 votes to be mayor of San Teodoro, so under the country's election code the two men flipped a coin five times and Feraren won.

DASH SMASH
Officials at the Mexico–U.S. border stopped a suspicious-looking car in 2001 and found a 135-lb (61-kg) woman squashed in the dashboard, peering out through the glove compartment.

Emperor Norton

On September 17, 1859, bankrupt San Francisco businessman Joshua Norton proclaimed himself Norton I, Emperor of the U.S.A. He reigned unofficially for the next 21 years, declaring the abolition of Congress, printing his own bonds, inspecting the city's drains and police officers, and later adding Protector of Mexico to his title.

Dressed in his ceremonial blue uniform with a pair of oversize boots slit at the sides to allow for his corns, and carrying a battered saber, Norton became a familiar figure around the city. Restaurants would put brass plaques at their entrances acknowledging the Emperor's patronage. When he was arrested for vagrancy, he received an apology the following morning from the chief of police. Norton took his duties very seriously and, at the outbreak of the Civil War in 1861, he wrote to President Lincoln and Jefferson Davis, president of the Confederate States, ordering them to attend talks with him in San Francisco. Neither man replied. When Norton died penniless in 1880, more than 10,000 people filed past his coffin to pay their last respects.

- People bowed and curtsied to him in the street
- Norton called himself Emperor of the U.S.A., "reigning" for 21 years
- He was so popular he often dined and traveled free of charge
- Every play opening in the city would reserve balcony seats for him
- He had his own portrait printed on his bonds
- He levied taxes and collected them from shopkeepers and businessmen

For all his eccentricity, Norton was the first person to suggest building a suspension bridge across San Francisco Bay. There have been recent campaigns to rename the Bay Bridge as the Emperor Norton Bridge in honor of the city's whimsical visionary ruler.

WALRUS MYSTERY

When London's St. Pancras train station was being renovated in 2003, archaeologists discovered a 19th-century burial site containing 1,500 human bodies and the remains of a 13-ft-long (4-m) Pacific walrus. The walrus bones were in a coffin with eight human skeletons.

WRONG FACE

A man who used counterfeit $100 bills to buy goods at a store in North Attleborough, Rhode Island, made the mistake of putting a picture of Abraham Lincoln on the notes instead of Benjamin Franklin.

POLICE SEARCH

Two four-year-old boys sparked a full-scale, five-hour search by police officers in Bremen, Germany, after pedaling more than 4 mi (6.4 km) from home on their toy tractors.

MILES AWAY

Four-year-old Jasmine Hudson threw a message in a bottle off the pier at Bournemouth, England, hoping that it would reach her aunt in nearby Guernsey, but instead five months later, she received a letter saying it had been found over 10,500 mi (17,000 km) away in Largs Bay, South Australia.

DIAMOND FIND

Twelve-year-old Michael Dettlaff from Apex, North Carolina, made $11,996 profit in just ten minutes thanks to an Arkansas diamond park's policy of allowing visitors to keep what they find. The boy scout paid $4 admission to the Crater of Diamonds State Park on July 31, 2013, and quickly found a 5.16-carat diamond valued at $12,000.

CARD CURRENCY

In 1685, soldiers in Quebec, Canada, were paid in playing cards, with promissory notes written on the back, after the French colonial government ran out of money.

Poop Guard

Larvae of the cereal leaf beetle crawl around with a pile of their own poop on their back to provide camouflage and prevent their body from drying out. They deposit black specks of their feces and globules of mucus on their back to form a fecal shield—this envelops their body and makes it appear brown, shiny and wet, and thus extremely unappetizing to predators.

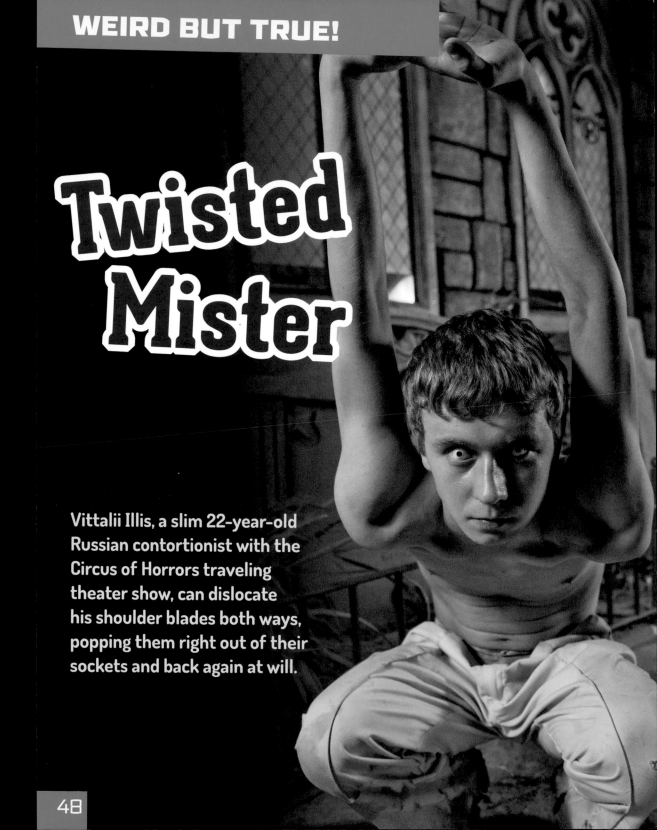

Twisted Mister

Vittalii Illis, a slim 22-year-old Russian contortionist with the Circus of Horrors traveling theater show, can dislocate his shoulder blades both ways, popping them right out of their sockets and back again at will.

He shocks audiences by dislocating his shoulders to rotate his arms back and around his body so that they meet at the front. He can also crawl around the stage on all fours in a creepy spider walk with his legs twisted in front of his body and his hands behind.

Vittalii, who also performs juggling, acrobatics and tightrope walking, was born with natural flexibility. He joined a circus in Russia when he was six as an acrobat, but his coach was so impressed with his ability to twist his body into seemingly impossible positions that he developed his act as a contortionist. Now, Vittalii does extensive stretching exercises every day to keep in whatever shape he chooses.

Do you train every day?
Yes, I do training every day, for about 1½ hours.

Does your act hurt at all?
No, thanks to my natural flexibility, and because I train every day, it is easy for me.

When you train, do you work on the same tricks?
Not every day. I like to discover something new, or I see what other contortionists do and try to replicate it.

Do you enjoy working in the Circus of Horrors?
Yes, the show is very unusual, not like an ordinary circus. I like the program very much, so I decided to come back and now it is my second year.

Does anybody else in your family work in a circus?
No, I am the only one. My family is quite ordinary. None of my family members has ever worked in a circus or as a rubber man.

What do you do in your time off?
I like soccer very much—I am a Chelsea fan. On weekends I like to watch films. I like comedies a lot—I like to have a laugh.

WEIRD BUT TRUE!

FOUR-YEAR RUN

Danish ultra-marathon runner Jesper Olsen has run around the world twice. Three years after completing his first run, he set off in July 2008 from Norway and, via South Africa and Argentina, arrived in Newfoundland in July 2012 at the end of his 23,000-mi (37,000-km) journey.

MUSCLE POWER

In India, where power supplies can be unreliable, fairgrounds can still run on clean energy, like a Ferris wheel powered by human muscle. Groups of men perform skillful and highly dangerous moves to keep the momentum going by swinging from seat to seat and hanging from the wheel as it rotates, which makes it function rather like a human hamster wheel.

FART BY MAIL

By using a nontoxic, fart-smelling formula sealed in a clear envelope, Fart By Mail, a California-based mail order service started by Zach Friedberg, allows people to send greetings that smell like real farts.

MISTAKEN IDENTITY

The Indian army recently spent six months keeping track of what it thought were Chinese spy drones, only to eventually realize that the distant specks in the sky were actually the planets Jupiter and Venus.

ZIP LINE

Instead of walking down the aisle at their wedding, Lauren Bushar and Ben Youngkin from Asheville, North Carolina, chose to fly into the ceremony on a zip line.

DARTH CHALLENGE

Since founding the Darth Valley Challenge in 2010, every summer Jonathan Rice from Longmont, Colorado, dons an all-black *Star Wars* Darth Vader costume and sprints 1 mi (1.6 km) across the Death Valley National Park near the California-Nevada border in sweltering 129°F (54°C) heat. He completed the 2013 run in 6 minutes 36 seconds and says the biggest problem is the mask, which hardly lets in any air.

PRISON IMPOSTER

A former inmate at New York's Rikers Island prison sneaked back into the jail disguised as a guard. Matthew Matagrano used a badge and I.D. card to gain entry and was spotted only when he moved inmates between cells.

Metro Surfing

"Metro surfing" is a highly dangerous new craze among some Russian teenagers that involves them jumping on the back of stationary trains on the Moscow subway and clinging on as they hurtle through narrow tunnels just inches from death. Some go a step further and climb on top of the train to ride it, but this can also prove deadly—tragically, two 19-year-old students were killed when they smashed into a low tunnel entrance while metro surfing.

Open Wide

In December 2012, a large carpet python was caught on camera in the gruesome process of swallowing its prey—a ringtail possum. The snake was hanging from a tree in Byron Bay in New South Wales, Australia, and eventually disappeared into the forest with its catch. The carpet python squeezes the breath out of its victim before stretching its jaws to swallow prey much larger than its own head.

LIVING MERMAN

Eric Ducharme from Crystal River, Florida, has been fascinated by mermaids since he was a child, so he now lives his life as a merman, often swimming underwater wearing a fake tail. He even runs his own business that designs custom-made mermaid tails from silicone and latex rubber. He says, "When I put on a tail I feel transformed."

HUMAN SNAIL

For more than five years, Liu Lingchao from Liuzhou, China, has carried his house on his back, like a human snail. His portable home is 5 ft (1.5 m) wide, 7 ft (2.2 m) tall and consists of plastic sheets attached to a bamboo frame—and because it weighs just 132 lb (60 kg), it is easy for him to carry it around with him while he travels the country earning a living by collecting discarded bottles.

POLICE INTELLIGENCE

A police officer in Stoke-on-Trent, England, was convinced he had caught four men using duplicate passports after thinking all the suspects were named Abu Dhabi. He had confused the names on the passports with the country from which the men had flown.

DRESSING DOWN

A 52-year-old woman from Paris, France, took a two-hour English exam posing as her 19-year-old daughter in an attempt to obtain a better grade for her. The mother wore thick makeup, low-cut jeans and Converse shoes in an attempt to pass herself off as a teenager, but a supervisor spotted the deception.

MESSAGE INTACT

Lucy Elliott, 12, from Coventry, England, threw a message in a plastic bottle out to sea off the coast of Cornwall in 1994, and 19 years later it washed up on a beach in Norway 750 mi (1,200 km) away. Incredibly, the handwritten message was still sufficiently legible for the finder to trace her.

HIDING IN AN AIRLINE CARGO CONTAINER

Roberto Viza Egües fled Cuba for Paris, France, in 2000 after hiding in an Air France cargo container at Havana Airport. After a 14-hour flight in freezing temperatures, he arrived in France where his application for asylum was denied.

Undercover Croc

To get up close and personal with deadly Nile crocodiles and hippos, American TV naturalist Dr. Brady Barr decided to dress up as them. Wearing a crocodile suit consisting of a prosthetic head attached to the front of a protective, canvas-draped metal cage, he was able to crawl on his hands and knees and get within touching distance of 13-ft-long (4-m) crocs in Tanzania without his cover being blown. Dressed in a heavy, armored hippo suit smeared with hippo dung to hide the human scent of the occupant, he slowly approached a 10,000-strong herd of hippos in Zambia's South Luangwa National Park, only to get stuck in the mud and be forced to radio for help.

Remotest Toilet

Perched on a cliff 8,500 ft (2,600 m) above sea level in the Altai Mountains, Siberia, this has got to be a contender for the world's most isolated toilet. It serves five workers at a weather station at Karaturek—a spot so remote that food and water are delivered annually by helicopter and their only other visitor is the postman who drops by once a month to collect the weather data.

SPORTING GUESTS

The three-bedroom Penthouse Real World Suite at the Hard Rock Hotel & Casino, Las Vegas, Nevada, has its own bowling alley. At the nearby Palms Hotel, the Hardwood Suite has its own basketball court!

QUEASY RIDER

Car mechanic Guenter Schroeder from Germany drank so much beer one evening that he ended up falling asleep on top of a horse. Having missed his last bus home, he stumbled across some stables and curled up on the horse's warm blanket even though the animal was standing up!

SECRET INSCRIPTION

Abraham Lincoln's pocket watch had a secret message engraved on the inside—and the president did not even know about it. The inscription describing the start of the American Civil War was engraved by jeweler Jonathan Dillon in 1861 but remained hidden until 2009 when Dillon's great-great-grandson contacted the Smithsonian's National Museum of American History, where the watch is kept, and told them about the rumored message. When an expert opened the historic watch, the secret was finally revealed.

FLYING DAGGER

After leaping from a helicopter, daredevil wingsuiter Jeb Corliss of Malibu, California, flew at a speed of 100 mph (160 km/h) through a mountain gap that was just 25 ft (7.6 m) wide at its narrowest point. The spectacular jump, known as the "flying dagger," was made through a fissure in China's 900-ft-high (274-m) Langshan Mountain.

FIRST BORN

In September 2013, Francesco Isella became the first baby to be born in 67 years in Lissa, Italy, and boosted the tiny village's population to six.

Tiger Woman

Katzen Hobbes is a real-life Catwoman with 90 percent of her body tattooed with black tiger stripes.

She used to have genuine tiger whiskers, which were sent to her by zoos around the world, implanted into her cheeks by means of specialist piercing rings. Now, her "whiskers" have been drawn on her face by scarification—scratches on the skin made deep enough to scar permanently.

It took over a decade for the mother-of-two from Austin, Texas (who is also known as Katzen Ink),

to acquire all her tiger tattoos, during which time more than 160 tattoo artists have worked on her, including 23 at the same time! Having so many artists filling in the black lines on her back, legs and stomach caused her such pain that she fainted more than once.

Even so, she loves being half woman, half big cat. "I can't imagine not being a tiger. I am a living, breathing work of art."

WEIRD BUT TRUE!

PARALLEL LIVES

Two British brothers, Ron and Fred Boyes, who had been separated for 80 years and were unaware of each other's existence, found when they finally met up that they had both reached the same rank in the Royal Air Force and played the same soccer position, and they both have a daughter named Wendy. The brothers were fostered separately in the 1930s and ended up in different parts of the U.K.— Ron in Derbyshire and Fred in Oxfordshire. They were reunited when a relative began researching their family tree.

CREMATION PRIZE

Baseball fan Matt Kratoville, 54, from Novato, California, won a free cremation by taking first prize in a "Funeral Night" contest at a San Rafael Pacifics game on August 23, 2013, in which he had to write his own obituary.

SLOW THIEF

After robbing a woman in the parking lot of a shopping mall near Melbourne, Australia, a 64-year-old man was arrested at the scene because he was too slow putting his walker into his getaway car.

UPSIDE DOWN

A 160-year-old four-anna (less than half a cent) Indian postage stamp with the head of Queen Victoria accidentally printed upside down is now worth more than $100,000.

CLOUD NINE

Five couples from New Zealand got married at an altitude of 41,000 ft (12,500 m). The group wedding ceremony took place in the business cabin of a Fiji Airways plane en route from Auckland to Nadi, Fiji.

Fan Power

A group of six *Star Wars* fans, led by Belgian Mark Dermul, traveled to Tunisia in 2012 to save the Lars Homestead— Luke Skywalker's home on the planet Tatooine that was featured in three of the *Star Wars* movies. They raised $11,700 and worked in 115°F (46°C) heat to restore the igloo-shaped building that had been ravaged by the desert climate and had fallen into disrepair since its last screen appearance in 2005.

Sleeping Partner

Guy Whittall enjoyed a peaceful night's sleep in Humani Lodge, Zimbabwe, unaware that an 8-ft-long (2.4-m) Nile crocodile was lying under his bed the whole time. In the morning, Guy dangled his bare feet over the edge of the bed, inches from the 330-lb (150-kg) monster's teeth. Later, the housemaid's screams alerted him to his unwelcome guest.

ANCIENT DEBT

A court in Glarus, Switzerland, finally wiped out a 655-year-old debt so that a farmer and his family no longer have to pay $70 a year to the Catholic Church to keep a sanctuary lamp burning. The debt dated back to 1357 when Konrad Mueller killed Heinrich Stucki, and to save his soul, he gave a lamp to the local church and vowed to fuel it with oil from his walnut trees for eternity—a promise that was kept by all subsequent owners of Mueller's land until the new ruling.

TWO'S COMPANY

Rudi Saldia cycles around the streets of Philadelphia, Pennsylvania, with his tabby cat Mary Jane perched on his shoulder. Using a sports camera mounted on his bike, he's recorded "Mary Jane's Co-pilot Adventures" and posted them on YouTube, where they picked up more than 1.2 million views in the first six months.

NOISY ANTS

When a 75-year-old woman from Offenburg, Germany, called police at 3 a.m. one morning to say that she could not sleep because her doorbell was always ringing, officers found that the cause was an ants' nest right next to the doorbell. The ants had built such a large home that their nest pressed the switching elements together, setting off the bell.

EXTRA BAGGAGE

Bisou, a seven-year-old Persian cat, made an unscheduled 3,400-mi (5,470-km) airplane and car journey after sneaking into owner Mervat Ciuti's suitcase as she packed at home in Cairo, Egypt, to visit her sister in England. Bisou, who normally never leaves the house, passed through airport security undetected and was stacked into the hold of the plane with hundreds of other bags, but she survived her ordeal unscathed.

PRICKLY PROBLEM

Sandra Nabucco was left with 272 spines painfully stuck in her scalp after a porcupine fell from a lamppost and landed on her head while she was walking her dog in Rio de Janeiro, Brazil. Surgeons used tweezers to remove the quills and gave her antibiotics to prevent the wounds from becoming infected. She said, "It was a huge shock. I felt a thud on my head and then felt spines with my hands. The pain was enormous." The porcupine survived because Sandra had broken its fall.

DUCK ESCORT

The busy A3 highway in Surrey, England, was closed during rush hour on August 15, 2013, causing a long traffic jam while 50 mallard ducks were given a police escort. The ducks were walked along the road before being steered with handfuls of corn to the safety of a nearby shed.

Resin Layers

Keng Lye from Singapore creates incredible 3-D paintings—such as this lifelike octopus—by using multiple layers of resin.

He pours resin into a container, then covers it with plastic wrap to protect it from dust and to allow it to harden. Once the resin is dry, he paints it in minute detail with acrylic paint. He adds layers of resin and acrylic paint, giving depth and realism to the composition, until the object is finished. The whole process is so laborious that even the simplest artwork can take him up to five days to complete, but the end result is worth all the effort.

STICKY FINGERS
Thieves in Bad Hersfeld, Germany, stole 5.5 tons of Nutella chocolate-hazelnut spread from a parked trailer.

YOUNG SCIENTIST
Jamie Edwards, a 13-year-old boy from Preston, England, successfully built a nuclear reactor in his school science class in March 2014.

COMPUTER ERROR
New Zealand electrical company Meridian Energy mistakenly sent a letter to a lamppost in Oakura and threatened to cut off its power unless it supplied them with its customer details within seven days.

Check This!

Although written and signed to the value of Australian $2,240, this giant billboard check looked worthless to most Australians until they realized it was actually legal tender. National Australia Bank put up four oversized checks to promote its mortgage rates, and once word spread that the checks could be cashed, there was a mad rush to rip them down from the billboards. Luka Pendes was one of four lucky winners fast enough to cash in on the offer.

BROTHER'S PRANK

While Dutch teenager Jamiro Smajic was on vacation in Italy, his older brother, Tobias Mathijsen, played a prank on him by tilting his bedroom 90 degrees. Over the course of two days, Tobias fixed furniture to walls, attached posters to the ceiling and even installed a light at an angle of 90 degrees. A series of pranks between the brothers started when Jamiro altered his brother's Facebook profile and Tobias responded by painting Jamiro's entire bedroom pink while he was away.

TOUGH GUY

At the 2013 World's Strongest Man competition in Sanya, China, Brian Shaw from Fort Lupton, Colorado, deadlifted over 975 lb (442.5 kg)—about the same weight as a horse. His biceps are nearly 2 ft (60 cm) in circumference, his neck is wider than most men's thighs and, when he used to play basketball as a teen, one opponent knocked himself out simply by running into Shaw's chest.

Palm Portraits

Spanish artist David Catá used a needle and different colored threads to sew more than 20 portraits of his friends and family into the palms of his hands. Using his body as a canvas, he pierces only the top layer of skin with a needle to avoid causing too much pain and then draws the thread through to make a stitch. Each picture takes him up to four hours to sew before he photographs it and then carefully picks out the thread to allow his skin to heal. The art project, which shows how people close to him are woven into his life, scars his palms for up to four weeks, after which he can start over with a new portrait.

STILL TICKING

The Beverly Clock, located in a foyer at the University of Otago in Dunedin, New Zealand, keeps ticking despite the fact that it has not been wound since 1864.

PHONE ACCESS

According to the United Nations, more of the world's population has access to cell phones than proper toilets.

Frozen Falls

As temperatures plunged to –34°F (–37°C) in January 2014, it was so cold that the U.S. side of the Niagara Falls froze before the water could reach the bottom, forming incredible 170-ft-long (52-m) icicles. The polar vortex that created the big freeze affected 240 million people in the U.S. and southern Canada.

DEATH WATCH

Fredrik Colting of Sweden has invented a watch that counts down every second to the wearer's death. The person's life expectancy is calculated based on medical history and lifestyle and when their current age is deducted, the countdown display starts on the Tikker, supposedly enabling them to make the most of the rest of their life.

MARRIED BRIDGE

Australian artist Jodi Rose loves bridges so much that in a special ceremony on June 17, 2013, she married a 600-year-old French bridge, Le Pont du Diable in Céret. Although the union is not legally recognized in France, Jodi invited 14 guests to attend, wore a traditional bridal gown and veil, and commissioned rings for both herself and the bridge.

WOOLY HAUL

In November 2013, thieves stole 160 sheep from a field near the aptly named village of Wool in Dorset, England.

LATE DELIVERY

The R.M.S. *Titanic* sank in 1912 with more than seven million pieces of mail on board, all of which the U.S. would be required to help deliver if they could be recovered.

Living Goddess

A 10-year-old Nepalese girl, Samita Bajracharya, is a living goddess or Kumari, believed to be an incarnation of Kali, the Hindu goddess of power. Kumaris, who are worshiped by both Hindus and Buddhists, are selected as toddlers by Buddhist high priests and must meet more than 30 criteria, including good health, a golden, unscratched skin and no missing teeth. Kumari means "virgin" in Nepalese, so when Samita reaches puberty, she will be considered unclean and will lose her title, but until then, she leads a privileged but sheltered life.

For her appearance at a chariot festival in Jawalakhel, Samita was dressed in the traditional costume that is passed down from one Kumari to the next. Before her arrival, workers hosed down her path and sniffer dogs were brought in to ensure her safety. Then, she was carried from her home by her family, making sure that her painted feet did not touch the ground, while devotees rushed forward to offer her flowers and money and to catch a glimpse of the child goddess.

Samita is not allowed to go to school, play outside or even touch her friends.

Freaky Fungus

Found high on the Tibetan plateau, a bizarre parasitic fungus known as "worm grass" infects the ghost moth caterpillar, consuming it from the inside, killing it, and then sprouting from its head. The fungus, *Ophiocordyceps sinensis*, has been regarded as a miracle ingredient in Chinese traditional medicine for centuries and is said to aid various ailments and to act as a powerful stimulant and aphrodisiac. Sold while still attached to the caterpillars, it can fetch prices upwards of $3,500 per pound—ten times the price of silver.

Fungus sprouting from caterpillar's head.

SUBWAY LOOT
Using dental floss and mousetrap glue, Puerto Rican native Eliel Santos makes around $150 a day by retrieving cash, jewelry and iPhones that have fallen down New York City subway grates.

SPY TREES
During World War I, engineers along the Western Front would cut down trees during the night and replace them with prefabricated observation posts that had been hand-decorated as highly detailed replica trees.

BANKER ERROR
A tired German bank clerk fell asleep with his finger on the number 2 key on his computer keyboard—and ended up turning a simple 62.40 euro transfer in to a customer's account into a withdrawal from the account of a whopping 222,222,222.22 euros ($293 million).

TIDY ROBOT
Researchers at the University of California, Berkeley, have taught a robot how to fold laundry. Faced with a pile of towels, the robot picks it up with its arms and uses a pair of high-resolution cameras to estimate its shape. Once it finds two adjacent corners, it starts folding, smoothing the towel after each fold to make a neat stack.

PICTURE PERFECT
Five years after losing her camera while scuba diving in Hawaii, Lindsay Scallan of Newnan, Georgia, learned that it had been found 6,000 mi (9,660 km) away in Taiwan. Although the camera was covered in seaweed and barnacles, her pictures were still intact on its memory card.

SHOCK REUNION
When Christine Greenslade, 66, decided to trace the whereabouts of her old schoolfriends in Penzance, England, in 2013, they were stunned to find she was still alive after a local newspaper had erroneously printed her obituary in 1980.

GLOWING COIN
In 2012, the Royal Canadian Mint released a 25-cent coin that featured a dinosaur with a glow-in-the-dark skeleton.

Wild Things

Snake Ball

Emerging from hibernation in spring, anaconda snakes form "mating balls," where up to eight males and one or two females congregate for as long as two hours in a tight, writhing, reproductive mass.

The males attempt to uncoil the female with a constant intertwining of their bodies through hers until their sexual organs are aligned for mating.

Flying Whippet

Davy Whippet, a dog owned and trained by Lara Sorensen in Alberta, Canada, ran and caught a Frisbee thrown a distance of 402 ft (122.5 m). After the Frisbee was launched, Davy sprinted the distance in about 10 seconds—that's nearly 25 percent faster than Usain Bolt—to catch it before it landed. Lara has a big field for Davy to run around in, yet she says, "He is a couch potato 99 percent of the day, but when you ask him to work, he is completely switched on."

PET ARMOR

To protect his vulnerable guinea pig Lucky, doting owner Sean McCoy from Fairfax, Virginia, made the pet a tiny suit of armor, consisting of an authentic miniature steel helmet and a chain mail suit.

DEADLY FISH

There are over 1,200 species of venomous fish—outnumbering the world's venomous snakes and all its other venomous vertebrates combined.

SKATEBOARDING GOAT

Happie, a Nigerian dwarf-cross goat owned by Melody Cooke, has spent hours riding around a parking lot in Fort Myers, Florida—on a skateboard. Happie took to skateboarding like a natural and has ridden the board nonstop for 25 seconds, covering a distance of 118 ft (36 m).

EARTHWORM ESCAPE

Earthworms pour out of the ground before a major flood, as they seek to escape rising groundwater.

FALLING TREE

While Lydia Bigras was walking with friends through Goldstream Provincial Park, British Columbia, Canada, her four-year-old Australian terrier Roo suddenly ran back the way they had come. The humans followed and seconds later a 60-ft (18-m) cedar tree crashed down where they had been standing. None of them had noticed that the tree was falling.

ATHLETIC COLLIE

Jumpy, an Australian border collie owned by Omar Von Muller of Los Angeles, California, lives up to his name by performing more than 20 agile tricks, including skateboard jumps, surfing, backflips, leaping off walls, playing Frisbee and riding a scooter.

HUNGRY BIRDS

Hummingbirds burn so much energy that, to avoid starving to death, they must eat their body-weight in food each day and slow down their metabolism as needed.

WARM NEST

After crawling into a rabbit burrow to make a kill, the European stoat will sometimes use the dead rabbit's carcass as a warm furry nest in which to raise its own young.

LIGHT BONES

Sharks do not have a hard bone skeleton. Instead, their skeleton is made from light, flexible cartilage—the same material that supports the human outer ear.

LIFE SAVER

When 17-year-old Ben Rees was home alone in the shower in Llanelli, Wales, his pet cockatiel Cookie flew into the bathroom, squawked noisily and dive-bombed him repeatedly to let him know that the house was on fire. Ben managed to escape through thick smoke, but sadly his feathered savior died in the fire and was later buried in the garden.

DRUNKEN PIG

A pig drank 18 cans of beer left outside at a campsite near Port Hedland, Western Australia, and then went on a drunken rampage during which it tried to fight a cow and swim across a river, before finally passing out.

Blind Chicken CPR

Roberta Rapo spent 3½ hours successfully resuscitating her daughter Rayna's (pictured here) blind pet chicken, Chooky Wooky, after a gust of wind had blown the bird into the family pool in Sydney, Australia, leaving it to drown. Finding the stricken chicken floating lifelessly in the pool, Roberta pulled it out and started mouth-to-mouth resuscitation and CPR, pumping the frail bird's heart until it finally began to revive. Chooky Wooky was later given a clean bill of health by a veterinarian and then laid a celebratory egg.

Insect Replica

This grasshopper in Indonesia took 40 minutes to cast off its exoskeleton—a hard outer shell—as it went through one of the stages in its two-month transformation from a nymph, which has no wings, into a fully grown adult grasshopper. As the nymph grows, the exoskeleton cannot stretch to match, so the young grasshopper must get rid of up to six different casings before it can grow wings.

PIG WHISPERER
Veterinarian Kees Scheepens from Brabant, Netherlands, hypnotizes pigs to measure their stress levels. An expert in pig body language and grunts, he estimates that he has seen more than five million swine while visiting stables in every country in Europe. To win the animals' trust, he sometimes eats from their troughs!

ATHLETIC DOG
Boogie the Labrador received a medal for completing a 13-mi (21-km) half-marathon for humans in Evansville, Indiana. After escaping from his leash the night before, he was found running in the race, which he finished ahead of more than half the competitors, before being reunited with owner Jerry Butts.

WHAT A SNITCH!
Driver Guillermo Reyes was arrested in Mexico City after his pet parakeet told police he was drunk. The officers had stopped Reyes during a routine check, but as he got out of his car to be tested, the bird inside the vehicle squawked, "He's drunk, he's drunk." Guillermo subsequently failed the breathalyzer test.

WONDER WEB

In the movie *Spider-Man 2*, the superhero shoots a web to prevent a runaway train from plunging to disaster—and a team of U.K. scientists has shown that this is not Hollywood exaggeration. The Darwin's bark spider, from Madagascar, creates webs that are ten times stronger than Kevlar, and if scaled up to Spider-Man proportions, its silk would be strong enough to halt a four-car subway train traveling at full speed.

SQUIRREL PROFIT

After 30 squirrels escaped from an enclosure at Japan's Inokashira Park Zoo, zookeepers combed surrounding parkland and recaptured 38!

RUBBER FLIPPERS

Yu, a loggerhead turtle that lost her front fins to a shark attack, swims around the Suma Aqualife Park in Kobe, Japan, wearing a pair of artificial flippers. The rubber limbs are attached to a vest slipped over the turtle's head.

Gone Fishing

The raft spider of Europe, which has a 3-in (8-cm) leg span, can dive beneath the surface to catch fish such as sticklebacks and can walk on water. The spider gets its name from the way it waits for its prey like a raft on the surface of the water—the minute hairs that cover its legs spread the spider's weight so it doesn't sink.

SEAL CROSSING

An elephant seal weighing more than half a ton stopped traffic for over an hour in the Brazilian beach city of Balneário Camboriú after waddling out of the Atlantic Ocean and across a busy street. The 10-ft-long (3-m) seal actually used a pedestrian crossing while police officers and firefighters splashed water on the animal to keep it cool.

Odd Lobster

Jeff Edwards from Owl's Head, Maine, caught this half-brown, half-orange lobster—a one-in-50-million genetic oddity resulting from a lack of pigmentation. The two-tone lobster is currently on display at the Gulf of Maine Research Institute in Portland. In a bizarre coincidence, a year earlier, fisherman Dana Duhaime caught a similar specimen off Beverly, Massachusetts. Split-color lobsters are often hermaphrodites, but Duhaime's catch was entirely female, making it even more rare.

FIERY SHRIMP

Acanthephyra purpurea, the fire-breathing shrimp, blinds and distracts its would-be predators by spewing out a blue-glowing bacterial cloud.

GUARDIAN ANGEL

A faithful dog has been trained to sniff out peanuts for seven-year-old Meghan Weingarth, from Suwanee, Georgia, who suffers from a serious nut allergy. Meghan breaks out in hives and could go into shock if she eats anything containing peanuts, but LilyBelle the goldendoodle now checks all of her food first and raises a paw to warn her if she is about to eat nuts.

MEMORY LANE

Decapitated flatworms regrow their old memories along with their new heads.

SNAKE BITE

Working at Werris Creek cemetery in New South Wales, Australia, 66-year-old Jake Thomas killed a venomous red-bellied black snake by cutting it in half with his shovel—but, amazingly, 15 minutes later the dead snake bit him on the hand and he had to spend two days in a hospital intensive care unit.

CROWD PLEASERS

Fighting male crickets are more violent—and more expressive in their victory dance—if other crickets are watching.

KILLER CATFISH

European catfish 5 ft (1.5 m) long living in the River Tarn in southwestern France have been seen lunging out of the water, snatching pigeons from the bank and then returning to the river to devour their prey.

CAT CANDIDATE

Hank, a Maine Coon cat, received over 6,000 votes in the 2012 U.S. Senate election in Virginia. Owners Matthew O'Leary and Anthony Roberts nominated Hank as a protest against regular political campaigns. Finishing third, Hank, who advocated spay and neuter programs, raised $60,000 for animal shelters.

PANDA VIDEO

Inexperienced female giant panda Colin kept rejecting male Yongyong until conservationists at the Panda Breeding and Research Base in Chengdu, China, played the pair a video of pandas mating to show them how it was done. "Colin took great interest in the film," said a vet at the center. "After that they mated successfully."

NASTY SHOCK

The shock from an electric eel is so powerful that it can knock a horse off its feet. The eels can generate an electrical charge of up to 600 volts—five times the power of a standard U.S. wall socket. Their bodies contain electric organs with cells that store power like tiny batteries, and when the eel feels threatened or is in attack mode, these cells discharge simultaneously.

SNAKE STASH

Discovering nine eggs in the yard of his home in Queensland, Australia, three-year-old Kyle Cummings put them in a plastic container and stashed them in his closet. By the time his mother found the container, seven of the eggs had hatched into venomous eastern brown snakes. The bite from these snakes, even as babies, can be fatal.

Death Trap

Measuring as much as 5 ft (1.5 m) in diameter and built up to 6 ft (1.8 m) above ground, the conjoined web of female red-legged golden orb spiders is so large, and is woven from such strong silk, that it can ensnare bats and even birds. This bird—a seafaring lesser noddy—was photographed by Isak Pretorius after it became trapped in a web on Cousine, an island in the Seychelles. Luckily for the bird, it was saved, but most perish. After a struggle, the web will eventually break, but as the birds fall to the ground their wings are still tangled in the web fibers, and they can't fly. They soon die from a combination of exhaustion and dehydration.

GOATS ARREST

Three goats were arrested and detained in Chennai, India, for vandalizing a new police car. The goats—part of a gang of 12—were accused of climbing on top of the vehicle, denting it, damaging the windshield and wipers, and scratching the paintwork.

CAT HAT

Seattle, Washington, designer Yumiko Landers has created a range of hats for cats that make them look like lions. The false mane—in a variety of colors—attaches around the cat's head with Velcro. Landers says, "Every cat believes they're the master of their domain. So I thought there's no better way to represent that than by making them look like a true lion."

FAKE POODLES

Dog lovers in Buenos Aires, Argentina, paid $150 for what they thought was a bargain price for a fashionable toy poodle, only to discover that they had been sold a ferret instead. The ferrets had been given steroids at birth to increase their size and then had their coats fluffed up to make them look like poodles.

Each cow is shampooed, blow-dried and styled—with oil added for shine and hairspray applied to keep the fuzzy look intact.

Fluffy Cows

Groomed and pampered dogs have long been a regular fixture in animal shows around the world, but now pampered cows are beginning to make their mark.

Phil Lautner of Lautner Farms in Iowa shows and sells his special-breed bovines at the National Western Stock Show, with one specimen being sold for an amazing $100,000. His cute cows undergo a meticulous beauty routine to create their unique look.

It takes months of special care, and up to two hours of preparation on the day, to get the cows ready for their moment in the spotlight.

Tough Nut

You might not fancy this little turtle's chances in the jaws of an alligator at the Okefenokee Swamp in Georgia, U.S.A., but it proved too tough a nut to crack. After trying in vain to pry open the shell with its powerful teeth, the gator eventually gave up, and when photographer Patrick Castleberry went over to see how the turtle was, he was delighted to find that it was still alive. So he flipped it over and it quickly swam off, none the worse for its brush with death.

BLOWN AWAY

When a deer became trapped on thin ice in Antigonish Harbor, Nova Scotia, Canada, helicopter pilot David Farrell remembered an old trick and used the wind created by the chopper's rotor blades to blow the stricken animal across the frozen water to safety.

MANURE FRESHENER

Indonesian high-school students Dwi Nailul Izzah and Rintya Aprianti Miki won first prize in the country's Science Project Olympiad with their air freshener made from cow dung. After leaving the manure to ferment for three days, they extracted the liquid and mixed it with coconut water to create a product from digested cow food that has a natural aroma of herbs.

MIRACLE MILK

Despite never having had puppies, Ba Boo, a three-year-old Shar-Pei dog owned by Sherry Brandt from Kodak, Tennessee, not only adopted an abandoned kitten, but also nursed it with her own milk.

HEAD HUNTER

Charlie Perito has a pet cat named Nicholas who sits on his head when they go out for walks together through the streets of New York City. Nicholas learned to perch on Charlie's shoulder as a three-month-old kitten and became so confident amid the busy traffic that he now jumps straight up from the ground onto his owner's head and expects to stay there so he can keep a lookout for low-flying pigeons.

PORKER WALKER

When piglet Chris P. Bacon was born with a congenital defect that meant he had no use of his hind limbs, his owner, Dr. Len Lucero of Sumterville, Florida, built him a two-wheeled harness out of a K'Nex building set. Now the little pig gets around in his cool customized wheelchair, has his own Facebook page with thousands of followers and has even become an inspiration to humans who have disabilities.

BEAR RESCUE

A 100-lb (45-kg) young bear spent at least 11 days with his head stuck in a plastic jar before being freed by a team of rescuers in Jamison City, Pennsylvania. The bear had apparently been attracted to the jar because it had once contained cooking oil.

CASH GUZZLER

Sundance, a 12-year-old golden retriever owned by Wayne Klinkel of Helena, Montana, ate $500 in cash (five $100 bills) when left alone in the car during a Christmas visit to Denver, Colorado.

GREEN GIANTS

Adult male mountain gorillas of East Africa can eat up to 75 lb (34 kg) of vegetation every day—equivalent to the weight of about 300 apples.

WHISTLING CATERPILLARS

Walnut sphinx caterpillars frighten off predatory birds by whistling from breathing holes in their sides. They pull their heads back to compress their body and then force air out of their abdominal spiracles as a whistling sound. Each whistle can last up to four seconds.

Overstuffed Bird

After attacking and devouring a small bird in Long Beach, California, this juvenile red-tailed hawk realized that it had eaten so much it was unable to fly. The bird of prey took half an hour to consume the bird and then managed to waddle just a few yards before falling flat on its back. Luckily, photographer Steve Shinn was on hand to call a local wildlife center, and by the next day, the hawk had recovered once it had fully digested its heavy meal.

Wolf Man

Former paratrooper Werner Freund has hand-reared and lived among wolves on his sanctuary in Merzig, Germany, for 40 years and is so close to them that they actually take meat from his mouth. To show the 29 wolves that he is their leader, he makes sure he is the first to get his teeth into some raw meat—in this case a dead deer—at feeding time. The wolves wait obediently until he has finished, and because he has earned their respect, they play with him rather than attack him, regularly licking his face as a sign of subservience.

UDDERLY BEAUTIFUL

An annual cow beauty contest—the German Holstein Show—takes place in Oldenburg, Germany. A dozen cow hairdressers use razor blades to groom more than 250 animals from across Europe in the search to find the most beautiful bovine.

POOCH HOOCH

Boneyard Brewery of Bend, Oregon, has created an alcohol-free beer for dogs. The brainchild of brewery taster Daniel Keeton, it is called Dawg Grog and is packed with vegetables, spices and honey to provide a nutritional, liquid treat for dogs.

TINY FLY

Euryplatea nanaknihali, a newly discovered species in Thailand, is the world's smallest fly, with a length of less than 0.02 in (0.5 mm)—and it reproduces by laying its eggs inside some of the world's smallest ants.

BAT CAVE

A cave in Austin, Texas, is home to 10 million Mexican free-tailed bats, crammed together on the walls at 400 bats per square foot.

EAGER BEAVER

In June 2013, a hungry beaver chewed through a fiber line and caused a 20-hour Internet and cell-phone outage in northern New Mexico, which affected more than 1,800 Web users.

Viewed from above.

Viewed from below.

Two-Headed Salamander

This two-headed fire salamander survived for only six months with a private breeder who had tried to feed it through both mouths. On its death, he donated it to a German university for research. The salamander's condition is called bicephaly, where each head has its own brain and they share control of the creature's organs and limbs. When snakes are born with bicephaly, one head may attack and even attempt to swallow the other.

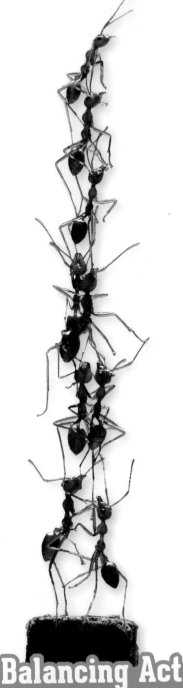

MONKEY BUSINESS

Sika deer on Japan's Yakushima Island find food by eavesdropping on the calls of feeding macaque monkeys.

STAR PIG

Ramona Flowers, a two-year-old female potbellied pig owned by Luis Bojorquez from Tijuana, Mexico, has furrows in her brow that make her look just like the character Yoda from *Star Wars*.

CELEBRITY COW

Big Bertha, a cow owned by Irish farmer Jerome O'Leary, died in 1993 aged 49—over three times the average lifespan of a cow. She produced 39 calves and became a local celebrity, leading noisy St. Patrick's Day parades after being given whiskey to calm her nerves. Following her death, she was stuffed and is now on display at Beaufort, County Kerry.

LIFE RAFT

If one dolphin becomes distressed, the other members of the pod will often join forces to form a raft with their bodies and keep the injured dolphin above the water so that it can breathe and regain its balance.

RESURRECTED FROG

Using cloning technology, scientists in Australia are bringing back to life the southern gastric-brooding frog, which became extinct in 1983. A few samples of the long-dead frog were found in a freezer, and this was enough to enable researchers to produce tadpole embryos.

MOTHER'S SACRIFICE

The female Japanese foliage spider allows her young to eat her to give them sufficient nutrients to survive.

KILLER WORM

Workers at an aquarium store in Surrey, England, were mystified by the disappearance of dozens of fish—until they found that a 3-ft-long (1-m) bobbit worm had been hiding in the tank for years. The sinister worm usually lives deep in the ocean but had been unwittingly introduced to the aquarium in a large rock and had been eating the fish ever since.

FISH FRAME

When Einstein the goldfish developed swim bladder disease, causing him to turn upside down and sink to the bottom of his tank, his owner, Leighton Naylor from Blackpool, England, built him a special life jacket to enable him to swim again. The jacket came in the form of a floating frame made from recycled tubing, fitting perfectly over the fish's body.

Balancing Act

These fire ants were pictured employing incredible teamwork and strength to escape a container in which they were being kept in Jakarta, Indonesia. Fire ants often work together in the wild to create unbelievable structures from their own bodies, such as towers, bridges and rafts on water.

Sea Monster

Members of the Catalina Island Marine Institute hold an 18-ft-long (5.5-m) oarfish that washed up off the coast of Southern California in 2013—a sea monster so huge that it needed 16 people to drag it ashore.

GATOR GUEST

A 2-ft-long (60-cm) alligator was found living under an escalator at Chicago's O'Hare International Airport. A startled maintenance worker discovered the reptile, which was captured when a police officer trapped it in a trash can.

AERIAL VIEW

Alphie, a tabby kitten owned by Vanessa Waite of Sheffield, England, made a full recovery after swallowing a 6-in-long (15-cm) TV antenna. He needed emergency treatment when the metal antenna, which was almost as long as his body, became lodged in his throat and stomach.

SURFING PIG

Every morning Matthew Bell takes his piglet Zorro surfing off the coast near Mount Maunganui, New Zealand. Matthew, who describes Zorro as a "phenomenal swimmer," first took him out on the waves when he was just three weeks old and plans to continue surfing with him until the pig is too big for the board.

BOOTYLICIOUS FLY

In 2011, a previously unnamed species of Australian horsefly with an attractive golden lower abdomen was named *Scaptia beyonceae* after the singer Beyoncé.

LADY TARZAN

A 14-year-old girl from Jharkland, India, talked to elephants that had settled in a residential area in 2013 and persuaded them to return to the forest. Nirmala Toppo, who is known as "Lady Tarzan," began talking to elephants after her mother was killed by a herd. She learned the techniques for driving them away and says elephants understand her tribal language.

THIRD EYELID

Woodpeckers have a third eyelid that keeps their two eyeballs in place as they ram trees with their beaks at great force at least 20 times a second.

RACCOON TAKEOVER

In 2012, Germany was invaded by more than a million raccoons, many of which nested in the attics of city houses.

DOZY OWL

As a romantic gesture at her wedding to Andrew Mattle in Wiltshire, England, bride Sonia Cadman hired a trained barn owl to swoop down during the ceremony with the rings attached to its feet. Alas, despite repeated attempts to coax it down, the bird fell asleep in the church rafters for an hour, forcing the minister to use a pair of backup rings.

DESIGNER DOGHOUSE

A St. Bernard dog named Wellington lives in an exact replica of his owner's home. Julian Kite, a former bricklayer, spent nearly £2,000 ($3,350) building Wellington's luxury kennel at a scale of 1:3 to his own detached house in Derbyshire, England. The 6½-ft-high (2-m) doghouse boasts stylish windows, a slate roof, fully functional guttering and even hanging baskets and potted shrubs outside. The interior has fully insulated floors and walls to keep out the cold, electric lighting and a fitted carpet to protect the pooch's paws.

FUR EXTENSIONS

An online company in the U.K. called Poochie Plumes offers hair extensions for dogs! Provided the dog's fur is at least an inch long, owners can pay £11 ($19) for extensions made from colored feathers. The plumes, which are attached individually using a micro ring, can be left in for six weeks, but the company warns the bright colors may run on white dogs.

DOG BOOTS

Police dogs in Germany have been issued Velcro-fastening shoes to protect their paws from broken glass during riots.

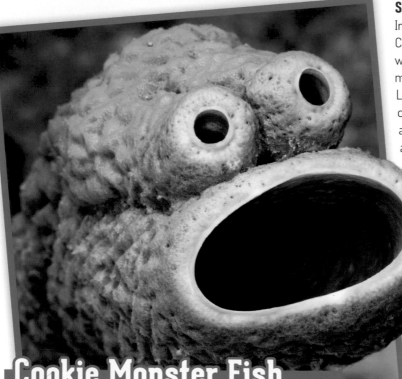

Cookie Monster Fish

This may look like Cookie Monster, the hungry Muppet, but it is in fact a trio of purple sea sponges (*Aplysina archeri*) that fused together near Curaçao in the Caribbean to form what appear to be a pair of wide eyes and a gaping mouth. The sponge is about 3 ft (0.9 m) tall. You can close its "mouth" simply by squeezing it gently between your thumb and forefinger.

SNAKE INVASION

In May 2013, the Louisiana State Capitol building in Baton Rouge was invaded by water snakes migrating from nearby Capitol Lake. Baby snakes were found curled up in closets, crawling across committee-room carpets and coiled in the corner of a bathroom.

HUGE HAIRBALL

Ty, a 392-lb (178-kg) tiger at Wildlife Rescue and Rehabilitation in Seminole, Florida, underwent surgery to remove a hairball the size of a basketball from his stomach. The 17-year-old tiger had been unable to hack up the 4-lb (1.8-kg) hairball because it was so big, and he hadn't eaten for two weeks.

AVIAN MARVEL

In January 2013, Wisdom, a Laysan albatross of the North Pacific, gave birth to her 36th chick—at age 62! The average Laysan albatross dies at less than half her age.

STOWAWAY FISH

In the wake of the 2011 Japanese tsunami, a striped beakfish, native to Asia, crossed the Pacific Ocean to Washington State in the U.S.A. aboard a small drifting boat. The fish survived the 5,000-mi (8,000-km) journey by feeding on organisms in the vessel.

FAKE SPIDER

A newly discovered species of small spider in Peru makes large fake spiders in order to ward off predators. It forms the decoy arachnids—right down to their eight legs—from pieces of debris and then vibrates its web to make the big spider seem alive.

DOG DETOUR

Hendrix, a six-year-old English springer spaniel, was supposed to be flying in cargo from New Jersey to Phoenix, Arizona, but instead ended up some thousands of miles away, across the Atlantic in Ireland, after the airline put him on the wrong flight.

NEW SPECIES

There are believed to be tens of thousands of olinguitos—relatives of raccoons—living wild in the treetops of Colombia and Ecuador, but until recently, no one knew they even existed. In 2003, Dr. Kristofer Helgen of the Smithsonian's National Museum of Natural History found some misidentified bones and skin in storage at a Chicago museum, but it took another decade for these to be identified and officially unveiled as the first new mammal species to be discovered in the western hemisphere for 35 years.

TRAVELING CAT

Ron Buss's cat Mata Hairi left her home in Portland, Oregon, for her usual short walk on September 1, 2012—and spent the next ten months traveling around the U.S.A. with a hitchhiker who picked her up in a café after thinking she was a stray. With Michael King, she hitched to California and Montana, becoming a local celebrity by riding on top of his backpack. It was only when she was taken to a veterinarian that a scan found a microchip, which led to her being reunited with Ron.

ABSTRACT ARTIST

Forced to stop racing after damaging a knee in 2009, racehorse Metro Meteor has since found fame as an abstract painter. Adopted by artist Ron Krajewski from Rocky Ridge, Maryland, the horse has sold more than 200 paintings for a combined sum of $20,000, and in 2013 was the best-selling artist at Gallery 30 in Gettysburg, Pennsylvania. For his large paintings, which can sell for up to $2,000, there is a waiting list of 120 customers.

Turtle Tears

This yellow-spotted river turtle in the western Amazonian rain forest is being mobbed by butterflies that have come to drink its tears. In a region where salt is rare, the turtles have a plentiful supply of the vital mineral sodium through their diet, prompting dozens of butterflies to flutter around the reptiles' heads for a fortifying drink. If no turtles are around, the butterflies will get their salt fix from animal urine or sweaty humans.

WILD THINGS

In the early 1970s, Hollywood actress Tippi Hedren and her family, including her then 14-year-old daughter Melanie Griffith, invited a full-grown lion, called Neil, into their California home for a photo shoot. Tippi and her husband Noel Marshall were in the process of sourcing a large number of exotic big cats for their movie *Roar*, an experience that would change their views on keeping exotic animals forever.

Tippi hired Neil from Ron Oxley, who lived in Soledad Canyon. She wanted to make a family movie, titled *Roar*, using 25 lions, tigers and other big cats, and in order to get to know lions, she and her family invited a number of young cubs to live at their house. Even small lions can be dangerous, however, and one scratched Melanie Griffith's face with its claws. They also tore up the house. Melanie later said, "She didn't mean to hurt me, but after seven years growing up with lions, I forgot you have to be careful. Just a blow can pop your head like a Ping-Pong ball."

The family then moved, with the lions, to a mountain ranch to film *Roar*. It was a painful experience. Tippi had her arm badly scratched by a leopard, and director of photography Jan de Bont survived a particularly dangerous incident resulting in 220 stitches. The cameramen had positioned themselves in a camouflaged pit, protected with football helmets. When the lions rushed by for the shot, one of the lions saw movement and lashed out with its paw, tearing off de Bont's scalp—he had removed his helmet to get a better shot. The original plan was to shoot *Roar* in nine months, but filming the big cats eventually took five years, and the film was not released until 1981.

Tippi playing with Neil at her home in Sherman Oaks, California.

Life with the Lions

A lion's paws are powerful enough to break a zebra's back—something to bear in mind when playing with them as pets.

Tippi's experience with big cats during the filming of *Roar* convinced her that such animals should not be in close contact with humans, so she turned the ranch where it was filmed into the Shambala Preserve, dedicated to the protection of exotic animals rescued from private collections. Since opening, Shambala has rescued 230 such animals. Although the lions in the pictures here appear to be tame, Tippi now warns that there is no such thing; they never lose their predatory instinct and can attack at any time.

Tippi and Melanie invited lions into their home at a time when the dangers of keeping such animals were not fully understood. Their experience taught them that even big cats are always extremely dangerous and should not be kept as pets. Since 1990, 254 big cats have escaped from captivity, with 143 killed, and exotic cats have killed at least 21 people while in captivity. Today, Tippi campaigns against the exotic animal industry and is lobbying the U.S. Congress to introduce laws restricting the breeding and buying of exotic predators by individuals, which is still legal in the U.S.A.

Melanie Griffith jumps into the pool, while Neil playfully grabs her leg.

Shrew Caravan

To avoid getting lost, young Asian musk shrews form a caravan behind their mother, lining up behind her as she walks and holding on to the fur of the animal in front with their teeth. If they lose contact, they reattach themselves to any moving object—in this case, a child's toy.

JELLYFISH INVASION

A mass invasion by jellyfish forced one of the world's largest nuclear reactors to shut down on September 29, 2013. Operators of the Oskarshamn nuclear plant in Sweden had to scramble the reactor after tons of jellyfish blocked the pipes that bring in cool water to the plant's turbines.

GUILTY LOCUST

In 1866, a locust was put on trial in Croatia for the damage caused by its swarm. It was sentenced to death by drowning.

STALKING CROC

New Zealand kayaker Ryan Blair was trapped on Governor Island off the coast of Western Australia for two weeks by a giant crocodile that he thought would eat him if he tried to escape. Having been taken to the remote location by boat, Blair had intended to kayak the 2.5 mi (4 km) back to the mainland, but every time he tried to paddle away, the 20-ft-long (6-m) crocodile stalked him, forcing him to return to the island. Desperate for water, he finally shone a light to alert a rescuer.

DOCTOR PARROT

Barbara Smith-Schafer from Lincolnshire, England, has a guardian angel watching over her in the form of her husband's African gray parrot, Dominic. Barbara has been diagnosed with a sleeping disorder called sleep apnea, which causes her breathing to be blocked, but Dominic has learned to recognize the heavy snoring that marks a possible attack and when he hears it, he wakes her by flapping his wings and pecking at her shoulder.

SENSING DANGER

A few hours before Hurricane Jeanne battered Gainesville, Florida, in 2004, butterflies in the University of Florida's experimental rain forest went into hiding, wedging themselves under rocks and disappearing into tree hollows. Eardrum-like organs on their abdomens may have alerted them to seek shelter when they sensed a marked drop in air pressure.

SNAKE INTRUDER

Police investigating a break-in at a charity store in Queensland, Australia, found the culprit was a 19-ft-long (5.7-m) python. Seeing a roof panel cut in half, clothing knocked over and crockery smashed, officers naturally suspected a human intruder until they discovered a smelly pool of vomit and the snake lying next to a wall. It is thought the 37-lb (17-kg) python entered the store through the roof, which was damaged in a cyclone in 2011.

CURLY TUSKS

The tusks of the babirusa pig of Indonesia grow up and curve backward over its eyes, often reaching a length of 12 in (30 cm)— so long that they sometimes pierce its forehead.

WAYWARD MOTH

A giant Atlas moth, which has a 12-in (30-cm) wingspan, was discovered by a family in their garden in Lancashire, England— more than 6,000 mi (9,600 km) from its Southeast Asian habitat.

EAGLE SELFIE

A sea eagle snatched a video camera that was positioned to take pictures of crocodiles in Western Australia and then recorded its two-hour flight, along with taking a couple of selfies. The 6-in-long (15-cm) camera vanished from a spot next to the Margaret River, but wildlife rangers had no idea of the thief's identity until the camera was retrieved 70 mi (112 km) away. When finally the film was played, the feathered culprit was seen poking its face into the lens.

Death Grip

Sloths can retain their grip on tree branches even after death. As they spend most of their lives in trees—sleeping, mating and giving birth while hanging upside down from branches—their claws and muscles have been developed for climbing, albeit slowly. This has made their grip so strong that sometimes when they die they are found still hanging from the branch hours later.

Trunk Snap

Looking for a quick bite, this ambitious Nile crocodile clamped its powerful jaws onto the trunk of a young elephant as it drank water from a pool in Zambia's South Luangwa National Park. The startled elephant trumpeted loudly, shook itself free and ran off into the bush, leaving the croc to search for a more modest meal. Lodge worker Ian Salisbury, who took the photo, said the same crocodile had earlier attacked a buffalo. The scene is a case of life imitating art, after the Rudyard Kipling story about the elephant that got its trunk when a crocodile bit it on the nose and stretched it.

PHONEY NAMES

Struggling to think up names quickly for 101 new beetle species that have recently been discovered in Papua New Guinea, scientists found inspiration by looking through the local phone book and choosing human family surnames at random.

SWEET REVENGE

When a fig wasp lays its eggs inside a fig but fails to pollinate it, the tree retaliates by dropping those unpollinated figs to the ground, killing the baby wasps inside.

RAT CATCHERS

A group of urban hunters—the Ryders Alley Trencher-Fed Society—meets regularly in New York to hunt rats with their pet dogs on the streets of Manhattan.

BATMOBILE

The New Zealand batfly cannot fly and does not even have wings—it hitches rides on bats instead.

MINE SEEKERS

Bees in Croatia are being trained to detect unexploded land mines, which have littered the country since the Balkan Wars in the 1990s. During four years of fighting in Croatia, 90,000 mines were planted all over the country, but now honeybees are being taught to seek out the smell of the explosive by associating it with food.

TWO HEADS

Yuri Yuravliov of Kiev, Ukraine, has a six-year-old female Central Asian tortoise with two heads, two hearts, one heart-shaped shell and six legs. The two heads even have different tastes in food. The left head is more dominant and opts for green vegetables, like lettuce, while the other prefers brightly colored food, such as carrots.

TIGER TRAINER

Animal trainer Randy Miller spends his days being attacked by a fully grown, 400-lb (181-kg) tiger—and he usually walks away without a scratch. Randy, who runs a facility in Big Bear, California, has trained big cat Eden to leap 15 ft (4.6 m) through the air at him and then pin him to the ground. The terrifying attacks are so realistic that Randy's animals have appeared in movies including *Gladiator*, *Transformers 2* and *The Last Samurai*.

ARTISTIC CHIMP

Brent, a 37-year-old chimpanzee who paints colorful pictures with his tongue, earned $10,000 for the Chimp Haven sanctuary in Keithville, Louisiana, by winning first prize in a national art contest.

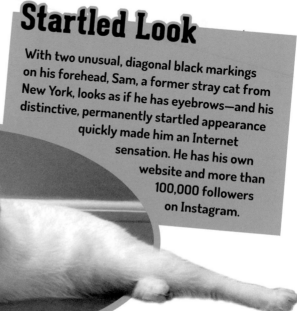

Startled Look

With two unusual, diagonal black markings on his forehead, Sam, a former stray cat from New York, looks as if he has eyebrows—and his distinctive, permanently startled appearance quickly made him an Internet sensation. He has his own website and more than 100,000 followers on Instagram.

Poop Disguise

Predatory birds and wasps usually give the bird-dung spider of Singapore a wide berth because its body looks like an unappetizing dollop of poop. The squat, brown spider hunts by night but spends most of its day huddled motionless on an exposed leaf or branch, and so it needs its disguise to avoid being eaten.

FLAT FACE

With his cute pie face and huge brown droopy eyes that give him a permanent air of innocence, Snoopybabe, a cat from Chengdu, China, has his own Facebook page and around half a million fans online. His owner, Miss Ning, regularly uploads dozens of new pictures of him, often dressing him in a range of designer outfits and even jewelry. Snoopybabe gets his distinctive appearance from his parents—he is a cross between an American short-hair and a Persian cat.

SKIN SURGERY

Veterinarians in Tualatin, Oregon, carried out an operation to remove 2½ lb (1.1 kg) of loose skin from a previously obese dachshund that had lost weight. Obie had once weighed a whopping 77 lb (35 kg), but after he shed 40 lb (18 kg) on an eight-month diet, the loose skin started to drag, so owner Nora Vanatta had it cut off.

CLEANEST CAT

Murli the cat ended up with an unexpected wash and blow-dry after being wedged behind the bumper of his owner's car when he drove it through a car wash. Reinhold Pratl of Hartberg, Austria, drove 15 mi (24 km) to the car wash and took the vehicle through the full cleaning cycle before he realized that his cat had come along for the ride. Cut free from the car, Murli was none the worse for her ordeal apart from the fact that she was soaking wet and smelled of shampoo.

BLIND FAITH

When their blind, eight-year-old dog Abby went missing from their home in Fairbanks, Alaska, during a heavy snowstorm, the Grapengeter family thought they would never see their beloved hound again—but a week later she turned up at the home of a local veterinarian 10 mi (16 km) away, having survived freezing temperatures of –40°F (–40°C) without even a hint of frostbite.

HURRICANE EVACUATION

Twelve hours before Hurricane Charley hit Florida in 2004, eight tagged sharks in Pine Island Sound fled abruptly to the open ocean. It is believed sharks sense the air and water pressure changes caused by an impending storm.

SIGN LANGUAGE

Angi and Don Holt-Parks from Toledo, Ohio, learned sign language and taught it to Rudi, their deaf pitbull mix, so they could communicate with the dog.

LION PASSENGER

A motorist who spotted an escaped lion roaming the streets of Kuwait lured it into the back of his car and then slammed the door shut to keep it secure. The man then got into the car with the angry lion to call the police.

MIRACULOUS SURVIVAL

Wasabi, a two-year-old cat owned by Stephanie Gustafson, survived a fall from the 11th floor of a housing block in Juneau, Alaska, after chasing a mosquito out a window. She escaped with a fractured leg and broken bones, which surgeons repaired in an operation.

LATE LUNCH

Baby adders go into hibernation shortly after they are born and often do not have their first meal until they are one year old.

Color Change

A dull olive-green color the rest of the year, the male Indian bullfrog (*Hoplobatrachus tigerinus*) dresses to impress in the mating season. To attract a female, his skin dramatically turns bright yellow while his prominent vocal sacs become a vivid blue. The Indian bullfrog has one other idiosyncrasy: despite being relatively large, it can jump over the surface of water the same as it does on land.

Bike Bird

No, your eyes are not deceiving you—Myles Bratter of Dover, New Hampshire, regularly rides his motorcycle at speeds of up to 80 mph (128 km/h) with Rainbow, his pet ruby macaw parrot, perched on his shoulder. Myles sent Ripley's this picture of him with speed-loving Rainbow, who is not tied down in any way, on the bike. The talented bird can speak over 160 words and phrases and has been photographed with dignitaries including George H. W. Bush as part of her fundraising work to help homeless people. Although she was born back in 1995, Rainbow has plenty of air miles left in her yet, as macaws can live to be over 100 years old.

CALMING PARROT

Jim Eggers from St. Louis, Missouri, suffers from bipolar disorder, but whenever he feels an episode coming on, he relies on his pet parrot, Sadie, to calm him down with a few wise words. She now accompanies him everywhere, carried in a backpack adapted to hold her cage.

TOAD VIBES

Common toads that had been breeding in a shallow Italian lakebed suddenly moved uphill in 2009—five days before a strong earthquake struck the region. The toads returned to the pool as soon as the quake's last aftershock had occurred.

HOMEWARD BOUND

After going missing on a family vacation in Daytona, Florida, Holly, a four-year-old cat owned by Jacob and Bonnie Richter, returned exhausted to within a mile of their home in West Palm Beach, having traveled 190 mi (306 km) in two months.

Vampire Cat

Lazarus, a kitten found wandering the streets of Johnson City, Tennessee, has a cleft palate that has left him looking like a vampire. With no upper lip, his lower fangs protrude, and he appears to be missing a nose, too. Yet, despite his condition, he is so loveable that his new owner, Cindy Chambers, is using him as a therapy cat to help change people's perceptions about animals and people with disabilities.

Walking Tall

Zarafa became such a sensation when she arrived in France that her image was painted on plates and embroidered into tapestries.

GIRAFFE Femelle.

In the 19th century, a giraffe called Zarafa rode on the back of a camel before walking 560 mi (900 km) across France from Marseille to Paris.

As the first giraffe ever to be seen in France, she was greeted by huge crowds throughout her epic 44-day walk. When she finally arrived in Paris, 100,000 people turned out to see her.

Captured in the Sudan in 1826, Zarafa was a gift from the viceroy of Egypt, Muhammad Ali, to the King of France, Charles X. The one-year-old giraffe was taken to Khartoum loaded onto the back of a camel. She was then transported down the Nile and across the Mediterranean Sea in the cargo hold of a ship. A hole cut into the ship's deck allowed her long neck to poke through. After 32 days at sea, she then had to walk from Marseille to Paris. She set off on hoof on May 20, 1827. All along her route people marveled at this strange 12-ft-tall (3.7-m) creature.

In Paris, fashionable ladies arranged their hair into towering styles, and spotted fabrics became all the rage. Zarafa remained the star attraction at the Jardin des Plantes zoo until her death in 1845.

AGENT SWAN
An Egyptian man arrested a swan and took it to a police station because he thought the bird was a spy. He became suspicious when he noticed the swan was carrying an electronic device, but it turned out to be a wildlife-tracking instrument.

WALKING SHARK
A previously unknown species of small shark, *Hemiscyllium halmahera*, uses its fins to walk along the ocean floor. The 30-in-long (76-cm) shark, which was recently discovered off the coast of Indonesia, wiggles along the seabed so that it can hunt for small fish and crustaceans.

ELEPHANT EXODUS
Just before the massive 2004 earthquake and tsunami devastated the Indian coast, elephants were seen breaking their chains and fleeing to higher ground.

SPOILED SHELLS
Fewer than 300 of Madagascar's ploughshare tortoises are living in the wild, prompting some conservationists to mark the animals' beautiful shells in order to reduce their value to poachers.

SILK THREAD
The silk used to form a silkworm's cocoon is actually hardened saliva that has been secreted from its mouth, and it can unravel into a single thread up to 1 mi (1.6 km) long.

STRETCH JELLY
Although its body is usually only about 6 ft (1.8 m) in length, the lion's mane jellyfish has tentacles that can grow up to 120 ft (37 m), making it longer than a blue whale.

DOGGED DETERMINATION
After his owner John Dolan of Bay Shore, Long Island, New York, was admitted to the hospital, Zander, a white Samoyed–husky mix, missed him so much that he sneaked out of the house and tracked his scent to the hospital 2 mi (3.2 km) away, crossing a highway and a stream to get there.

SINISTER SKULL
The pink underwing moth caterpillar of Australasia and North America has sinister face markings on its head that look uncannily like a human skull so that it can scare off predators.

Strange Markings

It is difficult to work out how many heads or legs Evita, a giant anteater at San Francisco Zoo, really has! The markings on her front legs could be mistaken for a panda's head. What is certain is that if the newborn baby on her back grows up to look like mom, she'll be easy to recognize.

ELASTIC NESTS

Long-tailed tits are small songbirds that deliberately weave stretchy spiders' webs into their nests to allow the structure to expand as their chicks grow.

FLAB LAB

Mike, an obese 133-lb (60-kg) labrador, lost 37 lb (17 kg) in seven months at a rescue center in Leicestershire, England, by going for regular walks in a tank of water—even though he was too big to fit in it at first. Before the hydrotherapy treatment, Mike was so heavy and unfit that he damaged a ligament in one of his legs and would be gasping for breath after waddling just short distances.

NEW LEGS

After losing his rear hooves to severe frostbite in Augusta County, Virginia, Hero the calf was able to walk again thanks to a pair of new prosthetic legs fitted by a company from New Jersey.

KILLER CROC

Over a 20-year period, Gustave, a 20-ft-long (6-m) Nile crocodile living in Africa's Lake Tanganyika, is thought to have killed more than 200 people and has so far resisted all attempts to be killed or captured.

ICY ESCAPE

Five donkeys narrowly escaped an icy death in rural Turkey in December 2013. The donkeys had huddled together for warmth in freezing temperatures in the Sanliurfa province in south eastern Turkey but were overcome by bad weather and had literally frozen stiff. Local officials sent a rescue team to save the animals, which had to carry the donkeys to safety, as they were too cold to walk. They were taken to a warm stable where they thawed out, and were fed and checked over by veterinaries.

WRONG CAT

Karen Jones of Kent, England, was heartbroken after the funeral of her beloved pet cat Norman, only to discover that she had buried the wrong animal. She was sure it was her black cat that she had found lying dead on a busy road, but a day after the backyard burial Norman turned up in the kitchen and began drinking his tea.

OH DEER!

The city center of Nara, Japan, is home to a herd of more than 1,000 sika deer who happily roam the streets among the busy traffic and pedestrians.

BEEFY BEETLE

The 6-in-long (15-cm) Hercules beetle of South America can lift 850 times its own body weight—the equivalent of a human lifting a 65-ton object. The male beetle also has fighting horns that are longer than its body.

BOTH ENDS

Despite being unremarkable to look at, woodlice can drink from both ends of their body—either through their mouth or their anus. They have tubelike structures on their posterior called uropods, which use capillary action to pull water up and into the anus.

RECORD BROOD

In 2013, a mallard duck at a wildlife reserve in Arundel, England, successfully hatched no fewer than 24 ducklings—which is three times the average number of hatches and the largest brood ever recorded.

SQUIRREL RAMPAGE

A gang of ten gray squirrels caused $21,000 worth of damage at a lawn bowling club in Edinburgh, Scotland, by eating part of a clubhouse. The rampaging rodents gnawed through 6-in-thick (15-cm) wooden joists and electrical wiring, causing the ceiling to collapse.

Squirting Blood

The short-horned lizard, which lives in the deserts and prairies of North America, shoots blood out of its eye as a defense mechanism to scare off predators. The blood is propelled from ducts in the corner of the eye and can spurt a distance of 3 ft (1 m). As well as warding off predators, the blood contains a chemical that is noxious to wolves and coyotes.

Easy Rider

In *Ripley's Believe It or Not! Download the Weird*, we told you about Norman, a shaggy Briard dog owned by the Cobb family of Canton, Georgia, who has been riding a scooter since he was a puppy and can cover 30 yd (27 m) in under 30 seconds. Well now Norman, who has his own Facebook page and over two million fans on YouTube, has learned to ride a bicycle, resting his front paws on the handlebars and pedaling expertly with his back paws.

DOG VACATIONS

The Paw Seasons holiday resort in Somerset, England, offers luxury two-week vacations for dogs—for a cool £47,000 ($70,000) a pet. The package includes a designer leash, collar and coat, a spa and grooming session, surfing on the beach, behavioral lessons, a custom-made doghouse in a replica of their owner's home, and screenings of *Lassie* and *101 Dalmatians* while chewing on dog-friendly popcorn.

SPLIT SHELL

An injured endangered green sea turtle that was washed ashore at Key West, Florida, had its fractured shell repaired by local dentist Fred Troxel using denture adhesive. He used the acrylic resin to bond two metal orthopedic plates across the 10-in (25-cm) split on the turtle's shell.

INFLATABLE SNAKE

Burmese pythons' hearts enlarge by up to 40 percent after they've eaten, and many of their organs, including the long digestive tract, double in size to enable them to swallow and digest large prey.

BOOMING BARK

Charlie, a golden retriever owned by Belinda Freebairn of Adelaide, Australia, has a bark that has been measured at 113.1 decibels—that's louder than a rock concert or a pneumatic drill.

TURTLE PEE

The Chinese soft-shelled turtle urinates from its mouth. The urine travels through the reptile's bloodstream to its mouth, where it has strange, gill-like projections. The turtle then submerges its head in a puddle of water and spits out the pee.

MUSICAL FISH

Japanese researchers have found that, although famed for their short attention span, goldfish can distinguish between the music of Johann Sebastian Bach and Igor Stravinsky.

FISH CANDLE

The eulachon, or candlefish, found on America's Pacific Coast, is so fatty during spawning that it can be dried, threaded on a wick and burned as a candle.

SLIME DEFENSE

A single hagfish can turn a bucket of water into slime in seconds. The fish is covered in slime glands, and when attacked, it releases the slime as a defense mechanism, choking the airways of predators as large as sharks.

SUPER SNAKE

Titanoboa, a snake that lived in South America 58 million years ago, grew up to 50 ft (15 m) long and had a mouth large enough to swallow a crocodile—whole.

RAM RAIDERS

A flock of 80 sheep invaded a ski shop in the Austrian resort of St. Anton. It is thought one sheep saw its reflection in a mirror and went in to investigate, and being sheep, the rest decided to follow.

JAMAICAN ICON

Biologist Paul Sikkel of Arkansas State University discovered a new species of parasite in the coral reefs off Jamaica's coast and named it *Gnathia marleyi* to honor Jamaican reggae musician Bob Marley.

Bizarre Bug

With its striped body and long "hair" sticking out of its rear, this planthopper insect looks just like a troll! The unnamed ¼-in-long (7-mm) creature may be a new species, one of 60 discovered by Conservation International researchers during a three-week trek through the South American rainforest in Suriname. The planthopper's hair-like excretions, which may serve to distract predators, are actually made of wax and are produced by specialized glands in the bug's abdomen.

DOLPHIN'S DINNER

A dolphin caught a huge 10-lb (4.5-kg) cod and then appeared to give it to a human family for their supper! Lucy Watkins and her grandparents were kayaking off the coast of Devon, England, when the dolphin surfaced with the fish and dropped it close to Lucy's boat. The friendly dolphin then nudged it to within 5 ft (1.5 m) of her before reappearing with its own dinner, a sea bass.

MOLE DIG

Archaeologists discovered a series of valuable 2,000-year-old Roman artifacts at an ancient fort in Cumbria, England, after the relics had been dug up by burrowing moles.

COLOR CHANGE

Reindeer change their eye color, from gold in summer to blue in winter. The blue color reduces the amount of light that is reflected out of their eyes, and this has the result of boosting their vision for the dark winters.

TWO-TONE LAMB

A lamb named Battenberg was born with black markings on one side of his face and white on the other—and while his front right and back left legs are black, the other two legs are white. His distinctive coloring helped save his life by ensuring that he was spotted in deep snow shortly after he was born in the Brecon Beacons National Park in Wales.

SIX-CLAWED LOBSTER

A mutant six-clawed lobster was caught off the coast of Massachusetts in 2013. Donated to the Maine State Aquarium in Boothbay Harbor, 4-lb (1.8-kg) Lola has a normal claw on one side, but instead of a singular claw on the other, she has five claws like a hand. The extra claws are either a genetic mutation or an unusual regrowth from a damaged or lost claw.

LARGER FEMALE

The female blanket octopus can be 40,000 times heavier and 100 times larger than a male—that's the equivalent to an average human standing next to a walnut. The female can reach 6½ ft (2 m) in length and weigh 22 lb (10 kg), but the male often measures just 0.9 in (2.4 cm) and weighs no more than 0.009 oz (0.25 g).

COBRA ALERT

In April 2013, police in Hanoi, Vietnam, arrested the driver of a car who was traveling with 53 live king cobras as passengers.

Bulldog Cow

It may have a head like a bulldog, but believe it or not, this is a calf that once belonged to Tom McVey of Texas.

De-FROG-sted

The wood frog survives a Canadian winter by effectively dying for weeks. Covered in ice, it looks dead but has simply frozen itself solid on the forest floor to cope with the intense cold, and when the temperature eventually rises, it thaws out and springs back to life.

Frozen

Defrosted

PET CAPYBARA
Melanie Typaldos and Richard Loveman keep Gary, a 110-lb (50-kg) capybara, as a pet at their home in Buda, Texas. They adopted the giant rodent after seeing capybaras while on vacation in Venezuela. They even let their pet sleep in their bed.

SKATEBOARDING DOGS
Biuf, a skateboarding bulldog, has become such an Internet star, with thousands of followers on Facebook, that his owner, Ivan Juscamaita, has opened a school in Lima, Peru, to teach other dogs to skate.

TOUGH GUY
The grasshopper mouse of North America can eat the highly poisonous Arizona bark scorpion without any ill effects because it is immune to the scorpion's venom, which instead acts as a painkiller to the mouse.

IRON SUPPLEMENT

Farmers sometimes feed their cows magnets that sit in their stomachs for their entire lives. The magnets attract any accidentally eaten metal, preventing it from causing harm to the cows.

TORTOISE TUNES

Celebrated pianist Richard Clayderman performed a selection of romantic tunes to Galápagos tortoises in London Zoo, England, in an effort to encourage them to mate.

CROC ESCAPE

After heavy rain allowed 15,000 crocodiles to escape from Rakwena Crocodile Farm in northern South Africa, one croc was found on a school rugby field 75 mi (120 km) away.

MEERKAT MIMIC

The African drongo bird can imitate the warning sound of meerkats. When the real meerkats run to the safety of their burrows, it swoops down and steals any food they have left behind.

WORKING DOG

Misty, Elaine Prickett's border collie, works for the administrative team at a quarry in Cumbria, England, handling bank notes and credit cards and returning them to customers. She also waits at the window for customers to arrive, then takes their ticket and finds a staff member to process the paperwork.

UNIQUE NOSES

Cows can be identified by their noseprints, which, just like human fingerprints, are unique.

Trapdoor Spider

The trapdoor spider lives in an underground burrow, the entrance to which is a cunningly camouflaged trapdoor made of vegetation and soil and hinged on one side with silk.

While waiting for prey, the spider holds on to the underside of the door and as soon as one of the silk "trip" lines are disturbed above ground, the trapdoor springs open and the spider leaps out to snatch its meal.

ARTFUL DODGERS

Ants can survive in the intense heat of a microwave oven because they are small enough to dodge the rays.

RAINING SPIDERS

Local people thought it was raining spiders when thousands of the creatures were found dangling from overhead power lines in one huge web in the Brazilian town of Santo Antônio da Platina in 2013. The spiders had temporarily joined thousands of individual webs together to form a massive web that extended more than 26 ft (8 m) above ground and up to 10 ft (3 m) in diameter. Strong winds have been known to pick up such massive webs, with the spiders, and carry them for miles until the wind drops, so the web falls and it seems to be raining spiders.

LONELY ROACHES

Cockroaches can suffer from loneliness and show signs of depression when separated from each other. If young cockroaches are not in constant physical contact with one another, they suffer isolation syndrome and take longer to develop into adults.

HITCHIN' A RIDE

While observing dolphins near Kalamos, Greece, in June 2012, researchers photographed an octopus riding on the belly of a dolphin as it leapt from the water.

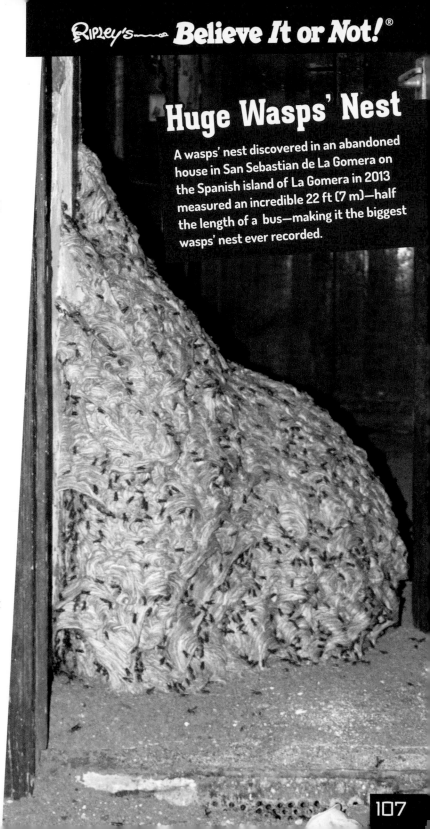

Huge Wasps' Nest

A wasps' nest discovered in an abandoned house in San Sebastian de La Gomera on the Spanish island of La Gomera in 2013 measured an incredible 22 ft (7 m)—half the length of a bus—making it the biggest wasps' nest ever recorded.

Beetle Revenge: Part 1

Frogs and toads consider beetle grubs to be a tasty snack, but Epomis ground beetle larvae have turned the tables and are able to eat amphibians many times their size. The baby beetle performs a dance with its antennae to lure the toad into launching an attack, but at the last minute, it dodges out of the way and quickly latches onto the toad with its spiked jaw. It then sucks the toad dry, eventually reducing it to just a pile of bones.

1. Lure!

2. Attack!

3. Eat!

WALKING UPRIGHT

Born with bones missing from his front legs, Harvey, a kitten at an animal rescue center in Glasgow, Scotland, learned to get around by crawling on his "elbows" or by walking upright on his back legs.

RENT-A-GOAT

In August 2013, the historic Congressional Cemetery in Washington, D.C., hired 58 goats for a week at a cost of $4,000 to act as lawn mowers and eat invasive plant species up to 7 ft (2.1 m) high.

BUMPER RIDE

A lucky black kitten nicknamed Pumpkin suffered nothing worse than a broken paw after being trapped for 22 hours and traveling about 100 mi (160 km) along upstate New York roads wedged behind the bumper of Stacey Pulsifer's Jeep.

DUNG ROAMIN'

Several species of frogs in Sri Lanka use mounds of fresh elephant dung as a moist, temporary home.

SPLIT PERSONALITY

A two-headed turtle named Thelma and Louise was born at San Antonio Zoo, Texas, in June 2013. The baby turtle ate with both heads but displayed a split personality, the right side being curious while the left was more aggressive.

GUARD CROCS

Instead of guard dogs, Awirut Nathip uses two adult crocodiles to protect his house in Thailand—and unsurprisingly, he has not been burgled in 15 years. He keeps Nguen under the house in a ditch because he is so aggressive, while Thong patrols the yard, often lying in front of the door as an extra deterrent.

ELUSIVE HIPPO

A hippopotamus spent over six months living in a sewage plant in Cape Town, South Africa, after escaping from a nature reserve. While on the run, the young male eluded capture for weeks in a city lake and also popped up in suburban gardens before setting up home in the sewage plant. He was finally caught and shipped to a game reserve.

DEVOTED DOG

For more than two months after his owner died, Tommy, a 12-year-old German shepherd dog, turned up every day at the church she used to attend. The dog headed to the church in San Donaci, Italy, as soon as the bells began to ring each afternoon, just as he had done for years when his owner was alive. Tommy even attended his owner's funeral, following her coffin as it was carried into the church. The local priest was so impressed by his devotion that he allowed him to sit in front of the altar during services.

LONG FUR

Colonel Meow, a Himalayan-Persian mix owned by Anne Marie Avey and Eric Rosario of Los Angeles, California, has hair that is an astonishing 9 in (23 cm) long. The cat, who has his own website, Facebook page and YouTube channel with more than two million views, has such long hair that it takes two people to brush it, which Anne Marie and Eric do three times a week.

Beetle Revenge: Part 2

The adult Epomis ground beetle continues this unusual behavior, biting, paralyzing and eating frogs larger than themselves.

Flesh-Eaters

Skulls Unlimited, a company based in Oklahoma City, Oklahoma, used thousands of tiny dermestid beetles to remove the flesh from this beached, dead 40-ft-long (12-m) humpback whale before reconstructing it as a skeleton.

The bones of the whale had to be separated and placed in containers for the beetles to be able to do their work . The whale was then degreased and chemically whitened, making the bones sanitary and ready to display at the Museum of Osteology, also in Oklahoma.

1

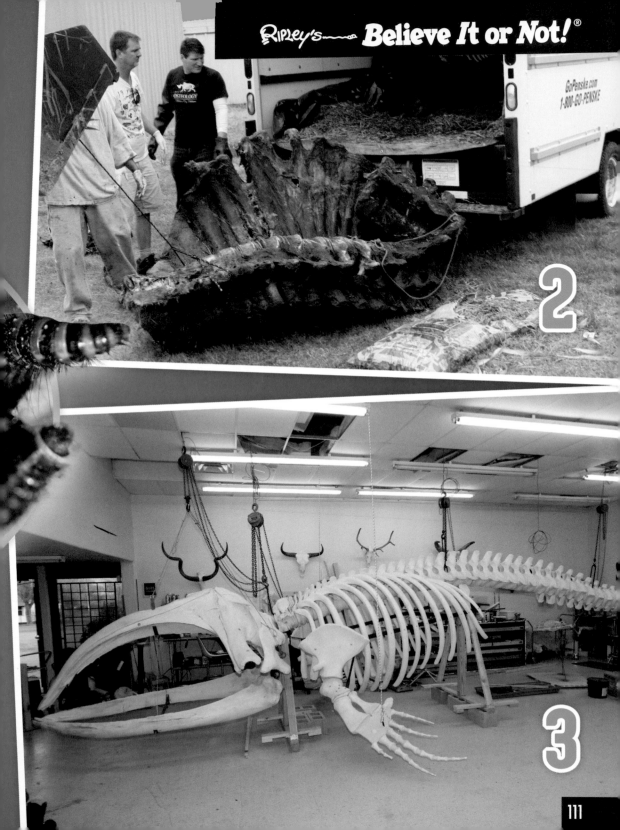

GoPenske.com
1-800-GO-PENSKE

2

3

Peculiar Bodies

Ayanna Williams has grown her fingernails for more than 20 years, and they now measure more than 18 in (45 cm) long. Seven years ago, she started growing her toenails, too. The nails on her big toes grew over 4 in (10 cm) long and those on her little toes grew 2 in (5 cm).

Nail Queen

PECULIAR BODIES

On the phone

Applying makeup

Brushing her teeth

Drinking a glass of water

Signing a letter

The 56-year-old grandmother from Houston, Texas, devotes several hours a day tending to her nails and admits she is a perfectionist when it comes to her "ten jewels." The nails are capped (painted on the top and around the edges) to help prevent them from breaking, and Ayanna is a regular at Spathena in Houston, where manicurist Athena Elliot works hard to keep the nails healthy.

When cooking in the kitchen Ayanna needs plenty of room because her fingernails get in the way, and she does not wash dishes by hand because her nails don't fit in the sink. Life can be difficult, but she just takes things at her own pace and eventually gets the job done—and she has plenty of family to help out.

Every morning when she wakes up, she asks herself if she should cut them—but it is easier said than done. She once said, "I love them. They are 50 percent of who I am. To cut them would be like losing a limb."

Toenail Loss

Ayanna eventually decided to cut her long toenails. It was not an easy decision, but life wasn't always easy with them. She had to walk slowly on her heels, like a penguin, and when going upstairs she had to walk sideways. She mostly wore flip-flops, as she couldn't wear socks or boots in winter and could only change into tennis shoes if she cut holes in the ends for her toenails to poke through. Despite these challenges, Ayanna did love her long toenails and is currently growing them again.

Horned Man

Colombian body modification artist Cain Tubal shows off his silicone horn implants and his metal facial piercings at the third annual International Tattoo Convention in Medellin, Colombia.

The convention showcased unconventional body-shock artists from all over the world, the most extreme of whom were suspended by metal barbs in their back or on razor-sharp hooks pierced through their skin.

HUGE TUMOR

Gemma Fletcher of Sheffield, England, had her daughter Ava delivered by emergency cesarean section only 32 weeks into her pregnancy after doctors discovered she had a kidney tumor that was even bigger than her baby. Little Ava weighed 6.4 lb (2.9 kg) at birth, but the tumor weighed 7.5 lb (3.4 kg).

FROZEN CORPSES

The Alcor Life Extension Foundation in Scottsdale, Arizona, provides safe storage for more than 120 frozen people, which it hopes one day to bring back to life.

MUMMIFIED ARM

In early 2012, an anonymous donor gave a mummified arm to the National Museum of Civil War Medicine in Frederick, Maryland. It is believed to have come from the 1862 Battle of Antietam and to have been found and preserved by a local farmer.

SLEEP TREK

Joy Grigg from Cornwall, England, disappeared after climbing out of her kitchen window while sleepwalking—and was later found unharmed in a hedge 6 mi (10 km) away. Two months earlier, in January 2013, she had walked 5 mi (8 km) in her sleep. Her husband kept calling her cell phone until the vibration in her pocket eventually woke her up.

BABY BLUE

Two-year-old Areesha Shehzad from Bradford, England, has to spend at least 12 hours a day under the glare of blue UV lights to save her from a one-in-four-million liver condition. Crigler-Najjar Syndrome means she is missing an enzyme that breaks down a toxic chemical found in red blood cells. Without the daily phototherapy treatment, she could succumb to fatal brain damage.

SIGHT TRICK

People who have been able to see during their entire life and are suddenly struck blind can develop Anton's Syndrome, in which they are mentally unaware that they have become blind.

BEARDED SCHOOLGIRL

A 16-year-old Chinese schoolgirl grew a full beard and mustache after the life-saving drug medication she was given to tackle a rare form of anemia produced unwanted side effects. As well as the tough black beard on her face, the girl's legs and arms became covered in thick hair—a condition called hirsutism.

EYES WRITE!

Tapan Dey of Kolkata, India, can write neatly by holding a pen with various parts of his body, including his eyes, nose, mouth and hair. He can also write with both hands and both feet simultaneously.

SLEEP EATER

Mother-of-three Lesley Cusack from Cheshire, England, eats up to 2,500 calories a night—in her sleep. She suffers from a sleep-related eating disorder and has no control over what she eats while sleepwalking. Her nighttime feasts have included an entire bowl of fruit, Vaseline, cough syrup, raw potatoes, soap powder and emulsion paint!

KNIFE BLADE

Billy McNeely of Fort Good Hope in Canada's Northwest Territories wondered why he suffered back pain and set off metal detectors—until he learned he had a 2¾-in (7-cm) knife blade buried in his back.

RARE BLOOD

James Harrison of New South Wales, Australia, has donated his rare type of blood 1,000 times. It contains an antibody that has saved over two million Australian babies from Rhesus disease, a serious form of anemia.

FOREIGN BODIES

Every year, about 1,500 patients in the U.S.A. have objects accidentally left inside their bodies during surgery. They have included surgical towels, sponges, tubes, a 7-in (18-cm) surgical clamp, a 13-in (33-cm) retractor, a section of a fetal heart monitor and a surgical glove.

Millie and Christine McKoy were born joined at the hip to slaves on a farm in North Carolina in 1851, the eighth and ninth of 14 siblings.

While still toddlers, they were sold to a traveling show and traded between various showmen before Joseph Smith became their manager. In another trade gone wrong, the sisters were stolen and taken to England, where they were abducted at least once more, before Smith and the girl's mother Monemia tracked them down four years later.

In 1899, renowned showman P. T. Barnum booked the twins for his American Museum in New York.

The Two-headed Nightingale

REMARKABLE HUMAN PHENOMENA!
THE AFRICAN TWINS.
(The Engraving by Permission of the Proprietors of the "Picture Times.")

(CHRISTINA AND MILLY.)

These extraordinary Children, only Five Years old, and whom Nature has linked by an Indissoluble Band, about 16 inches in circumference, having excited the most intense interest, and created the greatest sensation wherever they have been witnessed, **ARE NOW ON VIEW**, for a brief period only, at the

EGYPTIAN HALL, PICCADILLY,
From **TWO till FIVE**, and from **SEVEN till NINE o'Clock.**

They were born in Slavery; and their Guardian, appointed by the Orphan Court of Philadelphia, United States, legally apprenticed them to Mr. THOMPSON, of that City, who instantly freed them from their degrading Bondage, and determined to appropriate the Receipts arising from their Public Exhibition to the purpose of Emancipating the Parents of the Children, who are at this moment Slaves on a North-American Plantation. The better feelings of Humanity, as well as the Public Prints, they were feloniously abducted be jointly gratified by their inspection. As already stated in the man who had charge of them, and recovered in Dundee, from the Bedford Hotel, Covent Garden, by the Metropolitan Magistracy, having taken the warmest interest Scotland; the Scottish Authorities, as well as the Metropolitan that have been heretofore exhibited, these in their situation. Unlike most of these Eccentricities of Nature Pleasing and Attractive Appearance, and their **INTERESTING CHILDREN** have an extremely as to astonish every Visitor. They sing, with wonderful Extraordinary Conformation cannot fail to delight as well the unparalleled circumstance of a Duet, arising precision, the Native Melodies of their own Country, and thus be said to form the last, greatest, and most from Two Voices, but originating in the direction of One Mind, may **in the Annals of the Marvellous!**
Startling Novelty ever yet recorded **ADMISSION, ONE SHILLING.**
The immediate attention of the Public to this announcement is earnestly solicited, as they are now en route to the French Capital, where they have received a Special Invitation, and will thence return to Philadelphia to complete their Filial Mission.

When they were eventually returned to the U.S.A., Smith and his wife helped Millie and Christine learn to sing, dance, and play the piano and guitar, promoting them as the "Two-headed Nightingale"—one with a contralto voice, the other a soprano. The pair also mastered five languages and wrote their own poetry, talents that helped make the girls international stars.

The twins were exhibited in London when only five years old.

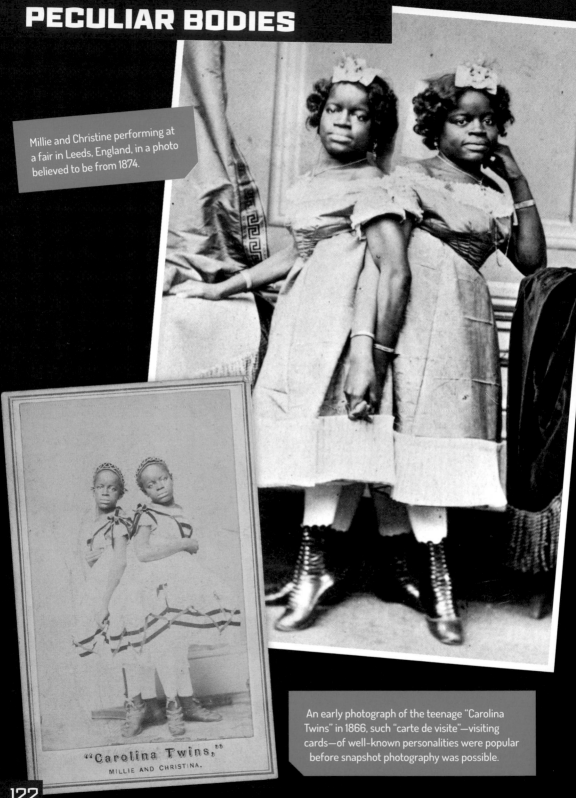

Millie and Christine performing at a fair in Leeds, England, in a photo believed to be from 1874.

"Carolina Twins,"
MILLIE AND CHRISTINA.

An early photograph of the teenage "Carolina Twins" in 1866, such "carte de visite"—visiting cards—of well-known personalities were popular before snapshot photography was possible.

At the height of their popularity, "Millie Christine"—the girls would often refer to themselves as a single person—was performing for thousands of people each day, and 150,000 spectators saw the pair when they visited Philadelphia. They soon earned enough money to buy a farm in North Carolina for their father Joseph—then a free man—and to support schools for black children. They performed at P. T. Barnum's famous American Museum in New York, appeared before Queen Victoria of England on a number of occasions and even received an invitation from the Pope.

They retired from show business in the early 1900s and survived until 1912, when they contracted tuberculosis and died within 24 hours of each other. They are buried at Welches Creek cemetery, North Carolina, where their descendants held a ceremony in 2012 to honor the centenary of their death.

The twins were so popular that they had their own music written for performances in England.

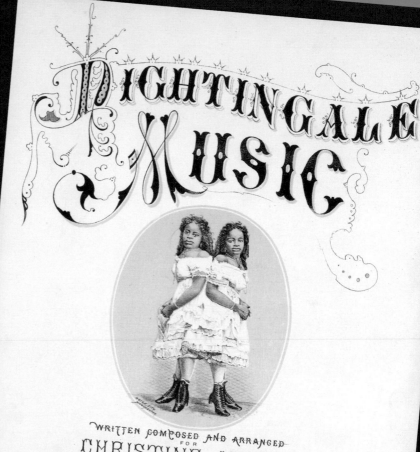

NIGHTINGALE MUSIC

WRITTEN COMPOSED AND ARRANGED FOR
CHRISTINE MILLIE
THE TWO-HEADED NIGHTINGALE.
BY
WILLIAM WILSON.

Nº1. THE DEAR, DEAR FRIENDS AT HOME 3/-
Nº2. (DUET) SISTERS WE, GAY & FREE. 4/-
Nº3. PUT ME IN MY LITTLE BED 3/-
Nº4. NIGHTINGALE SCHOTTISCHE. 3/-
Nº5. NIGHTINGALE MAZURKA 3/-
Nº6. (SONG.) WHIP POOR WILL. 3/-
Nº7. THE SONG OF THE NIGHTINGALE 3/-

PUBLISHED BY EMERY, 408, OXFORD STREET, LONDON, AND HIME & ADDISON, MANCHESTER.

WHISKEY DRIP

Doctors in Taranaki, New Zealand, saved the sight of a patient—Denis Duthie—who was suffering from methanol poisoning, by tube-feeding a bottle of Johnnie Walker whiskey into his body after they had run out of the medical alcohol that they usually use for this treatment.

TRUCK TATTOO

Fire-eater Miss Mena from Myrtle Beach, South Carolina, has a tattoo of a Ford F-150 truck on her upper arm—not because she likes them, but because she has been hit by one three times.

SEVERED ARM

When a Hungarian construction worker severed an arm in an accident in Purbach, Austria, he drove 10 mi (16 km) to the hospital—taking the arm with him. Despite blood pouring from his wound, he even stopped at traffic lights on the way. Then, he parked, walked into the hospital, placed his arm on the reception desk and asked for help.

ACTUAL SIZE!

[YOUR / UPLOADS]

Jar of Nails

Richard M. Gibson of Lafayette, Louisiana, has been saving his fingernail and toenail clippings since 1978. He keeps them in a 10-fl-oz (300-ml) jar, which is now 99 percent full.

HANDY APP

A Scottish company has created a prosthetic hand that can be controlled by a cell phone app. Touch Bionics's "i-limb ultra revolution" features a powered rotating thumb for increased dexterity and 24 different grip options, each activated by a single tap of the screen. This allows the wearer to adjust the hand for different tasks, such as writing, typing or even tying shoelaces.

LUCKY FALL

After Kevin Brockbank collapsed with a heart attack at work in Dundee, Scotland, his life was saved when his 210-lb (94-kg) friend, Martin Amriding, reached out to grab him but instead accidentally fell on him—and the impact kick-started his heart.

HEAD ADS

Brandon Chicotsky from Austin, Texas, sells advertising space on his bald head. He has founded BaldLogo.com where, for $320 a day, companies pay him to walk around town with their logo or brand name temporarily tattooed on his head.

BIG EYES

The eyeballs of people native to the Arctic Circle are 20 percent bigger than those of people from the Equator. This helps them to see better in a part of the world that receives little sunlight for large parts of the year.

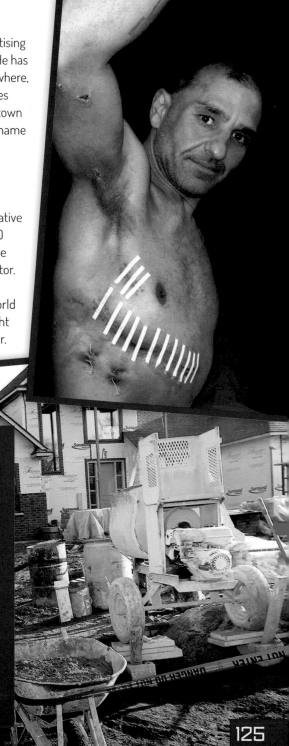

Mixer Mishap

Construction worker Shaukei Oliveira from Chatham, Ontario, Canada, miraculously survived when he was pulled into an operating cement mixer that ripped him open, crushing his bones and leaving his heart and a lung exposed. The 47-year-old had been scraping excess mortar from the edge of the mixing barrel when the paddle caught on his sweater and instantly dragged him inside the powerful machine. Luckily, his colleagues flipped the machine over and managed to free him before he was crushed to death. Even so, in just a few seconds he had suffered several broken ribs, a huge gash across his chest, serious cartilage and nerve damage and a collapsed lung. He was rushed to the hospital and placed on a respirator, but remarkably, two weeks later, he had recovered enough to return home.

Heavy Lifting

Weighing a colossal 1,345 lb (610 kg)—the same as five baby elephants—Khaled Mohsen Shaeri of Saudi Arabia was bed-bound for 2½ years. The country's King Abdullah took a personal interest in his situaton and ordered his evacuation to a hospital. This involved part of the apartment block where Shaeri lived being demolished so that he could be winched out of his home and wheeled onto a forklift truck before being airlifted to the hospital.

EYE WATERING

When archaeologists found the mummy of ancient Egyptian Pharaoh Ramesses IV in Egypt's Valley of the Kings in the late 19th century, they found that his eyes had been replaced with onions.

SCARY SCARS

It is customary for men living on the Sepik River in Papua New Guinea to have their backs cut to make deep scars that create the appearance of crocodile skin.

FOREVER AIRSICK

Since stepping off a plane in Turkey more than eight years ago, Catharine Bell from Northumberland, England, has been almost permanently airsick. She has been diagnosed with the neurological disorder Mal de Debarquement Syndrome, which leaves her with a spinning head and a churning stomach for months at a time.

LIVELY EYES

The focusing muscles of the eyes move about 100,000 times a day. To give your leg muscles the same workout, you would need to walk 50 mi (80 km) daily.

TATTOOED MAYOR

Ray Johnson of Campo, Colorado, is thought to be the U.S.A.'s most tattooed mayor. He has tattoos across his thighs, torso and arms.

TAPEWORM TRAUMA

Sherry Fuller from Essex, England, nearly died after pork tapeworms burrowed into her brain. The infestation, picked up while working in Madagascar, left her with larvae the size of a dime inside her head and dreams that haunted her for two years. She suffered headaches and seizures, her right eye turned black, and when she was given a worming tablet to kill the larvae, her arms, legs and back swelled up.

[YOUR / UPLOADS]

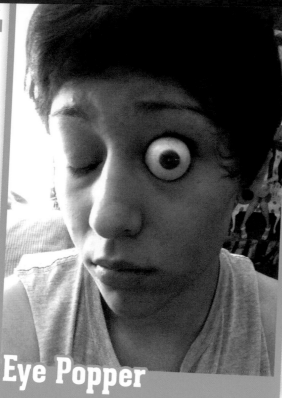

Eye Popper

A big Ripley's fan, 17-year-old Denise Salazar from Tracy, California, sent us these amazing pictures of her popping her eyes out of place. Her extreme and rare talent, which she has had since the age of eight, is called globe luxation and means that by pushing her eyelids back, she can squeeze her eyeballs out a long way. It looks spooky, but luckily she can pop them back in again at will.

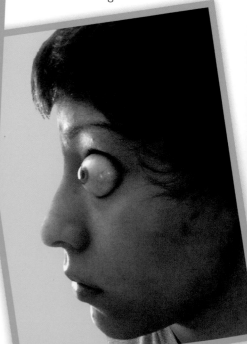

BLADDER BALL

After Amlesh Kumar of Delhi, India, had suffered stomach pains for 20 years, doctors removed a 1-lb (0.5-kg) bladder stone the size of a baseball from his abdomen.

HYPNOTIC MOM

Danielle Davies, from South Yorkshire, England, shed 84 lb (38 kg) and dropped ten dress sizes after her mother Bev hypnotized her into thinking she had been fitted with a gastric band.

LONG LOCKS

Eighty-six-year-old Nguyen Van Chien, from Tien Giang, Vietnam, has not cut his hair since he was in 12th grade—over 70 years ago. His hair now measures more than 13 ft (4 m) long and weighs about 4.4 lb (2 kg).

Human Tail

Vang Seo Chung from Hà Giang Province, Vietnam, has lived for over 40 years with a 1.6-ft-long (0.5-m) tail. The hairy appendage grows from his waist at a rate of 4 in (10 cm) a year. A few years ago, it was 10 ft (3 m) long and he could wrap it around his stomach, but his wife asked him to trim it back. He straps the tail to his body in a small bag when going on journeys. Vang Seo Chung was born normal except for the strange patch of furry hair on his waist. Once it grew, his tail was said to have brought good luck to his family. Whenever he has had it cut, he has become sick.

OLDEST DAD

Ramajit Raghav, a farmer from Sonipat, northern India, claims to have fathered a child at age 96, making him the world's oldest dad. He says he practiced celibacy until he met his wife Shakuntala, who is 44 years his junior, in 2000. He fathered his first son in 2010 at age 94 and had another child two years later.

PERMANENT SMILE

After suffering a stroke in 2004, Malcolm Myatt from Staffordshire, England, has been constantly smiling and laughing because he is no longer able to feel sadness. The stroke interfered with the part of the brain that regulates emotional responses, leaving him liable to start giggling at any time.

Black Scorpion

Performer Jason Black was born with the rare medical condition ectrodactyly (or lobster claw syndrome), which has left him with only two large pincer like fingers, a thumb on each hand and three toes on each foot.

He has turned his deformity to his advantage, however, by reinventing himself as the Black Scorpion, and touring the U.S.A. as a dynamic magician and sideshow performer who swallows balloons, escapes from handcuffs and walks on broken glass.

As well as working for over 15 years at the Austin, Texas, news station KEYE-TV, he is the creative director, writer and performer with the 999 Eyes Freakshow, a surreal sideshow founded by Samantha X and Dylan Blackthorn. The sideshow features body-modified performers and Vaudeville-style artists such as sword-swallowers and human pincushions, as well as artists with genetic anomalies such as Black himself. All of the acts are set to live music by That Damned Band under the musical direction of Dr. Sick. On tour, the show exhibits its grotesque "Mutantstrosities"—an authentic American Dime Museum featuring Patches the two-headed cow, pickled punks and oddities from around the world.

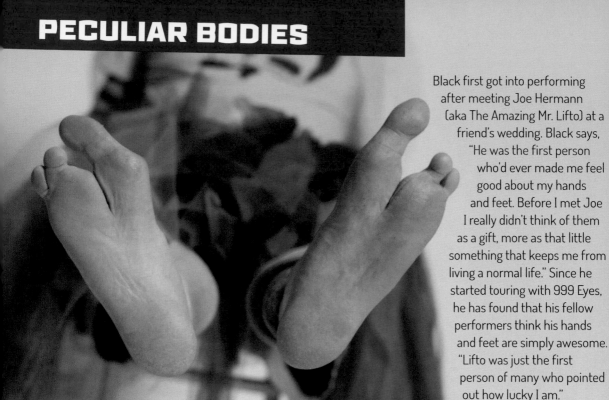

Black first got into performing after meeting Joe Hermann (aka The Amazing Mr. Lifto) at a friend's wedding. Black says, "He was the first person who'd ever made me feel good about my hands and feet. Before I met Joe I really didn't think of them as a gift, more as that little something that keeps me from living a normal life." Since he started touring with 999 Eyes, he has found that his fellow performers think his hands and feet are simply awesome. "Lifto was just the first person of many who pointed out how lucky I am."

LUCKY BREAK

Zoe Sievwright of Dundee, Scotland, survived a fall from 3,500 ft (1,067 m) when her parachute failed during a skydive, suffering only a broken ankle.

WAYWARD ARROW

While walking through a park in Moscow, Russia, Konstantine Myakush was shot through the neck by a sportsman's misfired arrow—yet survived. The 20-in (50-cm) arrow entered on the right side of his neck beneath his jaw and emerged through his throat on the left side. Surgeons removed the arrow successfully as it did not hit any major arteries.

MILLION-DOLLAR BABY

Rachel Evans of Sydney, Australia, was about to return home after a vacation in British Columbia when she went into premature labor at the airport. She gave birth to a daughter at a Vancouver hospital—and was presented with a medical bill for Canadian $1 million.

VILLANOUS VISAGE

Henry Damon of Caracas, Venezuela, has undergone several surgical procedures to make himself look like the villain Red Skull from the Captain America comic—including cutting off a part of his nose, subdermal implants on his forehead and facial tattoos.

RED FLAG

Thirteen-year-old Daniel Carr fell out of a tree and impaled himself on a 2-ft (0.6-m) flagpole in Suffolk, England, in 2005.

FOREIGN ACCENT

After suffering a serious head injury more than eight years ago, Leanne Rowe, an Australian woman born and raised in Tasmania, now speaks in a French accent—even though she has never been to France and has no French friends. She is believed to be Australia's second-ever case of Foreign Accent Syndrome, a condition linked to damage to the part of the brain that controls speech.

Wearing his trademark multicolored bandit mask and proudly displaying his claws, the Black Scorpion aims to change people's perceptions by making them realize that "freaks" are no different from any of the members of the audience.

Nose Job

A Chinese man whose nose was badly damaged in a road accident grew a new one on his forehead. After 22-year-old Xiaolian suffered severe nasal trauma and his nose became infected and damaged beyond repair, surgeons in Fuzhou decided to grow him a new one by implanting a tissue expander under the skin on his forehead. This was cut into the shape of a nose before cartilage from the patient's ribs was used to build the bridge of the nose. Lastly, surgeons constructed the nostrils. The nose grew on Xiaolian's forehead for more than nine months before being transplanted in place of the damaged nose.

VAMPIRE SALIVA

A new drug developed for treating stroke victims is made from Draculin, the saliva of vampire bats.

LENNON CLONE

After buying John Lennon's rotten tooth for $30,000 at an auction in 2011, dentist Dr. Michael Zuk, from Edmonton, Alberta, says he is hoping to extract the DNA and clone the former Beatle!

SKIN FALL

Teen sisters Emma and Stacey Picken from County Durham, England, shed all of their skin every day. They suffer from lamellar ichthyosis, a condition that accelerates their skin-cell turnover, causing the top layer to shed six times faster than most people. They constantly need to vacuum up their fallen skin, and the family washing machine keeps breaking down because it gets blocked with the residue of the skin cream they have to apply twice a day.

BLUE BODY

Jim Hall from Baltimore, Maryland, has his entire body covered in one huge bright-blue tattoo. When employed as a city planner, he kept his tattooed body hidden beneath his work suit, but once he retired in 2007, he was free to get his face and head inked, too. Over a 35-year period, Jim, who calls himself Blue Comma, has spent more than $135,000 on body modification.

SNAIL FACIAL

The Ci:z.Labo beauty salon in Tokyo, Japan, offers live snail facials to customers. The snails are placed on the customer's face and allowed to move around at random, their trail of slime helps to get rid of dead skin, heal the skin after sunburn, and generally moisturize it.

"BLIND" BARBER

Tian Hao, a hair stylist from Shaanxi Province, China, cuts his customers' hair with his eyes closed. He says he uses Zen meditation to feel the "aura" of the hair and to trim it perfectly while keeping his eyes shut. Once he has finished cutting the hair with sharp scissors, he uses a vacuum cleaner—rather than a blow-dryer—to style it.

SHOCK DIAGNOSIS

A 66-year-old Chinese man went to a hospital in Hong Kong seeking treatment for a swelling in his abdomen—and discovered that he was really a woman! The man's condition was caused by an extremely rare combination of two genetic disorders—Turner Syndrome, which causes women to lack some female features including the ability to get pregnant, and congenital adrenal hyperplasia, which makes the patient look like a man. Only six cases of a patient with both conditions have ever been reported.

Skin Ring

Icelandic designer Sruli Recht has produced a gold ring covered in a slice of his own skin. Surgeons removed a 4¼-in (11-cm) flap of skin from his abdomen, and the strip was then salted and tanned and then mounted on the 24-carat gold ring.

SHAKEN NOT HEARD

In 2008, British researchers discovered a 60-year-old woman who could recognize only one voice—that of James Bond actor, Sean Connery!

PERFECT MATCH

When Jonathan Woodlief of Dallas, Texas, needed a kidney transplant, he discovered that his wife of less than a month, Caitlin, was a match, overcoming incredible odds.

PIN NUMBER

Distracted by a phone call, an acupuncturist in Wiener Neustadt, Austria, locked up and went home, completely forgetting that a female patient was still in the treatment room covered in pins. Vivi Ziegler initially felt so relaxed that she fell asleep, but when she woke up alone in the dark and cold, she had to call police to rescue her through a window.

Eyeball Shaving

In China's Sichuan Province, barbers charge 80 cents to scrape customers' eyeballs with a sharp blade. Liu Deyuan is one of a few barbers who still practice the centuries-old tradition of eyeball shaving, which is said to enhance a person's view of life. He dips the blade in water and gently scrapes the insides of both eyelids. Then he pokes a thin metal rod with a smooth ball-shaped end beneath the eyelids and slides it back and forth like a windshield wiper. The whole process takes approximately five minutes, during which time the customer dares not move a muscle. Liu says he has never had an accident, attributing his success to a steady hand.

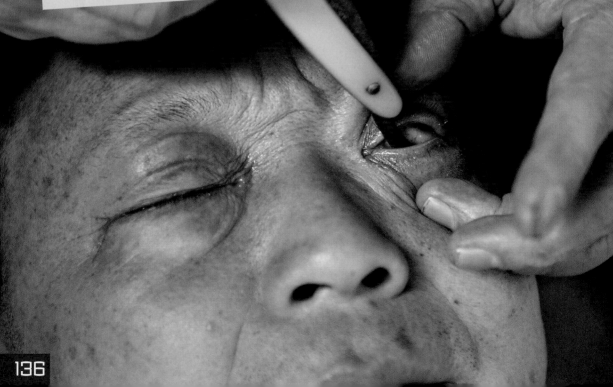

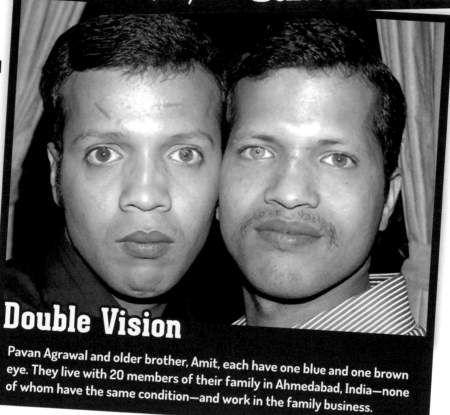

Double Vision

Pavan Agrawal and older brother, Amit, each have one blue and one brown eye. They live with 20 members of their family in Ahmedabad, India—none of whom have the same condition—and work in the family business.

SHOOTING BASKETS

While in a meningitis-induced coma, Maggie Meier of Overland Park, Kansas, was unable to walk, talk or eat, but the comatose high-school basketball player could shoot baskets from her wheelchair! Her neurologist explained that because basketball was ingrained as one of her basic instincts, her body remembered how to do it before it could stand or walk.

BIRD POOP

A Japanese beauty treatment, the Geisha Facial, uses a cream made from rice bran mixed with Asian nightingale excrement.

THROAT THREAT

A 55-year-old woman from Kattappana, India, suffering from a tickly throat, had a live, venomous centipede removed from her throat where it had been stuck for a week.

HEAD TATTOO

Left completely bald by alopecia, 60-year-old grandmother Ann McDonald from Edinburgh, Scotland, got fed up with wearing a wig and decided to have a full head tattoo instead. The £720 ($1,150) tattoo took 12 hours and consists of spiral shading with a black background and curls to represent hair.

FLESH-EATING MAGGOTS

After going on vacation to Peru, Rochelle Harris returned home to Derby, England, and began to hear scratching sounds and experience painful headaches. One morning she woke to find her pillow covered in fluid. When doctors investigated they found a writhing mass of flesh-eating maggots living inside her ear. A New World screwworm had laid its eggs inside Rochelle's ear, and the maggots had chewed a 0.5-in (12-mm) hole into her ear canal. Had the larvae reached her brain, the infestation could have been fatal.

FACE SLAPPING

Thai beauticians charge $350 to slap customers' faces—a treatment that is said to give a younger appearance by firming up flabby skin and helping to eliminate wrinkles and frown lines.

PERFECT MATCH

Gordon Henry from Berkshire, England, separated from his girlfriend Jo Macfarlane in 1993, but 20 years later they rekindled their romance after he came forward to give her one of his kidneys. She suffers from a chronic renal condition and was in desperate need of a donor. When her former partner heard about her situation, he offered his kidney and it proved to be a perfect match.

FACIAL PIERCINGS

Axel Rosales of Villa Maria, Argentina, has no fewer than 280 piercings on his face. The transformation took him 18 months, which averages out at a new piercing every other day.

LEFT BIAS

Although only 10 percent of the U.S. population is left-handed, three of the last four U.S. presidents—George Bush Sr., Bill Clinton and Barack Obama—have been left-handed. Before them, Ronald Reagan was also naturally left-handed but was forced to switch hands as a child.

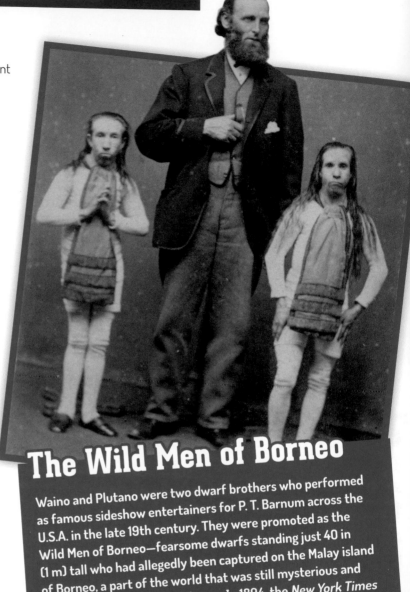

The Wild Men of Borneo

Waino and Plutano were two dwarf brothers who performed as famous sideshow entertainers for P. T. Barnum across the U.S.A. in the late 19th century. They were promoted as the Wild Men of Borneo—fearsome dwarfs standing just 40 in (1 m) tall who had allegedly been captured on the Malay island of Borneo, a part of the world that was still mysterious and exotic for most of their audience. In 1894, the *New York Times* called the pair "two of the strangest freaks ever exhibited in America." In reality, they were Hiram and Barney Davis, brothers from Ohio with learning difficulties who pretended to be wild "savages" on stage. They became famous when Barnum brought them to New York, where they earned large sums of money performing great feats of strength—it was claimed that they could each lift almost ten times their own weight.

Tattooed EYES

Jean Jabril Joseph, a poet from Fort Lauderdale, Florida, has had his sclera, the white part of the eye, tattooed black by means of a series of ink injections.

Although eyeball inking seems like a new trend, as early as the late 19th century, doctors routinely injected ink into patients' eyes to cover up disfiguring corneal scars.

Long Tongue

Philip Romano, a 21-year-old student from Armonk, New York, sent Ripley's this picture of his supersized tongue. One of the longest in the world, it measures an impressive 3.9 in (10 cm) from its tip to the middle of his closed lip.

BOUNCING BABY

Two-year-old Maria Kohler had an amazing escape when she fell 30 ft (9 m) from a fifth-floor balcony in Munich, Germany, bounced off a canvas canopy and landed on grass without suffering even a bruise or a scratch.

BACK FROM DEAD

Having been pronounced dead by doctors at a hospital in Syracuse, New York State, 39-year-old Colleen Burns was lying on the operating table about to have her organs removed for transplant when she suddenly woke up.

FROG DIET

William LaFever, 28, survived for three weeks in Utah's Escalante Desert by eating raw frogs and roots. He'd attempted to walk the 150 mi (240 km) from Boulder, Utah, to Page, Arizona, but soon began to suffer from starvation and dehydration in the intense heat. A rescue helicopter found him just in time—he would probably not have lasted another day.

Vampire Fangs

Sixteen-year-old Wang Pengfei from Chongqing, China, has grown two sharp front teeth that give him fangs like a vampire. He was born with very little hair and grew only these two pointy teeth from his upper gum and none on his lower jaw. His mother is desperate for him to undergo corrective surgery, but doctors say he must wait until he is an adult.

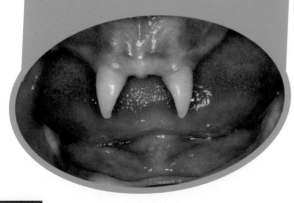

Mikel Ruffinelli's hips measure a staggering 100 in (2.5 m) in circumference, giving her the biggest hips in the world and making her so wide that she has to buy two seats to travel by plane and has to go through doorways sideways. Mikel can only drive a truck, uses a reinforced chair at her home in Los Angeles, California, and can't close the shower door—all because her hips get in the way.

Although her hips are huge, her waist measures just 40 in (100 cm) in circumference. Yet the 40-year-old plus-size model was an athletic teenager with no weight problems. Then, at 22, she put on 56 lb (25 kg) after giving birth to her first child. After three more children, her weight and hips ballooned further, and she now tips the scales at 420 lb (190 kg).

Mikel consumes on average 3,000 calories per day but has no wish to diet. "I don't have health problems," she says, "and anyway, men like an hourglass figure. Some people assume I've had surgery to enhance my body shape, but it's all natural. It's the result of having four children—but having large hips also runs in the family.

"Everywhere I go, I get attention for my hips—both good and bad. In the past, I was self-conscious, but as I got older I learned to love my body and now I'm not afraid to show it off. I don't want to get any bigger, but I don't want to lose my curves either. I look great!"

Happy Hippy

100 inches! (2.5 m)

A tattoo artist from Austin, Texas, has covered his entire body in more than 1,000 spots to become half man, half leopard.

Tattoo artist Larry retouches his spots himself as they start to fade.

Larry Da Leopard

Born Lance Brieschke, the 40-year-old big cat enthusiast has even changed his name to Larry Da Leopard. He began getting leopard tattoos at age 20, had his face inked five years later and is now covered head to toe in spots. In keeping with his character, he prowls the streets wearing little more than a Tarzan-like loincloth and a leopard-print jacket. If he goes out for walks with a friend, he is sometimes led around by a chain.

While many people love his look, his family cried when they first saw his spots and disowned him for ten years. He struggled to find a job, but now that he runs his own tattoo parlor, he uses his distinctive body as an advertisement.

Larry, what inspired your tattoos?

I got tired of society's expectations, so I started to become a manimal—half man, half animal. My leopard tattoos have given me special leopard powers, such as seeing in the dark, running really fast and hunting at night.

What kind of reaction did you get when you first had them all done?

My family has a military and Christian background so they didn't take to my tattoos very well. I was upset that they couldn't relate to my self-expression. What I saw as art, they saw as desecrating my body. It took them ten years to come around, but now we've got a better relationship. They can see I'm doing alright for myself.

Do you ever regret your tattoos?

No. I'm proud of my tattoos—few people look like me. When I look in the mirror in the morning, I like what I see. My tattoos will never be taken away from me. They could throw me in jail, but I'll always have this art on my body.

Do you have any plans for more body modification?

I top up my facial tattoos several times a year as they fade in the sun. I'd like to get my eyelids tattooed too, but I don't want to do it myself. It's hard to tattoo your own eyelids. And having your private parts tattooed really hurts—I wouldn't recommend it—but to me, the art is worth the pain.

Larry, seen here as a young boy, didn't always look like a leopard—he got his first tattoo at the age of 20.

PECULIAR BODIES

Larry in full leopard persona out with a friend in Austin.

This leopard certainly has no intention of changing its spots. He tops up his tattoos every few months as they fade and claims that they have somehow given him some of the traits of a big cat.

Larry stalks the streets of Austin, Texas, in little more than a leopard-skin loincloth!

SPEARED IN MOUTH

Elisangela Borborema Rosa came within a hair's breadth of death after being shot in the mouth with a spear gun as her husband cleaned the weapon in the kitchen of their home in Arraial do Cabo, Brazil. The spear went in through her mouth and pierced her spine, but if it had gone a fraction to either side, she would either have been killed or left paralyzed for life.

NASAL IMPALEMENT

Four-year-old Jiali Gang, from Gansu Province, China, survived after getting a metal screwdriver wedged deep into her nose. She was playing with the tool when she tripped and fell, impaling herself on the sharp spike. The screwdriver rammed up her left nostril, lodging itself just below her eye socket and only 0.08 in (2 mm) from her brain. Doctors were initially concerned that they might not be able to remove it safely, but eventually they managed to do so without causing long-term damage.

TALL FAMILY

The four members of the Kulkarni family from Pune, India, have a combined height of 26 ft (7.9 m). At just 16, Sanya is already 6 ft 4 in (1.9 m) tall, but it is no great surprise because she and older sister Mruga are the daughters of India's tallest couple, 7 ft 2 in (2.2 m) Sharad and 6 ft 3 in (1.9 m) Sanjot.

HONEYMOON HELL

Andrew Britton from Buckinghamshire, England, survived after dying six times while on his honeymoon in the Maldives. A few days after his wedding in November 2012, the 33-year-old contracted a heart-attacking virus, which caused him to suffer cardiac failure six times.

HEAVY HAIRBALL

Unable to eat or drink for a couple of days, a 19-year-old girl went to a hospital in Indore, India, where a 4-lb (1.8-kg) hairball was removed from her stomach. Later, she admitted that she had been eating her hair.

PEE TEETH

Scientists in Guangzhou, China, have grown teeth from human urine. The urine was used as a source of stem cells, which were then implanted in mice and within three weeks had developed into tiny toothlike structures with dental pulp and enamel.

EYE CATCHING

An assault trial in Philadelphia, Pennsylvania, was halted after the victim's prosthetic eye popped out in court while he was giving evidence. John Huttick was testifying about losing his eye in a fight when his prosthetic blue eye suddenly popped right out and he caught it as jurors gasped in shock.

PRECIOUS TONGUE

Beth Anderson, 25, from Wiltshire, England, was born with twice as many taste buds as most other people—and she puts her ultra-sensitive palate to good use by working as a baby food tester, where her tongue is insured for £1 million ($1.5 million).

DRANK URINE

Eighteen-year-old backpacker Sam Woodhead from London, England, survived for three days in searing 104°F (40°C) heat in the Australian Outback by drinking contact lens fluid and his own urine. Lost and disorientated after going for a jog from a Queensland cattle station, he shed 28 lb (12.7 kg) during his ordeal and was just hours from death when a search helicopter, which was just about to return to base because it was low on fuel, spotted a pair of brightly colored shorts that Sam had hoisted as a distress signal.

ENDLESS TUNE

For more than three years, Susan Root from Essex, England, has had an endless loop of the novelty song "How Much is that Doggie in the Window?" playing in her head. She suffers from a rare form of tinnitus where music and songs play in her head day and night—and the music she hears is often so loud it drowns out the sound of her husband Graham when he is speaking.

FREAKY LIPS

It looks like an eye, but it's really a mouth! By attaching false eyelashes to her upper lip and using tiny brushes to paint on a lifelike pupil, Sandra Holmbom from Pitea, Sweden, created a third eye on her mouth. She has also decorated her lips with images of roses, apples and even the northern lights.

SELECTIVE MEMORY

Different types of memories are stored in different parts of the brain, making it possible for a person to suffer amnesia that robs them of all the details of their life but still allows them to remember how to read and play music.

Hair Coat

British firm Arla commissioned the creation of a coat made entirely from men's chest hair. It took designers 200 hours to weave together about one million strands of hair. The limited-edition coat went on sale for £2,499 ($4,000).

ALWAYS LATE

Jim Dunbar from Angus, Scotland, suffers from a genuine medical condition called Chronic Lateness Syndrome, which means that his sense of time is warped, making him late for school, work, dates, vacations and funerals. He even arrived 20 minutes late for the medical appointment where he was diagnosed with the disorder.

BIKE MISHAP

Eleven-year-old Vignesh Nageshwaran from Delhi, India, impaled himself through the roof of his mouth with a toothbrush when he fell off his bicycle while cleaning his teeth in 2009.

SHEARED EYE

The right eye socket of 86-year-old Leroy Luetscher from Green Valley, Arizona, was impaled by a pair of pruning shears in 2011.

CHIMP FEET

A scientific study of visitors to the Boston Museum of Science in Massachusetts has revealed that about one in 13 people have flexible, apelike feet. Visitors to the museum were asked to walk barefoot, but whereas most had very rigid feet, a significant number had floppier feet—similar to the midtarsal break that enables chimpanzees to grip tree branches.

MASS HYSTERIA

In the fall of 2011, an outbreak of mass hysteria caused a dozen high-school students in LeRoy, New York, to suffer symptoms of painful shaking and verbal outbursts.

HEALTH BENEFIT

Members of a remote community in Ecuador with a rare form of dwarfism called Laron syndrome are almost totally immune to cancer and diabetes.

CRASH LANDING

Skydiver Liam Dunne from Taupo, New Zealand, cheated death when his main parachute failed and a reserve chute only partially worked after he had jumped from 13,000 ft (4,000 m). He hit the ground at such a speed that he bounced, but his life was saved by landing on soft earth.

HARPOON HORROR

Fisherman Bruno Barcellos de Souza Coutinho accidentally shot himself in the face with a harpoon and survived even though the spear pierced his left eye and traveled 6 in (15 cm) into his skull before becoming lodged in his brain. He was cleaning the gun in Petrópolis, Brazil, when it went off, firing a 12-in-long (30-cm) spear into his head, but he suffered no brain damage and was even conscious enough to get help.

STAR STUDENT

Twelve-year-old Irene Nthambi of Thika, Kenya, who is blind and has no sense of touch in her fingers, is able to join in lessons at her school for the visually impaired by using her tongue to write and her lips to read. She writes by gripping a stylus with her tongue and uses her lips to read a Braille machine. Despite having to adapt, she is always top of her class.

Topsy-Turvy World

Bojana Danilovic from Užice, Serbia, has an extreme form of spatial orientation phenomenon whereby she sees the entire world upside down. She has to turn books, newspapers, her cell phone and even her TV upside down. At work she uses a special upside-down computer screen and keyboard. Usually the eyes see the world upside down, and the brain flips the image when processing it, but in Bojana's case, this correction doesn't happen.

Teeny Waists

ACTUAL SIZE!

Nerina Orton has a waist that measures just 15¾ in (40 cm). The student from Birmingham, England, has shrunk her abdomen by tying herself into smaller and smaller corsets, a method known as "tightlacing," eventually displacing the intestines, stomach and liver.

Nerina wears a corset almost all day every day, even in her sleep, and removes it only to shower. She reports that when she takes the corset off, she can feel her internal organs moving back to their original position as her waist returns to a svelte 24 in (61 cm). Nerina, who first started wearing corsets as a teenager and now owns 78 of them, makes regular visits to a doctor to ensure that the extreme effect of the corset on her body is not causing long-term damage to her health.

15¾-inch (40-cm) waist!

Nerina Orton wears a corset for 23 hours a day.

Queen of the Corset

Ethel Granger (1905–1982) of Peterborough, England, had possibly the smallest waist of all time, just 13 in (33 cm) around!

Ethel wore a corset for decades, but she did not gain public attention until the 1950s and achieved her tiniest waist in the 1960s, by which time her natural size had shrunk by 10 in (25 cm). She would sleep in her corset and gradually tighten the laces over the course of each day, until her waist was so small that she had to make her own clothes.

Polaire (1879–1939), real name Emilie Marie Bouchard, was a French vaudeville performer famous in Paris in the early 20th century for her tiny 16-in (40-cm) "wasp waist"— shrunk by years of wearing a corset for hours every day.

When Polaire played on Broadway, she was billed as "The Ugliest Woman in the World," yet she was renowned in Europe for her beauty.

Electric corsets were advertised as the latest miracle cure in the late 19th century. It was claimed that electricity running through the corset— actually magnets—could treat a wide range of medical conditions, strengthen the internal organs and "weak backs" and even cure obesity.

PECULIAR BODIES

STRUCK OUT
Chicago Cubs's Tyler Colvin was impaled in the chest by a broken baseball bat while running from third base in a 2010 game against the Florida Marlins.

HAND-WALKER
Ten-year-old Yan Yuhong from Yibin, Hubei Province, China, has been walking on his hands during his journey to and from school every day for more than four years. Paralyzed by a childhood illness, he learned to walk on his hands when he was four and now finds it faster walking that way than if he uses crutches. He still has to get up earlier than his classmates, because his journey to school takes him 90 minutes each way.

NO JOKE
A person who suffers from laughter-induced syncope can completely lose consciousness just from laughing.

PENCIL PUZZLE
A 24-year-old Afghan man unknowingly spent 15 years with a pencil in his head following a childhood accident. After suffering for years from constant headaches, colds and deteriorating vision in one eye, the man sought help from doctors in Aachen, Germany, and a scan showed that a 4-in (10-cm) pencil was lodged from his sinuses to his pharynx, damaging his right eye socket.

STRONG GIRLS
Teenage sisters Haylee and Hannah Smith of Lebanon, Oregon, lifted a 3,000-lb (1,362-kg) tractor off their father Jeff after it flipped over while he was driving it and pinned him underneath.

SLIP AND IMPALE
Eight-year-old Lewis Todd from Manchester, England, slipped while climbing a gate in 2013 and was impaled above the thigh on a metal spike.

LEAKING BRAIN
Joe Nagy of Phoenix, Arizona, thought he had a chronic runny nose for 18 months—only to learn that the clear liquid was actually his brain leaking! The brain, which is located directly above the nose, produces up to 12 oz (350 ml) of fluid a day, and doctors found that the membrane surrounding Joe's brain had a hole in it, causing fluid to trickle out. Having located the leak, they repaired it with surgery.

TOUCHING SHOULDERS
Krystal Dickson from Boston, Massachusetts, is able to twist her body so that she can touch her shoulders together.

SLIP OF THE PEN
Eight-year-old Veronica Valentine was pierced 3 in (7.5 cm) into her chest by a pen when she fell down the stairs at her home in Coral Springs, Florida, in 2001.

BOY BONANZA
Jay and Teri Schwandt from Grand Rapids, Michigan, have 12 children—and they're all boys. Furthermore, Teri's sister, Kate Osberger, who lives in Detroit, has ten children—and they're all boys, too!

BACK TO HER SENSES
Thanks to a three-hour operation, 66-year-old June Blythe from Norfolk, England, can taste and smell things for the first time in nearly 40 years. She lost her senses in 1975 after suffering from chronic rhinosinusitis, a severe inflammatory condition of the nasal sinuses. Amazingly, she went on to win prizes for her cooking (which she couldn't taste) and became an aromatherapist, using fragrant plant oils (which she couldn't smell).

JAVELIN JOLT
French long jumper Salim Sdiri was impaled in the side by a Finnish competitor's javelin thrown from the other side of the arena during a 2007 track-and-field meet in Rome, Italy.

NAIL OLYMPICS
More than 200 competitors converged on Rome, Italy, to take part in the 2013 Nail Olympics—a two-day nail art competition showcasing outrageous designs featuring feathers and figurines on perfectly manicured fingernails.

Beard Bowl

Isaiah Webb can eat ramen noodles from his beard! The San Francisco, California, beard enthusiast—also known as Mr. Incredibeard—began growing his facial hair long in 2012.

After six months, his wife Angela started molding his beard into weird and wonderful creations. He now boasts over 28 different designs, including one that holds five cups and another that can accommodate a burger, fries and a shake. He shapes his beard with hot curlers, hair spray and a blow-dryer, and posts a new creation online every other Monday.

Unusual Novelties

Barbie World

Stanley Colorite of Hudson, Florida, owns 2,000 Barbies and 1,000 Ken dolls.

His collection is so big it takes up four rooms of his house, including his bathroom. He bought his first doll in 1997 and now buys up to 20 dolls a month, estimating that he spends $30,000 a year on his hobby.

FLOATING CINEMA

For a 2012 film festival, German architect Ole Scheeren designed a floating movie theater in a lagoon on the coast of Thailand. The Archipelago Cinema consisted of a floating screen mounted on wood and foam rafts and a separate floating auditorium, to which filmgoers were transported by boat.

HOGWARTS MODEL

The 50-ft (15-m) model of Hogwarts Castle that was used for every *Harry Potter* movie contained more than 2,500 fiber-optic lights and was so detailed that if all the hours spent on construction by the 86 artists and crew members were added up, it would total 74 years.

READING PAJAMAS

A hi-tech pair of pajamas can be used to read bedtime stories to children. The Smart Pajamas are printed with 47 clusters of dots—each cluster linked to a different story—which act like barcodes when scanned by a smartphone or a tablet.

BIRD SCARER

Workers at Staverton Airport in Gloucestershire, England, keep troublesome birds off the runway by mounting a loudspeaker to the roof of a van and playing Tina Turner songs at full volume.

NAVAJO VERSION

Using authentic Native American speakers, *Star Wars* has been dubbed into Navajo to help preserve the language. A team of five Navajo people labored over translating the original script, hampered by the fact that there is no direct translation for famous phrases such as "May the force be with you."

CHILDREN'S CLOWN

Before he became famous, Hugh Jackman, star of the *X-Men* and *Wolverine* movies, worked as a clown at children's birthday parties in his native Australia for three years, charging $50 per show.

BURNING TOPIC

Nearly one million people tuned in to watch an eight-hour primetime program on Norwegian TV showing nothing but a burning fireplace—and some viewers called in to complain that the wood fuel was stacked facing the wrong way! The show was inspired by Lars Mytting's book about chopping and burning wood, which spent more than a year on the Norwegian best-seller list.

ALIEN STREETS

Klingon Court and Romulan Court are two streets that meet at an intersection in Sacramento, California. They were named in 1977 by civil engineer and *Star Trek* fan Ted Colbert.

GOLDEN OLDIE

In September 2013, Fred Stobaugh, a retired truck driver from Peoria, Illinois, had a hit on the Billboard Hot 100—at age 96. "Oh Sweet Lorraine," a poem set to music about his late wife to whom he had been married for 72 years, entered the list at number 42, ahead of the likes of Bruno Mars and Avril Lavigne. The great-great grandfather also reached number 5 in the U.S. iTunes chart.

DESIGNER LABEL

Jason Hemperly of Dennison, Ohio, created his own suit for his high-school prom from the labels of 120 Mountain Dew soda bottles.

AERIAL VIOLINIST

Janice Martin from Racine, Wisconsin, is the world's only aerial violinist, acrobatically playing the instrument upside-down while suspended in midair.

SHEEP IDOL

The most popular TV program in Senegal is an American Idol-style reality show to find the nation's most beautiful sheep. *Khar Bii*, or "This Sheep," has been running for over four seasons, airs several times a week and its Facebook page has nearly 17,000 likes.

Pay Raise

More than 60 employees at New York real estate agency Rapid Realty earned higher commission splits for life by agreeing to get the company's logo tattooed somewhere on their bodies. CEO Anthony Lolli came up with the idea, which can earn agents a pay raise of up to 60 percent, after doing business with a tattoo artist. Employees have had tattoos on their arms, ankles and backs, and one employee, Robert Trezza, had his done despite working at the company for only a month.

DOLLY'S DEFEAT

Country singer Dolly Parton once lost a Dolly Parton look-alike contest in Santa Monica, California—to a man!

MOVIE REMAKE

Arizona amateur filmmakers Jonason Pauley and Jesse Perrotta spent more than two years creating their own 80-minute, scene-for-scene live action remake of the entire *Toy Story* movie using official merchandise toys and real actors.

LOW HEELS

Women require a license to wear shoes with heels more than 2 in (5 cm) high in the Californian town of Carmel-by-the-Sea.

TAG MATCH

Stephanie Watson from Melbourne, Australia, made her wedding dress from 10,000 plastic bread expiration tags that she had collected over a ten-year period.

QUICK CHANGE

Vanna White has been the hostess on the TV game show *Wheel of Fortune* since 1982, and in that time she has worn over 6,000 dresses, never wearing the same outfit more than once.

SPENDING SPREE

Five-year-old Danny Kitchen from Bristol, England, ran up a $2,500 bill on his parents' iPad in just 10 minutes after downloading a free game and then ending up in its online store.

PHONE AUDITION

English actor Eddie Redmayne did an audition for the role of Marius in the 2013 movie *Les Misérables* on his iPhone. Wearing his cowboy outfit from the movie *Hick* that he was shooting at the time in North Carolina, he filmed himself singing in his trailer on the set and sent it to his agent.

Living Dolls

Valeria Lukyanova and Justin Jedlica are a real-life Barbie and Ken. The slim 28-year-old Ukrainian model is every inch a Barbie doll, enhancing her Barbie looks with clever makeup and colored contact lenses. Justin, 33, from Chicago, has spent over $150,000 on 140 cosmetic procedures to transform himself into Ken, including nose jobs, pectoral, buttock and bicep implants, and facial surgery. He says he treats himself as a human sculpture.

Comic Capers

Artist Andrew Vickers from Sheffield, England, made this papier-mâché sculpture using old comics he found in a dumpster, only to discover that they were actually rare editions worth £20,000 ($30,000). Unbeknownst to him, his Paperboy figure contained pasted sections from classic Marvel Comics books, including a valuable 1963 first edition of *The Avengers*, worth £10,000 ($15,000) alone. As a result it would have been cheaper for him to have created the sculpture out of Italian marble!

Shiver Me Timbers!

An anonymous multimillionaire has built his own private pirate island in a lake on his estate in Cambridgeshire, England. Featuring wooden buildings in an 18th-century design, Challis Island reflects its owner's love of all things piratical and has its own inn, The Black Dubloon, as well as a guesthouse, beach, waterfall, lagoon and boat dock.

COLONEL'S SUIT
Masao Watanabe, the President of Kentucky Fried Chicken in Japan, bought the trademark white suit of "Colonel" Harland Sanders for $20,750 in June 2013.

OLD RAPPER
Jeanne Calment of Arles, France, made a rap album in 1996 when she was 120 years old.

FOUR GUITARS
E.N. Burton from Raleigh, North Carolina, plays four guitars at the same time—lead guitars with each hand and bass guitars with each foot.

DIVORCE DRESS
Fifteen-year-old art student Demi Barnes from Sussex, England, made a wedding dress from more than 1,500 divorce papers. After constructing a wire bodice frame, it took her ten hours to staple on the genuine—but blank—divorce papers that she had downloaded from the Internet.

HARD WORK
In a single year (1932), U.S. author Walter Gibson, whose pen name was Maxwell Grant, wrote 28 books using a grand total of 1,680,000 words.

TALK SHOW
Nepalese talk show host Rabi Lamichhane broadcast for over 62 hours continuously in April 2013, talking for so long that as he neared the end of his third day he had started to grow a beard.

FALL GUYS
Three friends from Logan, Utah, collected 1,462 trash bags full of leaves to create a pile 17 ft (5.2 m) high and 60 ft (18 m) in circumference. They then filmed themselves jumping onto the pile from a nearby rooftop and posted the video on YouTube.

In 1905, retired Kansas City Fire Chief George C. Hale came up with the idea of making short "phantom ride" travelogues showing film shot from the front of a moving train.

His Hale's Tours films were screened in mock railroad cars, which would rock, vibrate and tilt to simulate real train travel. Sound effects, including steam whistles and thundering wheels, added to the illusion, while painted scenery rolled past the side windows. By 1907, there were 500 Hale's Tours theaters in the U.S.A., but with the rise of movie theaters and a limited amount of footage, their popularity proved short-lived and most had vanished within four years.

Cameraman Billy Bitzer perched precariously on the front of a moving train while filming the action for a Hale's Tours travelogue.

Railroad Cinema

TAKE A TRIP
THROUGH
RUGGED SCOTLAND
VIA
KYLES- STROME FERRY
NEAR OBAN

RIDE THROUGH
THE
ROCKY MOUNTAINS
OF
WESTERN CANADA

HALE'S TOURS
AND SCENES OF THE WORLD.
TRAINS EVERY 10 Minutes.

Hale's Tours films were screened in a mock railroad car.
Up to 72 passengers sat facing the screen where they
saw and felt the movements and heard the sounds
that made them believe they were on a real train.

LOST FOR WORDS

Actress Jori Phillips from Vancouver, British Columbia, spent months tearing pages out of a thesaurus, then folding and gluing them together to make a strapless paper dress. Lined with fabric and featuring a bodice for support, her recycled dress consists of hundreds of pages of synonyms from A to O.

DOG LEADS

New York City band Caninus made three records with two pitbull terriers, Budgie and Basil, on lead vocals. Caninus was formed in 2001 by metalcore band Most Precious Blood, who replaced its vocalists with dogs. The band played until 2011 when Basil died.

ORIGINAL MEMBERS

Texas rock band ZZ Top have had the same line-up—Billy Gibbons, Dusty Hill and Frank Beard—since they formed in 1969.

TOWER DRUM

U.S. composer Joseph Bertolozzi turned Paris's famous Eiffel Tower into a giant drum kit. Using conventional drumsticks, latex mallets and even a large log wrapped in wool, he explored every surface of the 1,062-ft (324-m) tower, hitting its railings, panels and girders with varying intensity to create 2,000 different sounds for a percussion piece titled Tower Music. It is not the first monument that Bertolozzi has sampled—in 2007, he composed Bridge Music by repeatedly hitting New York State's Mid-Hudson Bridge.

TEXT ERROR

A 33-year-old Sussex, New Jersey, man was arrested after sending a text message to a police detective by mistake saying he had drugs to sell and wanted to meet at a pizza parlor.

SPEEDY TWEETER

On August 3, 2012, Joseph Caswell from Cary, North Carolina, sent 62 tweets in a minute—that's faster than one every second.

[YOUR / UPLOADS]

Cymbal of Faith

Reverend Mark Temperato from New York owns a giant drum kit consisting of more than 900 pieces—and he can hit every drum, cymbal or cow bell without moving from his seat, although some pieces are 8 ft (2.4 m) apart. Temperato, who plays under the stage name RevM, spent over 20 years building up his collection, which weighs in excess of 5,000 lb (2,270 kg) and requires 17 hours of maintenance per week.

HOMING SHOES

U.K. designer Dominic Wilcox has created shoes with computer-linked GPS technology, which send the wearer in the direction of home. The left shoe has a built-in compass and flashing arrows, while the right shoe has a distance gauge.

SKY WALKERS

Kung fu movie fans can run through the air or over the water at a martial arts theme park in Kunming, China. The park has the same computerized wire-lifting system that is used on the big screen, allowing visitors to copy the sky-walking stunts seen in movies such as *Crouching Tiger, Hidden Dragon*.

TWEET PANIC

More than half of stock market trading is done by computers that automatically sift through news, data and even tweets to carry out trades in fractions of a second without any human input. So, on April 23, 2013, when a hoax news agency tweet reported explosions at the White House, the Wall Street computers reacted by unloading $134 billion worth of stocks in just ten minutes.

GOLD SHIRT

Millionaire Datta Phuge from Pune, India, spent $235,000 on a shirt crafted out of 7 lb (3.2 kg) of 22-carat solid gold. It took a team of 15 goldsmiths two weeks to construct the shirt, which contains 14,000 gold flowerings interwoven with 100,000 gold spangles all sewn into a velvet lining, as well as six Swarovski crystal buttons.

MOUSE MARRIAGE

Wayne Allwine (1947–2009), the voice of Mickey Mouse from 1977 to 2009, was married to Russi Taylor, who has provided the voice of Minnie Mouse since 1986.

Tattoo Roulette

American singer Ryan Cabrera had to get the face of actor Ryan Gosling inked on his leg after losing a game of tattoo roulette where blindfolded friends get to pick a tattoo for each other.

Human Skin Rug

New York City artist Chrissy Conant turned herself into a human skin rug. She made a life-size, flesh-colored, silicone rubber cast of herself to form the Chrissy Skin Rug, which looks like a bear-skin rug—but with her as the animal.

To make the controversial piece, which has been exhibited in galleries and museums, Chrissy had to shave her body, cover herself in Vaseline and lie perfectly still for several hours while being coated with buckets full of gelatinous mold making material.

SPIDER STRINGS

Shigeyoshi Osaki of Japan's Nara Medical University makes violin strings from woven spiderweb silk. More than 300 spiders are used to generate the 5,000 individual strands of silk needed to make up each string.

BIKINI BLING

U.S. designer Susan Rosen and Steinmetz Diamonds created a bikini that used 150 carats of flawless diamonds set in platinum and had no fabric. Tiger Woods was rumored to have bought it in 2010. Price: $30 million.

SVELTE BELT

U.K. department store Selfridges commissioned a belt featuring 70 pyramids crafted from 18-carat gold and mounted on white leather. Priced at $32,000 for anyone with a waist under 28 in (71 cm)—each additional inch added $1,300 to the price.

COOL RECEPTION

In November 2012, English rock guitarist Charlie Simpson, formerly with the band Busted, played a 15-minute outdoor gig in Siberia while enduring temperatures of –22°F (–30°C).

LOST TALE

The Tallow Candle, a 700-word fairy tale penned by Danish writer Hans Christian Andersen in the 1820s, remained unknown for nearly 200 years until a copy of the manuscript was discovered at the bottom of a filing box in 2012.

EGYPTIAN DESCRIPTION

Nileen Namita, a mother-of-three from Brighton, England, underwent more than 50 cosmetic surgeries—including eight nose jobs and three facelifts costing a total of $360,000 to fulfill her dream of looking like the ancient Egyptian queen Nefertiti.

HUMAN SCARECROW

After graduating from university with a music degree, 22-year-old Jamie Fox landed a £250-a-week ($400) job as a human scarecrow on a farm in Norfolk, England, playing the ukulele, accordion and cowbell to scare away troublesome partridges.

BIEBER DUPLICATE

Toby Sheldon, a 33-year-old songwriter from Los Angeles, California, has spent $100,000 on cosmetic surgery trying to transform himself into his idol Justin Bieber, including $30,000 to acquire the singer's baby-faced perma-smile. He has also had eyelid surgery, chin reduction and face fillers and has had his hairline lowered.

HOT TOPIC

The futuristic 1953 novel *Fahrenheit 451* by U.S. author Ray Bradbury (1920–2012) was originally called *The Fireman*, but both he and his publishers thought it was a boring title, so he called his local fire station and asked what temperature paper burned at. The fireman put Bradbury on hold, went away to burn a book and then reported back with the relevant temperature—451°F (233°C).

NAME CHANGE

Jason Sadler of Jacksonville, Florida, agreed to allow a website to become his official last name for $45,500, so that for the whole of 2013 he was legitimately known as Jason HeadsetsDotCom.

WORKERS' BALLET

As part of the Ural Industrial Biennial of Contemporary Art, a Russian theater put on an experimental one-act ballet in a car factory, involving factory employees in their work clothes alongside professional dancers.

REAL RACER

Available to just one customer, the video game *Grid 2: Mono Edition* by Codemasters was priced at a cool $190,000—because as well as the racing game itself and a PlayStation 3 console to play it on, the special package included a real 170-mph (275-km/h) BAC Mono supercar, helmet and race suit.

Musical Shell

This Bolivian musical instrument-maker is working on *charangos*—a traditional South American stringed instrument similar to a lute that is sometimes made from the backs of armadillos.

MILK JEWELRY

Allicia Mogavero from Wakefield, Rhode Island, makes jewelry from women's breast milk. Mothers from around the world send her their breast milk in sealed bags, and she then plasticizes a sample and molds it into miniature shapes—hearts, moons, flowers or tiny hands—which are then set into pendants.

MOOD MUSIC

A Japanese company has invented a set of mind-reading headphones that play music based on the wearer's mood. The headphones contain a forehead sensor that analyzes brainwaves to detect the person's mood and then connects to an iPhone app that selects the song best suited to that state of mind.

FAST FAIL

A YouTube video showing a South Korean woman failing her driving test within just seven seconds quickly notched up half a million views. Moments after starting the engine, the woman drove up a bank and overturned the car, while the instructor yelled at her to put her foot on the brake instead of the gas.

HEALTH APP

A Facebook app called "Help, I Have the Flu" scans your friends' status updates for words like "sniffles" and "coughing" to suggest which people you should avoid for a couple of weeks.

MULTI-TASKING

Ukrainian virtuoso Oleksandr Bozhyk can play four violins at once. Using two bows, he rests two violins on his left arm, tucks another under his right arm and a fourth beneath his chin.

BEAT THAT!

At an extreme drumming event in Nashville, Tennessee, in July 2013, Tom Grosset from Toronto, Ontario, recorded 1,208 single strokes in 60 seconds—more than 20 beats per second.

ROLLING FINE

Rolling Stones's guitarist Keith Richards has racked up a library fine of $5,000 (£3,000) after failing to return books he borrowed more than 50 years ago from a public library in Kent, England.

TRASH SOUNDS

The child musicians of the Cateura Orchestra from the Cateura slum of Paraguay play instruments— including a violin, cello, flute and drum—which are all made from landfill trash. In such an impoverished area, a real violin costs more than a house.

LIGHT TRICK

A team of scientists at the Massachusetts Institute of Technology have created a camera that can take photos around a corner, using reflected light.

High Voice

OHO Digital KaraOK Center unveiled a fully functional golden microphone measuring 9 ft (2.8 m) high and 22 in (56 cm) in diameter in Urumqi, China. The microphone is so tall that you need to stand on steps to sing into it.

DRESS CODE

Visitors to Chessington World of Adventures safari park in Surrey, England, have been banned from wearing fake leopard-print and tiger-stripe clothes in case they confuse or frighten the animals.

LOST LOTTERY

In 2010, an elderly man in England threw away a winning lottery ticket that was worth $181 million.

GAME CURE

Doctors at McGill University, Montreal, Canada, treat patients with a lazy eye by getting them to play the video game Tetris because it trains both eyes to work together.

SHOE MEAL

In 1978, German filmmaker Werner Herzog cooked and ate his shoe in public after losing a bet.

COMIC TEMPLE

Chalermchai Kositpipat spent more than a decade building the Wat Rong Khun Buddhist temple near Chiang Rai, Thailand, which is decorated with cultural figures from comics and movies—including Superman, Batman, Neo from *The Matrix* and the aliens from the *Predator* movies—as well as more traditional religious icons.

Toad Fashion

Inspired by the fairy-tale idea of a toad transformed into Prince Charming, Paris-based Polish designer Monika Jarosz has turned the whole skins of thousands of real cane toads into top-of-the-range fashion accessories. The toxic toads are a major pest in Australia, so, with the help of a taxidermist, Monika recycles their dyed skins into belts, bags and purses, the largest of which sell for up to $1,600. The toad's skin goes through 14 stages before it becomes high-quality leather. Then, the eyes are replaced with semiprecious stones.

Ostrich Pillow

The Ostrich Pillow is a lightweight cushion hat that lets you take a power nap anytime, anywhere... if you don't mind getting strange looks from passersby. Designed by Key Portilla-Kawamura and Ali Ganjavian, who met in college in London, England, the hat is made from ultra-soft jersey padded out with polystyrene micro-balls so that you can comfortably lean your head against any surface. There are even holes on either side of the helmet so that you can keep your hands warm while dozing.

SLOW BURNER
Published in 1851, Herman Melville's novel *Moby Dick* was initially trashed by reviewers and sold only 3,700 copies in his lifetime. It is now widely regarded as one of the 100 best books of all time and has sold millions of copies worldwide.

RAPID AGING
U.S. filmmaker Anthony Cerniello made a video showing a young girl aging a lifetime in less than five minutes. Attending the girl's family reunion, he and photographer Keith Sirchio took portraits of her female relatives of all ages. These were then morphed slowly before animators brought the pictures to life by adding blinks and mouth movements.

Star Trek House

Steve Nighteagle Doman spent four years turning the front room of his home in Guffey, Colorado, into a *Star Trek*-themed Federation Room.

Driven by 14 computers, his starship was created for $25,000 by recycling ordinary household objects, including parts of old printers, pieces of cutlery, hair dryers, air filters from trucks, plumbing and drainage pipes, bottle caps, Christmas lights, old cassette players, curling irons and vacuum cleaner hoses. Now the sci-fi fan and carpenter plans to give the rest of his house a 23rd-century makeover.

Klingon Wedding

In October 2012, at a convention in London, England, 1,063 *Star Trek* fans dressed up as characters from the show. The convention also hosted the wedding of Swedish couple Jossie Sockertopp and Sonnie Gustavsson, who got married wearing full Klingon attire. Their service was conducted in the Klingon language.

MOM'S WATCHING
Canadian pop star Justin Bieber has a large tattoo of his mother's eye inked into the crook of his left arm.

BEAT IT
Mikki Jay from St. Helens, England, spent $16,000 on having her nose, chin and cheeks remodeled so that she could become a professional Michael Jackson impersonator.

FISHY THEORY
Italian opera singer Enrico Caruso (1873–1921) used to wear anchovies around his neck in the belief that they protected his voice from his heavy smoking habit.

TWICE THE KONG
When *King Kong* was sold to television in 1956, New York's WOR-TV screened it twice every day for a week.

ADRENALINE RUSH
Watching an adrenaline-charged horror movie can burn more calories than 30 minutes of lifting weights.

FOREVER CLEAN
U.S. company Wool&Prince has developed an odor-resistant, wrinkle-free wool shirt that can be worn for 100 days straight without being washed.

Diamond Bra

Lingerie-maker Victoria's Secret designed a $2.5-million bra adorned with 5,200 precious gems, including a 20-carat diamond and a huge ruby.

HAIR GLASSES

Two graduates from London's Royal College of Art, Alexander Groves and Azuka Murakami, have designed a collection of fashion glasses with frames made from discarded human hair bound together with bioresin.

RARE COMIC

Among the old newspapers used to insulate a wall of the house that he had just bought in Elbow Lake, Minnesota, construction worker David Gonzalez found a rare copy of *Action Comics* No. 1, a June 1938 comic book featuring the first appearance of Superman. He later sold the comic at auction for $175,000—more than 17 times the price that he paid for the house.

IN STITCHES

In 2013, Norwegian TV's public broadcasting network announced it was devoting five hours of airtime to live knitting—preceded by a four-hour documentary on how the wool shorn from a sheep's back is turned into a sweater.

GIANT TV

A giant TV made by Porsche in Austria has a 201-in (510-cm) screen and costs more than $600,000—four times as much as a Porsche 911 sports car. The C SEED 201 is made up of more than 787,000 LEDs, which display 281 trillion colors, and is so big it has to be used outdoors.

MULTITASKING

Ben Lapps from Mason, Ohio, can play the guitar and basketball at the same time. A YouTube video, which attracted 300,000 views in a single day, shows him maintaining a tune on his guitar while bouncing a basketball and shooting hoops.

SNEAKER MUSEUM

Jordan Michael Geller's ShoeZeum in Las Vegas, Nevada, includes one of every model of Nike Air Jordans ever made and in total houses a collection of more than 2,600 pairs of sneakers. Only a few of the shoes have been worn, but they include a pair that Michael Jordan himself laced as a rookie for the Chicago Bulls basketball team.

PAPER APP

Thousands of Venezuelan people downloaded a smartphone app that helped them find toilet paper—a commodity that was in short supply in the country during much of 2013.

COSTLY ERROR

In 2005, a broker for Mizuho Securities in Japan wanted to sell off a single share for 610,000 yen, but instead he ordered 610,000 shares to be sold for 1 yen each. The typing error cost Mizuho $224 million.

SOCCER DRESS

Karen Bell, a bride from Manchester, England, made her wedding dress by sewing together the groom's collection of Manchester City soccer jerseys, some dating back to the early 1980s.

GIRL POWER

The Japanese all-girl pop group AKB48 has 130 members—and because they can't all fit on stage at the same time, before each show they hold a rock-paper-scissors contest to select a limited number of singers to perform.

GAMING FAN

Brett Martin from Denver, Colorado, has over 8,000 items of video game memorabilia, worth an estimated $100,000.

Roadkill Fashion

Fashion designer Jess Eaton from Brighton, England, created a range of wedding clothes from roadkill, including this bridal cape made from swans' feathers. She also made a necklace out of human bones after sourcing a ribcage from a university medical department.

Doctor Who

British sci-fi phenomenon *Doctor Who* first aired on television on November 23, 1963, and has now been running for more than 50 years, making it the world's longest-running sci-fi show.

As of July 11, 2016, a total of 826 episodes had been broadcast, and the show is now seen in more than 50 countries every week. Ripley's wanted to celebrate this achievement by introducing some of the world's more unusual "Whovians," as *Doctor Who* fans are known, and their tributes to the show.

Dalek Collector

A fan of *Doctor Who's* robotic adversaries since the age of seven, Rob Hull from Doncaster, England, has now collected over 1,200 Daleks. It has taken him 25 years to acquire Daleks in every size from tiny miniatures to a life-size model, and they have virtually taken over his family home. Two of his children have also started their own Dalek collections.

- There have been 12 Doctors in total—the First Doctor appeared on November 23, 1963, and the Twelfth Doctor made his first appearance on December 25, 2013.

- The total number of years traveled by all the Doctors is 204,272,560,259,444.

- A total of 52 percent of the Doctor's adventures are set in the future, 22 percent in the past and 16 percent in the present day.

- The Daleks are the most popular adversary in the series, appearing in 22 stories with 9 cameos. The Cybermen come a distant second with 14 stories and 5 cameos.

- The longest journey through time was taken by the Tenth Doctor between Utopia and The Sound of Drums, which was 99.99 trillion years.

- Up to 2013, the Daleks said "Exterminate!" 469 times and killed 210 people on screen.

- The Doctor has appeared in *The Simpsons* TV show four times but has never spoken a word.

- Tapes containing nine episodes of *Doctor Who* from the 1960s that were thought to be lost to the world were discovered in 2013 in a TV station cupboard in Nigeria.

- The most well-traveled Doctor is the Eleventh, with 70 journeys through time on screen.

- The Doctor speaks five billion languages, including Baby and Horse.

- It would take 371 hours 19 minutes 25 seconds to watch every *Doctor Who* episode until the end of 2013.

Whose Nails?

Nail artist Kayleigh O'Connor from Birmingham, England, has designed a range of beautifully painted fingernails celebrating *Doctor Who*, depicting some of the Doctor's arch enemies as well as the TARDIS. She has also created nails portraying characters from *Harry Potter* and the TV series *Breaking Bad*.

BESSIE

HERE WE GO AGAIN

THE TALONS OF WENG-CHIANG

GENESIS OF THE DALEKS

IT'S THE END...
...BUT THE MOMENT
HAS BEEN PREPARED FOR

THE DE...

CITY OF DEATH

Cyberman Groom

A Cyberman marries his bride at a mass *Doctor Who* wedding ceremony in London, England, in November 2013 to mark the 50th anniversary of the show. Fifty "Whovian" couples married or renewed their vows in costume before a congregation of Daleks and different incarnations of the Doctor, after which they were given commemorative rings and *Doctor Who* tattoos. Fans flew in from as far afield as Canada and the U.S.A.

Baywheux Tapestry

Cartoonist Bill Mudron from Portland, Oregon, drew this superb artwork in the style of the Bayeux Tapestry to chronicle the Doctor's entire adventures over 50 years. The 6-sq-ft (0.5-sq-m) design begins with the First Doctor, William Hartnell, in 1963 and continues through every regeneration up to Matt Smith, the Eleventh Doctor, in 2013.

TARDIS Cake

Baker and *Doctor Who* fan Lisa Wheatcroft from England made this amazing 4-ft-tall (1.2-m) TARDIS cake. Taking three weeks to make, it was constructed from over a dozen blocks of cake held together by a puffed rice and marshmallow mix, chocolate ganache, and icing painted the exact shade of blue.

Maize Maze

Farmer and *Doctor Who* fan Tom Pearcy created a 1,000-ft-long (300-m) image of a Dalek that covered an 18-acre (7-ha) field containing more than one million maize plants near York, England. The design takes the form of a giant maze consisting of 6¼ mi (10 km) of pathways.

REVERSE VIDEO

Israel's Messe Kopp filmed himself walking backward while interacting with passersby through the streets of Jerusalem—and then ran the film backward so that he appears to be going in the right direction while everything else, including such things as water spilling back into a bucket, is in reverse.

PSY STYLE

On April 14, 2013, South Korean singer Psy's single "Gentleman" racked up an incredible 38 million views in 24 hours when the video was first posted on YouTube.

$5-MILLION LETTER

A letter written by English scientist Francis Crick to his 12-year-old son Michael in 1953 about the discovery of DNA sold at a New York City auction for $5.3 million in 2013.

Cat Bearding

One former Internet craze is cat bearding, where pet owners are photographed positioning their cat in front of their face so that it looks as if they have a beard! The craze began on Tumblr when a user uploaded a snap of his fake feline beard and the trick quickly spread across the world. Tumblr even hosts a cat bearding website showing the best pictures of the wacky trend.

Dogs too!

SMALLEST LIBRARY

The library in Cardigan, Prince Edward Island, Canada, sits in a building that measures just 11 x 11 ft (3.5 x 3.5 m) and is home to 1,800 books, making it the smallest public library in the world. A lifetime membership costs just $5.

GOWN TRASHING

The latest trend in bridal photography is called Trash the Dress—and it involves the bride deliberately wrecking her wedding gown straight after the ceremony by getting it wet, dirty, splattered in paint or even partly set on fire!

FIRST YEAR

Using more than 1,200 one-second clips recorded on his iPhone, proud father Sam Cornwell, from Portsmouth, England, produced a seven-minute film capturing moments from every single day of his son Indigo's first year of life.

CAMERA HAPPY

Kong Kenk from Ho Chi Minh City, Vietnam, has uploaded more than 115,000 photos onto his Facebook page.

PET LEOPARD

In the 1930s, dancer and singer Josephine Baker (1906–1975) walked a pet leopard called Chiquita around Paris, France, on a diamond-studded leash.

PIGEONS FIRED

Police in the Indian state of Orissa employed a fleet of 1,400 carrier pigeons to deliver messages until 2005, when e-mail and cell phones made the pigeons redundant.

Rose Petal Dress

Xiao Fan arranged for 9,999 red roses to be made into a flowing gown before making a Valentine's Day proposal to girlfriend Yin Mi at the Guangzhou, China, amusement park where they had first met three years earlier. The gown had a 5-ft-long (1.5-m) train made from individually stitched blooms. The number of roses used to make the dress was also symbolic, as the number nine in Chinese culture represents "forever."

Trash Fashion

Ripley's staged a "Trashy Fashion Show" in March 2012 with entrants creating imaginative dresses from discarded items such as magazines, bottle caps, grocery bags, paper cups, trading cards, snack wrappers and even an old shower curtain. All three winning designs were acquired for display at its Ripley's Odditorium in St. Augustine, Florida.

DIAMOND DENIM

Secret Circus created a pair of women's jeans with 15 large, high-quality diamonds sewn into the back pockets. Price: $1.3 million.

ROAR ROAR

King Kong's roar was a lion's and a tiger's roar combined and run backward.

BARBIE WORLD

Over 20 years, Sarah Burge, a mother from Cambridgeshire, England, has undergone hundreds of cosmetic surgeries and spent more than $130,000 to turn herself into a real-life Barbie.

THE BORROWER

Louise Brown from Stranraer, Scotland, borrowed more than 25,000 books from local libraries over a period of 63 years.

Analise Barnard and Amani Grant designed this gown and headband made entirely of coffee filters.

Masha Sardari in a formal knee-length gown made from used paint brushes and paper bags.

Kennedy Trugter wore a sleeveless top adorned with newspaper flowers and ruffles, and a triple-tiered skirt made with hundreds of pleated paper sections.

SCI-FI SHRINE

Steve Sansweet's Rancho Obi-Wan museum in Petaluma, California, houses his collection of more than 300,000 items of *Star Wars* memorabilia, including toys, models and life-size exhibits, and it includes an entire room of pinball and arcade machines.

TWITTER WEDDING

When Cengizhan Celik married Candan Canik in Turkey, they exchanged their wedding vows via Twitter. Mustafa Kara, mayor of Istanbul's Uskudar district, conducted the ceremony by sending tweets to the couple, asking them to respond on their iPads.

MIXED MESSAGES

The sounds made by the brachiosaurs in Steven Spielberg's 1993 movie blockbuster *Jurassic Park* were a combination of whale songs and donkey calls.

WITCH ANCESTOR

A female ancestor of *Harry Potter* actress Emma Watson was convicted of witchcraft in 16th-century England.

WRONG WAY

In the space of three weeks in September 2013, two motorists drove across a runway at Fairbanks International Airport, Alaska, which is used by 737 airplanes, after their smartphone satellite navigation apps gave them wrong directions.

Human Transformer

This guy's a real-life Transformer! Drew Beaumier from Fountain Valley, California, had always been a fan of the alien robots, so when he bought a used Power Wheels toy car for $300, he decided to take it apart and turn himself into a human Transformer. He pieced the car back together at the hinges and then glued it to a sports undergarment so that he could wear it like a suit. To make it look really authentic, he fixed wheels to his arms and legs so that when he curls down he can roll along the street like a car.

Who's the Little Lady?

Billed in contemporary U.S. sideshows as the "World's Smallest Lady," Margaret Ann Robinson was so tiny she could stand in the palm of your hand.

When she was 19, she stood just 21 in (53 cm) tall and weighed 18 lb (8.1 kg), making her smaller than the average two-year-old. No wonder Shrine's Circus billed her in 1936 as a "Living, Breathing, Walking, Talking Human Doll."

She was born Margaret Ann Meek in Denver, Colorado, in 1916 and weighed a respectable 6 lb 8 oz (2.9 kg) at birth. Both her parents were of normal stature, with her father, a coal miner, standing 5 ft 11 in (1.8 m) tall. When it became apparent that Margaret Ann suffered from dwarfism, she went into show business, and at the 1934 World's Fair in Chicago, she and Captain Werner, "the smallest man in the world," were pictured standing together in a leather carrying case at the gates of "Midget City," a colony of 187 little people living in miniature houses with tiny furniture.

The seat of a standard adult chair was too high for Margaret Ann's tiny frame. She lived with other dwarfs in a colony that had specially made tiny furniture and houses.

21 in (53 cm) tall.

IN PERSON
MARGARET ANN ROBINSON
The Smallest Adult
Ever Born to Live!
Height 21 ins. - Age 19 yrs. - Weight 18 lbs.
This Living, Breathing, Walking, Talking Human Doll
Will Appear Twice Daily At

MELHA TEMPLE A.A.O.N.M.S
SHRINERS' CIRCUS
PRESENTING
The Morton-Hamid Circus
MAY 4TH TO 9TH INCLUSIVE 1936 STATE ARMORY

Printed in U.S.A.

To emphasize her diminutive stature, on her 19th birthday, at the California Pacific World's Fair, a waiter carried Margaret Ann on a tray along with her birthday cake.

Often traveling with her mother, Margaret Ann went on to perform with circuses for more than 40 years. At the height of her fame, she advertised Johnson's Glo-Coat floor cleaner to show housewives how easy it was to keep their kitchens spotless. By the age of 50, she still wowed audiences billed as "Princess Ann, The Tiny Lady."

Margaret Ann with Captain Werner, the "Smallest Man and Smallest Woman in the World," posing inside a traveling bag outside "Midget City" at the Chicago World's Fair in 1934.

Margaret Ann Robinson regularly appeared with Singer's Midgets, a troupe founded in 1912 by Austrian Leopold von Singer and his wife. Recruiting little people wherever they went, Singer's Midgets performed in U.S. vaudeville theaters after World War I, and some of his artists appeared in movies, including *The Terror of Tiny Town* (1938), the world's only musical Western with an all-dwarf cast. Also in 1938, Singer signed a contract with MGM to provide 124 proportionately sized little people to play Munchkins in *The Wizard of Oz*, although Margaret Ann was not among them.

THE MOST MARVELOUS AND ONLY ATTRACTION OF ITS KIND IN THE WORLD
SINGER'S MIDGETS
3 MIDGET ELEPHANTS 30 WONDERFUL MIDGETS 20 PONIES

Start (Photo 1)

Finish (Photo 4,514)

Selfie Series

Photographer Noah Kalina from Brooklyn, New York, took a self-portrait every day for over 12 years—making a total of 4,514 photos. He then put them together in a rapid time-lapse video, which soon went viral, that shows him aging from 19 to 31 in just seven minutes. What's more, Noah plans to continue taking pictures indefinitely.

Just some of Noah's 4,514 selfies taken for his time-lapse YouTube video.

BIRTHDAY TREAT

Travis Schwend paid $300 to hire the Sun-Ray Cinema in Jacksonville, Florida, for five hours so that his son Jonah could celebrate his 13th birthday by playing video games with his friends on a huge screen, with unlimited pizza, popcorn and soft drinks.

HEAVILY EDITED

The total footage shot for Stanley Kubrick's 1968 sci-fi adventure *2001: A Space Odyssey* was around 200 times the final length of the movie.

FINED HIMSELF

After his own smartphone went off and disrupted a courtroom hearing at Ionia, Michigan, Judge Raymond Voet held himself in contempt and paid a fine of $25.

PERSONAL SUPERHERO

In 2012, Marvel Comics specially created a new superhero, Blue Ear, to encourage Anthony Smith, a hearing-impaired four-year-old boy from Salem, New Hampshire, to wear his hearing aid to school. After the young comic-book fan protested that superheroes never wear hearing aids, his mother wrote to Marvel, and they responded by inventing a new action figure—named after Anthony's nickname for his aid—who owed his superpowers to his listening device.

PANTS HATS

For a book signing by *Captain Underpants* author Dav Pilkey at Napierville, Illinois, 270 people—adults and children—wore underpants on their head.

YOUNG PROGRAMMER

Zora Ball from Philadelphia, Pennsylvania, created her own mobile video game—featuring ballerinas, jewels and vampires—at age seven. She used the Bootstrap programming system, which is usually taught to students twice her age.

Zip Tie

For men who struggle to fasten their tie, designer Josh Jakus, from Oakland, California, has created an idiotproof, wool felt tie with a zipper sewn down the middle that does up in seconds and eliminates the need for tying knots. Finding that his company, Actual, had a surplus of felt and zippers from manufacturing other products, Josh tried to think of ways of making use of the extra material. He began experimenting with a necklace but ended up with a novel necktie instead.

DOTING HUSBAND

Paul Brockman from Lomita, California, has bought his wife Margot 55,000 dresses over the past 56 years, and he chose them all himself.

MICRO BOOK

Japanese publisher Toppan Printing has created a book with pages measuring just 0.03 x 0.03 in (0.75 x 0.75 mm). The 22-page book, which contains names and illustrations of flowers, is so small it can be read only with a magnifying glass.

MUSICAL COFFIN

Swedish inventor Fredrik Hjelmquist has created a coffin with a built-in stereo system. It allows people to compile their own personal playlist before they die so that their favorite music can be streamed into their grave. Relatives can even update the songs by using an app and a touchscreen that is built into the headstone.

HARP TWINS

Camille and Kennerly Kitt—the world's only known identical twin professional harpists— play rock classics by Metallica, The Rolling Stones, Bon Jovi and AC/DC on harps. They also perform in unusual locations including graveyards, desert tracks and highway interchanges.

TUBE SONG

Guitar-playing comedian and singer-songwriter Jay Foreman from London, England, has penned a rhyming song in which he mentions the names of all 270 of London's Underground stations. The song takes just over three minutes to perform.

Musical Skateboards

Juhana Nyrhinen from Finland makes $500 electric versions of kanteles and other traditional stringed Finnish folk instruments from ordinary skateboards. Players can hold the instrument on their lap and achieve a distinctive tremolo sound effect by leaning on the wheels.

Prize Artist

Laura Tyler, who used to work as an artist at the Ripley's Believe It or Not! art department in Orlando, Florida, won the $100,000 first prize in season five of SyFy channel's reality show *Face Off*, where contestants compete for the title of Best Special Effects Make-Up Artist.

Laura made wax figures for Ripley's Odditoriums around the globe and, as you can see here, she displayed her talents to the full on the show, skillfully applying prosthetics and face paint to create imaginative figures such as the Grim Reaper, a face-ripping, blood-soaked Wrath Monster and, in the finals, an Italian Renaissance-inspired swan-sorcerer.

Feats to Beat

Extreme Therapy

People in Russia stand on a bed of razor-sharp nails as a way of confronting their biggest fears head-on. The tortuous trial is part of a two-day course called "Life Without Fear" that helps participants overcome their phobias by undertaking a series of extreme activities. These include stopping falling knives with their bare stomach, walking on hot coals, breaking wooden poles with their neck, sitting on broken glass, allowing giant bugs to crawl over their face, walking on knife blades, eating pieces of burning cotton, swimming in freezing water and being buried alive.

TOUGH TEETH

Hungarian strongman Zsolt Sinka pulled a 55-ton Airbus A320 airplane nearly 130 ft (40 m)—using just his teeth. Sinka, who has previously used his teeth to pull fire engines and trains, achieved his latest feat in just 52 seconds at Liszt Ferenc Airport in Budapest.

COCONUT CRACKER

Keshab Swain of Odisha, India, can crack open 85 green coconuts with his elbow in just 60 seconds. He can also smash 18 coconuts in one minute with his forehead.

NO FEAR

Peter Sheath from Southampton, England, has been water-skiing for over 25 years despite being blind since the age of 30. Now age 74, he still takes to the water twice a week and says that his disability helps him in the sport because, as he is unable to see, he never feels scared.

CATHEDRAL CROSSING

In May 2013, Austrian tightrope walker Christian Waldner became the first man to walk a 164-ft (50-m) slackline between the two towers of Vienna's famous St. Stephen's Cathedral. He made the perilous crossing, some 200 ft (60 m) above ground, not just once, but four times.

Wheelchair Jumper

Lonnie leaps from a 1,150-ft-high (350-m) bridge in Hunan, China.

Canadian BASE jumper Lonnie Bissonnette throws himself off 1,000-ft-high (330-m) bridges in his wheelchair.

He has been paralyzed from the waist down since a 2004 BASE-jumping accident. Doctors told him he would never jump again, but within 12 months, he was back traveling the world fulfilling his passion. He is unable to walk but has enough strength in his right arm to be able to pull the parachute chord for a safe descent and landing. He is the first and only paraplegic BASE jumper to jump off all four BASE objects—Buildings, Antennae, Span (bridge) and Earth (cliff).

The Great Blondin

Charles Blondin, born Jean-François Gravelet in France in 1824, was the greatest funambulist—tightrope walker—of the 19th century.

In 1859, a crowd of several thousand people thronged the shores of the formidable Niagara Gorge to watch him make the first-ever tightrope crossing over the Niagara River, on a 1,300-ft-long (396-m) rope that was just 2 in (5 cm) thick. Blondin never used a harness, or even a net, as he believed that to use safety devices was to tempt fate. As a result, bookmakers took large amounts of money betting against the man who had only a 26-ft-long (8-m) balancing pole to stop him from tumbling nearly 175 ft (53 m) into the waters below. On his first crossing, Blondin terrified onlookers by stopping halfway across to haul up a bottle of wine for refreshment from a tourist boat, before continuing to the other side and returning with a large daguerreotype camera and taking a snapshot of the watching crowds!

Blondin's manager posted newspaper adverts to drum up spectators for his client's daring feats of balance. People would pay up to 50 cents to watch the daredevil perform.

NIAGARA FALLS,

NEW AND DARING FEATS BY THE INTREPID

BLONDIN.

EXTRAORDINARY FEATS

OF

BALANCING.

—ON—

Wednesday, Aug. 1st, at 4 P. M.

ON this occasion Mons. Blondin will perform the world renowned

Chair Feat,

Sitting and standing in various postures, with only one leg of the chair resting upon the rope : placing the chair upon the rope before him, and climb over the back and stand erect in the chair. Also numerous other feats of balancing with the chair

Mons. Blondin will also, as he returns from the Canada side, take with him an instrument, and when in the centre of the rope take a

Stereoscopic View

Of the Thousands upon the American Side.

☞ This view will positively be made by Mons. Blondin, while he is standing upon the rope. Extraordinary as it may appear, he will balance the instrument steady enough to make a perfect picture.

☞ Tickets 25 cents ; Reserved Seats 25 cents extra
Doors open at 3 o'clock P. M.

HARRY COLCORD.

Blondin on his first-ever tightrope walk across the Niagara Gorge in 1859.

Not content with getting only himself across the tightrope, Blondin showed his strength as well as his agility by carrying someone on his back. On more than one occasion, Blondin wheeled a stove across his tightrope and stopped to cook on it midway. He once did this while crossing Niagara and lowered food down to passengers who were waiting in a boat in the waters below.

During subsequent Niagara crossings, merely walking along the rope wasn't enough, and he went on to perform increasingly outlandish stunts such as walking backward, turning somersaults, walking blindfolded, standing on his head, being locked in chains, and standing on stilts.

Blondin became a sensation and performed in China, Australia, India and the U.K., where he later settled, altogether clocking up an estimated 10,000 mi (16,000 km) of tightrope walking. By the end of his slip-free career, he had crossed Niagara Falls no less than 300 times. He died at the age of 72.

Blondin could cross the tightrope by balance alone— here he has a sack placed over his head, so that every footfall relies upon his agility, skill and instinct.

Blondin successfully carried his manager, Harry Colcord, on his back across Niagara Falls on more than one occasion.

FEATS TO BEAT

BIG BOUNCE

Thirty-year-old Jay Phoenix completed 150 bungee jumps in 21½ hours from a 130-ft-high (40-m) crane in Brisbane, Australia, averaging seven jumps an hour. He maintained his energy levels by snacking between jumps, and as he found he was often still chewing on the way down, he discovered that he could swallow while bouncing.

MARATHON HIKE

Matt "The Walker" Livermanne from Salt Lake City, Utah, walked 10,000 mi (16,000 km) around the U.S.A.—including the old Route 66 from Los Angeles, California, to Chicago, Illinois, a mammoth 2,400-mi (3,862-km) hike—in just 19 months. He clocked up more than 20 million steps.

HYBRID SPORT

Originating in the Netherlands, footgolf is a new sport where players kick a soccer ball into holes on a golf course in as few shots as possible—and in June 2012 the first Footgolf World Cup was held in Budapest, Hungary, attracting players from countries as far away as the U.S.A., Argentina and Mexico.

VETERAN RACER

Hershel McGriff from Portland, Oregon, drove in a NASCAR West Series race at Sonoma Raceway, California, on June 23, 2012, at the age of 84. He finished a respectable 18th in a field of 30 drivers.

RARE CARD

As an investment for his son, Jason LeBlanc of Newburyport, Massachusetts, paid $92,000 at a 2013 auction in Maine for a 148-year-old baseball card. The 1865 card showed a photograph of the all-conquering Brooklyn Atlantics amateur baseball club.

HELPING HAND

Brazilian soccer team Aparecidense were thrown out of the Fourth Division play-offs in 2013 after club masseur Romildo da Silva stepped onto the field from behind the net and blocked two goalbound shots in the dying minutes to prevent opponents Tupi from snatching victory. Da Silva, who was chased from the field by enraged Tupi players, was fined $250 and suspended for 24 matches.

FROG LADY

Thayer Cueter (aka The Frog Lady) of Edmonds, Washington State, has built up a collection of over 10,000 items of frog-related memorabilia, including 400 Kermit the Frog toys, 490 plush frog toys and 20 different pairs of frog pajamas.

36 OFF

A referee at a junior league soccer match in Paraguay between Teniente Fariña and Libertad brandished 36 red cards—sending off the substitutes as well as all the players—after a mass brawl broke out in the closing minutes.

PUDDING RACE

At the Yorkshire Pudding Boat Race in Brawby, England, competitors paddle giant traditional Yorkshire puddings—made of flour, water and eggs and coated in varnish—across a lake.

TREE THROWING

Every January, people living near Weidenthal, Germany, get rid of their old Christmas trees by staging a competition to see how far they can throw them. There are three disciplines in the World Christmas Tree Throwing Championships—weitwurf (javelin-style), hammerwurf (hammer-style) and hochwurf (high-jump-style)—and all trees must first be stripped of lights and other decorations.

KILLER BALL

In 1920, Ray Chapman of the Cleveland Indians died after the ball pitched to him struck him on the head—he is the only player to be killed by a baseball during a Major League game.

BUBBLE POP

On January 28, 2013, 336 pupils at Hawthorne High School, New Jersey, popped over 8,000 sq ft (743 sq m) of bubble wrap in two minutes. The event celebrated Bubble Wrap Appreciation Day—Marc Chavannes and Al Fielding invented bubble wrap in Hawthorne in 1960.

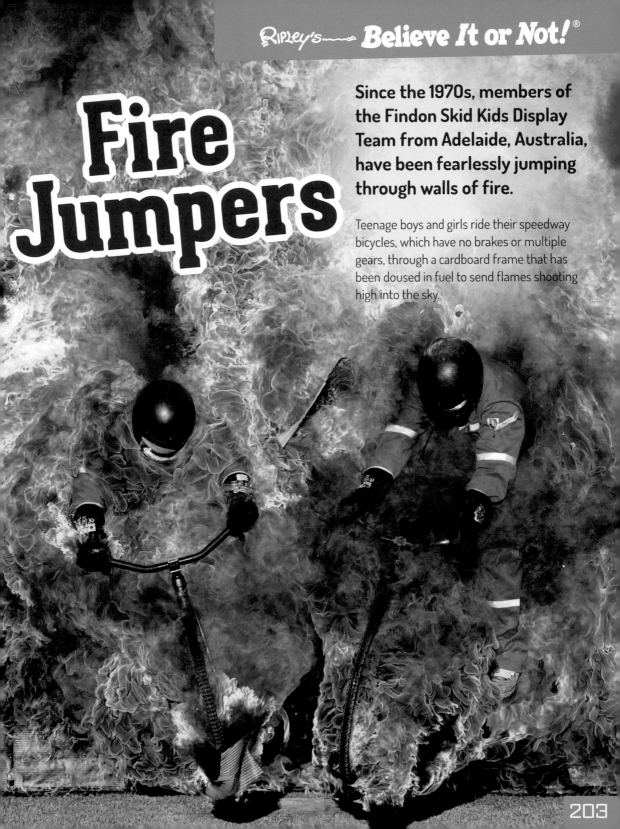

Fire Jumpers

Since the 1970s, members of the Findon Skid Kids Display Team from Adelaide, Australia, have been fearlessly jumping through walls of fire.

Teenage boys and girls ride their speedway bicycles, which have no brakes or multiple gears, through a cardboard frame that has been doused in fuel to send flames shooting high into the sky.

Everest BASE Jump

In May 2013, Russian extreme sports star Valery Rozov BASE jumped off the north face of Mount Everest 23,688 ft (7,220 m) above sea level. He flew for nearly a minute at 125 mph (200 km/h) along the north face before landing safely on the Rongbuk glacier at an altitude of 19,521 ft (5,950 m). He made his daring jump to celebrate the 60th anniversary of the conquest of Everest.

LUCKY BOUNCE

Former National Football League quarterback Brad Johnson is the only person in the league's history to complete a touchdown pass to himself. He did it playing for the Minnesota Vikings against the Carolina Panthers in 1997 when he caught his own deflected pass and then ran three yards for a unique touchdown.

OPEN WIDE

Dinesh Shivnath Upadhyaya from Mumbai, India, can fit 800 drinking straws in his mouth at the same time.

Flaming Football

Played in parts of Indonesia to celebrate the holy month of Ramadan, *sepak bola api* is just like soccer—except all the players are barefoot and the ball is a red-hot fireball! The ball is actually an old coconut shell, which has been soaked in 5 gal (20 l) of kerosene for up to a week to ensure it will stay alight for the duration of the game. So that players can kick and even head it without suffering severe burns, they undergo a pre-match ritual that is supposed to make them impervious to fire and includes a 21-day fast and avoiding eating any foods cooked with fire.

SLAND SWIM

In 2013, Anna Wardley from Hampshire, England, became the first person in nearly 30 years to swim nonstop around the Isle of Wight. She completed the 60-mi (97-km) challenge in just over 26½ hours, making some 87,500 strokes in the process.

FLYING HIGH

Professional kiteboarder Jesse Richman from Maui, Hawaii, was towed by a boat and lifted an unprecedented 790 ft (240 m) into the air above the Columbia River Gorge in Oregon—more than 20 times the height that kiteboarders usually reach when their kite is caught by the wind.

BATTERY POWER

As part of a recycling enterprise, the region of Durham, Ontario, Canada, collected 11,288 lb (5,120 kg) of batteries in just 24 hours.

GLOBAL RUN

Starting and finishing at Sydney Opera House, Australian athlete Tom Denniss circumnavigated the world on foot by running the equivalent of a marathon a day for 622 days. Visiting five continents and going through 17 pairs of shoes, he ran 16,250 mi (26,000 km) in just under 21 months from December 2011 to September 2013. His scariest moment came during his run over the Andes mountain range, when he slipped on a snowcap and nearly fell down a 1,000-ft (300-m) ice cliff.

SHARP PRACTICE

Sword-swallower Aerial Manx from Melbourne, Australia, can do cartwheels with a sword in his throat.

MARTIAL ARTS

On June 9, 2012, 10,000 students of kung fu gathered in Henan, China, to put on a martial arts display for the country's Cultural Heritage Day.

A man uses a baseball bat to smash a coconut placed on a fellow Bir Khalsa member's forehead. The group recently broke 59 coconuts in one minute in this way.

Stunt Team

Members of a stunt group called Bir Khalsa ("The Brave Pure") perform daring feats for villagers in the Punjab region of India. They chew glass tube lights, play with fire, fight with swords and spiked maces, and allow themselves to be run over by cars. The 450 members, whose ages range from young children to men in their thirties, practice the ancient Sikh martial art of ghatka. The group's founder, Kamaljeet Singh Khalsa, says that children are initially trained to perform ghatka using wooden swords, but when they reach the age of six, they graduate to iron ritual daggers—but always under adult supervision.

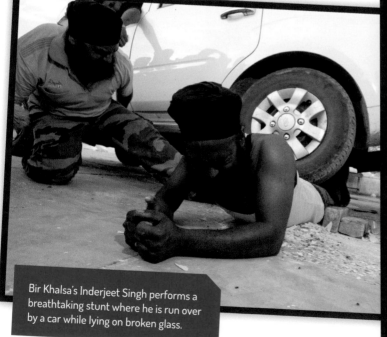

Bir Khalsa's Inderjeet Singh performs a breathtaking stunt where he is run over by a car while lying on broken glass.

WORLD WALK

Masahito Yoshida from Tottori, Japan, walked 25,000 mi (40,000 km) around the world in 4½ years. He set off from Shanghai, China, at the start of 2009 with a two-wheeled cart carrying 110 lb (50 kg) of luggage and walked across Asia and Europe to Portugal. He then flew to the east coast of the U.S.A. before walking from Atlantic City, New Jersey, to Vancouver, Canada. After hiking across Australia, he ended his epic trek walking from the southern tip of Asia back home.

LAST DOG

The last hot dog and bun sold at the last Montreal Expos baseball game in 2004 sold for $2,605 on eBay—more than 700 times its original price.

OLDEST FAMILY

In 2012, nine brothers and sisters of the Melis family from Ogliastra, Sardinia, boasted a combined age of 818—this works out to an average age of 91 and makes them the world's oldest living family. The siblings, who ranged in age from 78 to 105, attribute their longevity to minestrone soup.

SPIN MASTER

Eighteen-year-old Michael Kopp from Germany is able to spin a basketball on a toothbrush held in his mouth.

NO RUNS

The Detroit Tigers and Pittsburgh Pirates baseball teams played a pair of nine-inning scoreless games in three days in May 2013—only the fifth time this has happened in over 100 years of Major League history.

RED SOCK

A bloody sock worn by Boston Red Sox pitcher Curt Schilling in the 2004 World Series sold for $92,613 at an auction in February 2013.

HUMAN FLAG

A total of 26,904 residents of Vladivostok gathered on the city's Zolotoy Bridge and held aloft red, white and blue flags to create a living image of the Russian flag.

Greasy Pole

Every August in St. Julian's, Malta, hundreds of brave young men attempt to climb a 65-ft-long (20-m) greasy pole and retrieve a flag at the end for a game called gostra, which dates back to the Middle Ages. Some competitors prefer to run along the wooden pole as fast as possible in the hope of grabbing a flag before inevitably slipping off into the water below.

The Mighty Atom

The Mighty Atom could bend iron bars using his hair.

Breaking a chain purely by the expansion of his chest.

Joseph Greenstein was born prematurely in Poland in 1893. A small child, he never grew over 5 ft 4 in (163 cm) in height and weighed just 145 lb (65.7 kg).

However, his small stature did not prevent Joseph from becoming "The Mighty Atom," one of the strongest men in the world—perhaps even the strongest, pound for pound.

In his youth, Joseph was befriended by a Russian wrestler and circus strongman who helped him become a top wrestler billed as "Kid Greenstein"—a name that would take him to Asia, where he honed his physical prowess and developed the mental powers he would later use in his strongman performances.

An iron grip, strength and concentration helped the Mighty Atom bend steel bars as if they were wire.

Two gentleman help the Atom bend an iron bar over his nose.

The Atom lying on a bed of nails, with the added weight of 17 members of a band!

He believed that the power of the mind was just as important as the power of physical strength. It was in America that Joseph became the Mighty Atom and made his name devising unique and seemingly impossible feats of strength for his comparatively small stature. He could lift 500-lb (225-kg) weights with his teeth, bite nails in two, and bend iron bars into different shapes.

In 1934, he broke a rib during an act in New York, but when the ambulance was called, he offered to pull it to the hospital with his hair. He performed at Atlantic City and Coney Island, and after wowing crowds with his brawn, he would sell them tonics that promised to maximize their own muscle power.

His other feats included changing a car tire with no tools and lying on a bed of nails while supporting a 17-piece band on his body.

The Mighty Atom had a surprisingly long career, given the extreme demands placed on his body, and he continued to perform into old age, appearing at Madison Square Garden, New York, in his eighties. His incredible story is thought to be the basis for the long-running DC Comics character "Atom," who first appeared in 1940.

All photos courtesy of Eastwind One Corporation, Ed Spielman Pres.

Biting a chain in half with his teeth was a regular trick.

GIANT SNOWBALL

The Silver Star Mountain Resort at Vernon, British Columbia, made a snowball that was nearly 12 ft (3.6 m) tall and weighed 40,000 lb (18,000 kg).

EXPLOSIVE TARGETS

The traditional Colombian sport of tejo involves throwing metal disks at gunpowder-filled targets that explode on impact.

WHEELY CRAZY!

Originating in the U.S.A., the sport of extreme mountain unicycling, described as a cross between mountain biking and rodeo riding, sees thrill-seekers pedal, pivot and bunny-hop from rock to rock as they try to ride all the way down steep mountain faces on their custom-made unicycles without falling into deep chasms.

BLIND VAULTER

Fifteen-year-old pole-vaulter Charlotte Brown from Emory, Texas, qualified for the 2013 state championships even though she is legally blind. She has cleared a height of 11 ft 6 in (3.5 m) and is able to vault by counting her steps on her run-up and listening to her coach yell when it is time to launch. She also places an 80-ft (24-m) strip of dark artificial turf adjacent to the approach lane to create a light/dark contrast she can follow in order to keep running in a straight line.

DEADLY WATERS

On September 2, 2013, 64-year-old American endurance swimmer Diana Nyad became the first person to swim the treacherous waters from Cuba to Florida without a shark cage. She swam without a wetsuit or flippers, but wore a silicone mask to protect her face from the jellyfish stings that had foiled two of her four previous attempts. Diana completed the 110-mi (176-km) crossing in just under 53 hours. She had first attempted the swim 35 years earlier, in 1978.

Berry Boarding

Believe it or not, this intrepid wakeboarder is being pulled through a bog of cranberries at the 2010 Red Bull Winch Sessions in Tomah, Wisconsin. To harvest cranberries, the beds are flooded with up to 1 ft (30 cm) of water above the vines, and because the berries are filled with air, they readily float to the surface and present a fresh, fruity challenge for wakeboarders.

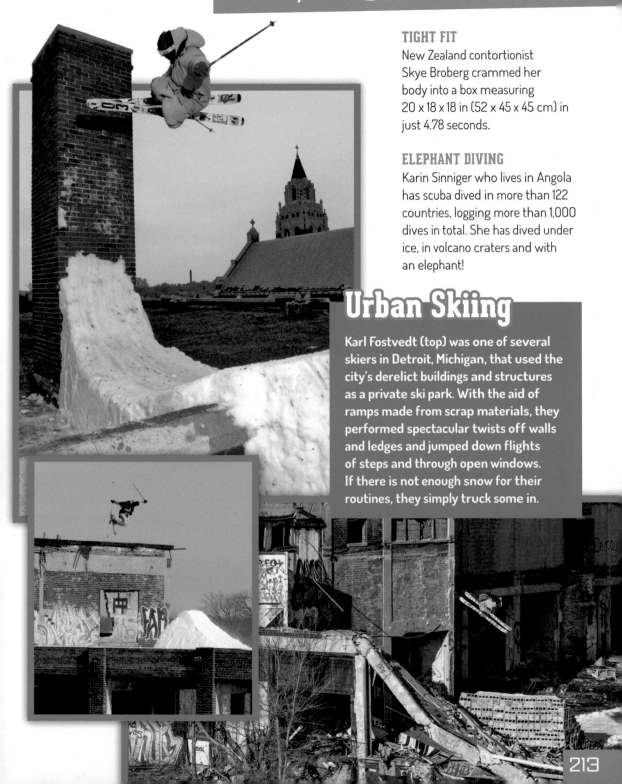

TIGHT FIT
New Zealand contortionist Skye Broberg crammed her body into a box measuring 20 x 18 x 18 in (52 x 45 x 45 cm) in just 4.78 seconds.

ELEPHANT DIVING
Karin Sinniger who lives in Angola has scuba dived in more than 122 countries, logging more than 1,000 dives in total. She has dived under ice, in volcano craters and with an elephant!

Urban Skiing

Karl Fostvedt (top) was one of several skiers in Detroit, Michigan, that used the city's derelict buildings and structures as a private ski park. With the aid of ramps made from scrap materials, they performed spectacular twists off walls and ledges and jumped down flights of steps and through open windows. If there is not enough snow for their routines, they simply truck some in.

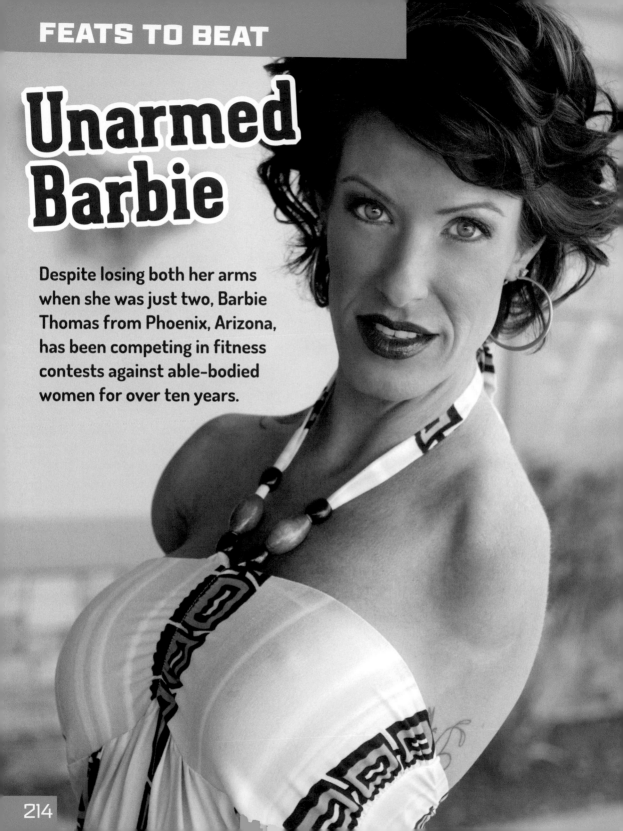

Unarmed Barbie

Despite losing both her arms when she was just two, Barbie Thomas from Phoenix, Arizona, has been competing in fitness contests against able-bodied women for over ten years.

214

Barbie Thomas's arms were burned to the bone by a supercharged electric shock at the age of two after she had climbed onto a transformer and grabbed the wires with both hands. "They were like charcoal," she said. "They were completely dead and had to be amputated at the shoulders."

Young Barbie was not expected to live. However, not only did she survive against the odds, but she also quickly learned to adapt by holding out her legs to hug her mother and using her legs and feet to get dressed. As a young girl, she entered dance and swimming competitions, as well as played soccer, before turning to fitness. Now the inspirational mother-of-two trains at the gym six days a week, doing weights and leg exercises and practicing her routine, which includes splits, high kicks, and an incredible ninja kip up where, from lying on her back, she bounces straight up into a standing position.

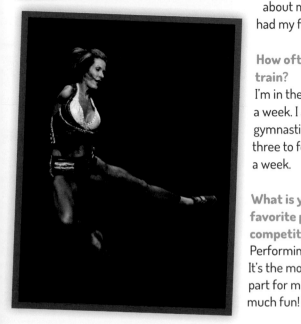

What made you become a fitness fanatic?
I've always been "fit." I was very active growing up but got serious about my fitness after I had my first baby.

How often do you train?
I'm in the gym six days a week. I also go to gymnastics practice three to four days a week.

What is your favorite part of the competition?
Performing a routine. It's the most challenging part for me, but it's so much fun!

What inspires you?
Knowing that I'm inspiring others and hearing their stories. Also, people who have it harder than I do—they inspire me!

Do you have particularly dextrous feet?
My feet ARE my hands. I wish my toes were a little longer, but yes . . . they have a lot of dexterity, especially my right foot. I'm right footed!

What has been your greatest challenge, and how did you overcome it?
Besides backflips, caring for my boys when they were babies, especially when they were newborn. The first time I learned by trial and error, but by the time I had my second baby, it was a piece of cake.

FEATS TO BEAT

BIG PUSH

U.S. Marine Sgt. Enrique Treviño from Dallas, Texas, completed one million push-ups in 2012—that's an average of nearly 2,740 per day.

HEAD SMASH

Scott Damerow, a student at the Georgia Institute of Technology, U.S.A., cracked 142 eggs in one minute, using only his forehead.

LETTER OPENERS

William L. Brown of Gainesville, Florida, has collected more than 5,000 letter openers. He bought his first letter opener in Rome, Italy, in the late 1950s and became hooked.

DARING DORIS

Great-great-grandmother Doris Long from Hampshire, England, celebrated her 99th birthday in May 2013 by bravely rappeling down the side of a 110-ft-high (34-m) building.

CAN CASTLE

The Toyohashi Junior Chamber from Japan re-created a corner tower of Yoshida Castle from 104,840 aluminum cans. The cans, which were held together by glue, formed a tower measuring 16 ft (5 m) high, 21.6 ft (6.6 m) wide and 18 ft (5.5 m) long.

BIG BUBBLE

Canadian bubble artist Fan Yang encapsulated no fewer than 181 people in a single bubble that measured 164-ft-long (50-m) and 13-ft-high (4-m) in Vancouver, British Columbia, Canada.

HOMEMADE SHOES

Since 1971, George Walter from Pittsburgh, Pennsylvania, has traveled the world on foot, visiting more than 40 countries and wearing sandals he makes himself from tire treads, nails and nylon straps.

Man in a Bag

Bulgarian Jane Petkov swam 1¼ mi (2 km) across Lake Ohrid in Macedonia while tied up in a bag. With his arms and legs strapped to his body, the 59-year-old swam on his back "like a dolphin" for nearly three hours, averaging 0.4 mph (0.7 km/h).

SKATEBOARD SPEEDSTER

Daredevil South African professional skateboarder Decio Lourenco hit a top speed of 68 mph (109 km/h) as he raced down a hill and through traffic on a busy Cape Town highway, passing within just a few feet of oncoming vehicles. His high-speed stunt angered the police, who say he triggered a speed camera in an area where the limit is just 37 mph (60 km/h).

GARDEN COURSE

Desperate to build a snowboarding course in the back garden of his home in Aviemore, Scotland, Mikey Jachacy and nine friends made several trips 2,000 ft (600 m) up the Cairngorm Mountains and collected eight tons of snow. They then built a 200-ft-long (60-m) course, complete with ramps, jumps and even a cable-operated ski lift, which ran off an old motorcycle engine.

TEAM TOILET

In 2012, Toronto Maple Leafs fan Jim Vigmond paid $5,300 for a toilet from the hockey team's locker room at their old Maple Leaf Gardens arena.

SAND SKIER

Henrik May from Germany prefers to ski on sand rather than on snow and has reached a top speed of 57 mph (92 km/h) on a dune in the Namibian Desert.

STRONG TEETH

Former circus strongman Mike Greenstein of Queens, New York, can still pull cars with his teeth at the age of 92.

SAFE HANDS

Cincinnati Reds fan Caleb Lloyd caught two home-run balls in the same inning during the Reds' win over the Atlanta Braves in May 2012.

MILES AHEAD

Sixty-nine-year-old Larry Macon from San Antonio, Texas, completed an unprecedented 255 marathons in 2013, averaging three a week, which made a total of over 4,110 mi (6,614 km). He wears out 13 pairs of running shoes a year and, working as a full-time attorney, has even held conference calls while running.

OLDEST WINNER

Sixty-five-year-old Bill "Spaceman" Lee of San Francisco, California, became the oldest pitcher to win a pro baseball game when his San Rafael Pacifics beat the Maui Na Koa Ikaika on August 23, 2012.

ATLANTIC FLIGHT

Bernard Chambers released his prize-winning racing pigeon Percy in Brittany, France, expecting him to fly the 303 mi (485 km) home to Staffordshire, England—but instead the bird turned up 3,200 mi (5,150 km) away in Quebec, Canada.

HELICOPTER DROP

In July 2013, Zack Hample of New York City caught a baseball dropped from a helicopter flying 1,050 ft (320 m) above him at Lowell, Massachusetts. The ball plummeted toward him at 95 mph (152 km/h) on its 12-second journey into his mitt.

COW COSTUMES

A total of 470 people turned up for a restaurant-sponsored event in Fairfax, Virginia, dressed as cows, wearing one- or two-piece black-and-white costumes complete with heads and matching shoes.

SURFBOARD BALANCE

Doug McManaman of Nova Scotia, Canada, balanced a 9-ft-long (2.7-m), 20-lb (9-kg) surfboard on his chin for 51.47 seconds.

FAST HANDS

Bryan Bednarek, from Chicago, Illinois, can clap his hands together more than 800 times in a minute—that's an incredible 13 times a second.

BIKE CLIMB

Without his feet ever touching the ground, Italian Vittorio Brumotti cycled up 3,700 steps to the top of the tallest building in the world—the 2,715-ft-high (828-m) Burj Khalifa in Dubai. He jumped his way up the 160 floors in 2 hours 20 minutes.

Barnstormers

The Barnstormers were daredevil pilots and stuntmen who performed outrageous airplane stunts for traveling air shows, flying circuses and Hollywood movies in the U.S.A. in the 1920s.

Named after entertainers that performed in rural New York barns in the early 19th century, many Barnstormers caught the flying bug from when they were pilots in World War I, and they often flew ex-Air Force Curtiss biplanes. Barnstormers were famous for their death-defying wing-walks, where stuntmen and women would climb from the cockpit and perform stunts on the wings, usually completely unsecured, at flying speeds of up to 90 mph (145 km/h). The moves didn't just look dangerous, they could be genuinely deadly, and many Barnstormers lost their lives in the pursuit of ever-more imaginative stunts to thrill crowds on the ground or while shooting Hollywood movies.

By the late 1920s, the Barnstormers' casualty rate was so high that the government stepped in and made it illegal for stunt aircraft to fly within 300 ft (90 m) of each other.

Legendary pilot Charles Lindbergh, the first man to fly solo nonstop across the Atlantic in 1927, was a Barnstormer early in his aviation career.

Al Wilson made a dangerous leap onto a plane from a car traveling at 80 mph (129 km/h) in 1927.

FEATS TO BEAT

Ivan Unger and Gladys Roy playing tennis on a plane in 1925. Roy was later killed when she backed into a spinning propeller.

The 13 Black Cats were a troop of Hollywood stuntmen and women specializing in madcap airplane and automobile exploits in the 1920s. They flew on barnstorming tours when not shooting movies and proudly kept to the motto on their calling card— "We'll do anything!"

"Spider" Matlock, Al Johnson and "Fronty" Nichols strike a pose on a plane piloted by Bon MacDougall. Nichols would later die in a parachute accident, and Matlock was killed in a motor race.

In 1924, Al Wilson became probably the first man to drive a golf ball from the wings of a plane.

13 Black Cats Price List

The Cats provided a price list for Hollywood movie producers looking to hire their services.

General stunt rate per hour	$35	A plane crash into an automobile	$250
Fire on plane	$50	Upside-down plane-to-plane transfer	$500
Plane-to-plane transfer	$100	A plane crash into a house or trees	$1,200
A loop with man standing on wing	$150	Explode a plane midflight	$1,500

Chief White Eagle would hang from planes at 5,000 ft (1,525 m) attached by only his hair, a stunt that would later kill him when the pilot attempted a loop the loop and his locks came loose.

TAPE BALL

A ball built from various tapes—including masking, electrical and duct—by the Portland Promise Center in Louisville, Kentucky, weighed 2,000 lb (908 kg) and had a circumference of 12¾ ft (3.9 m)—more than five times the size of a standard basketball.

COLD COMFORT

In February 2013, six competitors—four men and two women—perched for 48 hours on 8¼-ft-high (2.5-m) blocks of ice in temperatures that dipped to below –18°F (–28°C) to become joint winners of a national ice pole-sitting contest that takes place in Vilhelmina, Sweden.

DISNEY DAYS

Southern Californians Tonya Mickesh and Jeff Reitz visited Disneyland every day during 2012—a total of 366 trips. They each walked up to 4 mi (6.4 km) per visit, meaning that between them they clocked up a total of nearly 3,000 mi (4,830 km) in the course of the year. They also posted more than 2,000 photos of their adventure on Instagram.

Ram Race

In a novel twist to the 100-meter race, competitors in Yiwu County, China, race along a course while carrying a full-grown sheep whose legs are bound to prevent escape. The "Running with Sheep" event is part of an annual harvest celebration, which also includes a sheep beauty contest.

All Fours

Running on all fours, Japan's Kenichi Ito scrambled 100 meters in a speedy 16.87 seconds at Tokyo's Olympic athletic track in November, 2013. He beat six other competitors in an all-fours 100-meter race and said that he's been developing his distinctive running style, which is based on the movements of the African Patas monkey, for more than a decade.

HOT LIPS
Fire-eater Carissa Hendrix of Calgary, Alberta, can hold a flaming torch in her mouth for more than two minutes.

GIANTS STADIUM
New York Giants fan Don Martini, 75, spent two years and $20,000 building a replica scale model of the team's old stadium in a garage behind his Blairstown, New Jersey, bagel shop. He made 65,000 seats and even included working lights and elevators in the model, which measures 20 ft (6 m) long and 17 ft (5.2 m) wide.

QUICK CHANGE
During the 2012 Formula-1 German Grand Prix, the McLaren team changed all four tires on driver Jenson Button's car in just 2.3 seconds.

FLORAL JERSEY
German Bundesliga soccer club Borussia Dortmund launched their new jersey for the 2013–14 season by planting 80,645 flowers—mainly yellow marigolds—to replicate the design on nearby parkland.

JACKET POTATOES
At the Kiplingcotes Derby, a 500-year-old, 4-mi (6.4-km) cross-country horse race in Yorkshire, England, the amateur jockeys achieve the required riding weight of 140 lb (63.5 kg) by putting potatoes into their jacket pockets.

VETERAN CLIMBER
On May 23, 2013, Japanese mountaineer Yuichiro Miura reached the summit of Mount Everest at the admirable age of 80 years 223 days.

BLOOD DONOR
Edward Kisslack of Waynesboro, Pennsylvania, has donated 30 gal (114 l) of blood in the last 50 years— enough to replace the blood in his own body 20 times.

BUTTER KNIFE
Schoolteacher Claes Blixt from Skene, Sweden, made a giant wooden butter knife that measures 97.63 in long (248 cm) and weighs 62 lb 13 oz (28.5 kg).

MASSIVE MURAL
Amanda Warrington spent more than 1,000 hours solving a 24,000-piece jigsaw puzzle. When she had finished, she glued the 14 x 5 ft (4.3 x 1.5 m) montage to a wall of her home in Gloucestershire, England.

FEATS TO BEAT

YOUNG WING-WALKERS
Reaching speeds of up to 100 mph (160 km/h) and flying only yards apart, schoolgirls Rose Powell and Flame Brewer performed wing-walking stunts in formation—at age nine. When they took to the skies over Gloucestershire, England, the cousins, from London, became the third generation of their families to wing walk on two of their grandfather's vintage biplanes.

HEAVY BURDEN
Jim "The Shark" Dreyer from Grand Rapids, Michigan, swam 22 mi (35 km) in 51 hours across Lake St. Clair, near the U.S.–Canada border, hauling a ton of bricks.

STIFF UPPER LIP
Saddi Muhammad pulled a 1.9-ton truck that was attached to his mustache for 200 ft (60 m) in his hometown of Lahore, Pakistan, in October 2012.

CAPITAL KNOWLEDGE
At just 18 months old, Aanav Jayakar from Cleveland, Ohio, could correctly identify 21 countries on a map of the world and recite 61 capital cities.

Model Car

As a tribute to the Aston Martin DBR1 that won the 1959 Le Mans 24-hour Endurance Race, the Evanta Motor Company, from Hertfordshire, England, has produced a life-size model of the famous sports car in the form of an Airfix construction kit. The $38,000 kit measures 21 ft (6.35 m) long and 11 ft (3.4 m) high and consists of the car's body shell, lights, screens, four 16-in (40-cm) wire wheels with race tires, race seats and steering wheel. Also included is a replica of the Le Mans trophy and an Aston Martin cap signed by the two victorious drivers from 1959, Briton Roy Salvadori and American Carroll Shelby.

DITCH PLUNGE

Extreme kayaker Ben Marr from Mallorytown, Ontario, somehow kept upright as he paddled furiously down a steep concrete drainage ditch called the Lions Bay Slide in British Columbia at nearly 35 mph (56 km/h) before splashing into a reservoir.

BATTING MARATHON

Overcoming fatigue, muscle pain and hunger, 52-year-old baseball fanatic Mike Filippone, president of the North Babylon Youth League, New York, batted for 24 hours straight in June 2013, during which he hit close to 10,000 balls.

WRONG ROUTE

Of the 5,000 runners that took part in the 2013 Marathon of the North in Sunderland, England, only one competitor—Leicester's Jake Harrison—completed the correct course. Organizers accidentally sent everyone else on a wrong route, which meant that their total run was in fact 289 yd (264 m) short of the full 26 mi 385 yd (42.2 km) marathon distance.

Full Hand

Philip Osenton, a U.K. wine consultant based in Beijing, China, can hold 51 wine glasses in one hand at the same time. He learned his skill while working as a wine steward at top London hotels.

PIER PRESSURE

Jay and Hazel Preller from Somerset, England, traveled 7,000 mi (11,265 km) over the course of two years visiting all 60 seaside piers in the U.K.—and kissed on the end of each one. They first met on Weston-super-Mare's Grand Pier and got married on Brighton Pier.

MARATHON BOUNCE

Phoebe Asquith, 24, from Yorkshire, England, bounced 4.1 mi (6.6 km) on a Hippity Hop (Space Hopper) toy. The journey took her 4½ hours at an average speed of just under 1 mph (1.6 km/h).

FANCY DRESS

In June 2013, David Smith from Derbyshire, England, ran an incredible 69 mi (110 km) along Hadrian's Wall in the north of England in 14 hours 24 minutes—wearing a full Roman centurion costume. Previously, he competed in marathons wearing outfits such as handcuffs, a straitjacket and a gingerbread-man costume.

CROSS COUNTRY

Star Wars fan Jacob French raised more than $100,000 for charity by walking 3,100 mi (4,960 km) from Perth to Sydney, Australia, dressed in a stormtrooper costume. The walk took him nine months, during which time he lost over 26 lb (12 kg) in weight and wore out seven pairs of shoes.

MATCHSTICK MARKER

Shourabh Modi of Madhya Pradesh, India, wrote the name of Madhya Pradesh chief minister Shivraj Singh Chauhan 11,111 times on 2,778 matchsticks—four times per match—in 30 days.

JUGGLING GENIUS

Ravi Fernando, a math undergrad at Stanford University, California, can solve a Rubik's Cube puzzle in 1½ minutes while juggling it and two small balls.

DELAYED DIPLOMA

More than 80 years after dropping out of high school despite needing only one credit to graduate, Audrey Crabtree of Cedar Falls, Iowa, finally received an honorary diploma—at age 99. She had left Waterloo East High School in 1932 following an accident that caused her to miss some school and because she also had to care for her sick grandmother.

Defying Death

A Ukrainian daredevil who calls himself Mustang Wanted hangs hundreds of feet in the air from a skyscraper in Moscow, Russia, just by the fingertips of one hand. The 26-year-old gave up his desk job as a legal advisor to become a skywalker, balancing without a safety harness on the edge of tall buildings and cranes, knowing that the slightest slip would mean certain death. His exploits as a real-life Spider-Man have brought him thousands of followers on social network sites. Although he has performed pull-ups on a metal girder 300 ft (90 m) above the ground, he says his greatest fear is being caught by the police.

Artistic License

BEAN PORTRAIT

Malcolm West from Surrey, England, used more than 5,000 jellybeans in 20 different flavors to create a 4-ft-high (1.2-m) portrait of the Duchess of Cambridge. He used licorice and chocolate pudding flavors for her hair and candy floss and pink grapefruit for her complexion, gluing each bean into place.

BODY-PAINTING

A team of artists body-painted 316 people in just five hours at Cork, Ireland. The models removed all their clothes apart from their underwear before paint was applied to every exposed part of their bodies except for the soles of their feet.

CHEWED GUM

Ukrainian artist Anna-Sofiya Matveeva creates portraits of celebrities such as Elton John and the late Steve Jobs from hundreds of pieces of chewed gum. After separating the gum into different colors and shades, she warms it up in a microwave. Each finished artwork can weigh up to 11 lb (5 kg).

SPACE FILLERS

Swedish artist Michael Johansson creates large Tetris-like installations filled precisely with diverse everyday objects including wardrobes, filing cabinets, household appliances, suitcases and even cars, caravans and tractors. His colorful, compartmentalized artworks have occupied spaces in abandoned storefronts, between buildings and between stacked shipping containers.

CORN MURAL

Murals made from 275,000 ears of corn of different colors, including blue, orange and black, decorate the exterior and interior of the Corn Palace building in Mitchell, South Dakota. The corn murals are changed annually and have portrayed such iconic American images as Mount Rushmore and cowboys riding horses.

ART OF REGURGITATION

Los Angeles, California, artist John Knuth feeds ordinary houseflies water and sugar mixed with watercolor pigments and lets them paint by regurgitation. He harvests hundreds of thousands of flies from maggots he orders online and, after feeding them the mixture, he simply allows nature to take its course. Sure enough, within a few weeks his entire canvas is covered with millions of tiny colorful specks of fly vomit.

Wrapper's Delight

Artist Laura Benjamin from East Hampton, New York, used dozens of torn and cut candy wrappers to make this multi-layered collage of Miss Piggy, part of her Wrapper's Delight collection.

BOUNCY CHAIR

Preston Moeller from North Carolina might have made the world's bounciest office chair—out of 65,000 rubber bands. The chair weighs 35 lb (15.8 kg), and it took him 300 hours to loop the bands together to make the chair.

BARGAIN BUY

Russian artist Ilya Bolotowsky's painting *Vertical Diamond* sold at an auction for $34,375—five months after Beth Feeback from Concord, North Carolina, had bought it at a Goodwill store for $10.

WORD ART

Artist Michael Volpicelli from Stillwater, Oklahoma, makes portraits of famous people using only written words relating to their life. Using pen and ink, he draws inspirational figures such as Pope John Paul II and Malala Yousafzai, the 16-year-old Pakistani girl shot by the Taliban for going to school, from hundreds of words linked to their lives.

Tree Hole Paintings

Art student Wang Yue uses tree trunks as her canvas to brighten up the streets of Shijiazhuang, China, a city with one of the worst levels of air pollution in the world. Once she has found a tree with a suitable hole, she composes a digital drawing before painting the image onto the exposed bark. Wang Yue has already created more than a dozen images, including pictures of raccoons, pandas, birds and botanical landscapes.

Invisible Bodies

Passersby do a double take when they see these bronze sculptures on the waterfront at Marseille, France, because the subjects' vital organs appear to be missing. They are part of a collection of ten quirky, life-size human statues by sculptor Bruno Catalano that are without large chunks of their bodies. He says the invisible bodies represent the part of a person's life that is often missing. Working from original clay carvings, each statue takes him about 15 days to make.

MINIATURE WORLD
Nichola Battilana from Brighton, Ontario, makes miniature landscapes in thimbles. She sculpts tiny houses with paper clay, uses tufts of moss to represent a garden and then carefully positions them in the thimble.

SHOE ANIMALS
Kenya's Ocean Sole company has made more than 100 different sculptures from old flip-flops that have been discarded on the country's beaches, including elephants, warthogs and an 18-ft-tall (5.5-m) rubber giraffe.

LINT FIGURES
Cheryl Capezzuti from Pittsburgh, Pennsylvania, sculpts dryer lint into animals, angels and life-size human figures. She gets lint sent to her by people from all over the world and mixes it with glue to form her fluffy sculptures.

Snot Shots

Photographer Ulf Lundin invited models to his studio for an unusual and unflattering photo and video session—he asked them to sneeze into his camera and captured each nose explosion in graphic detail for a project named *Bless You*.

The Swedish artist was inspired by the drama and loss of control that everybody displays when they sneeze.

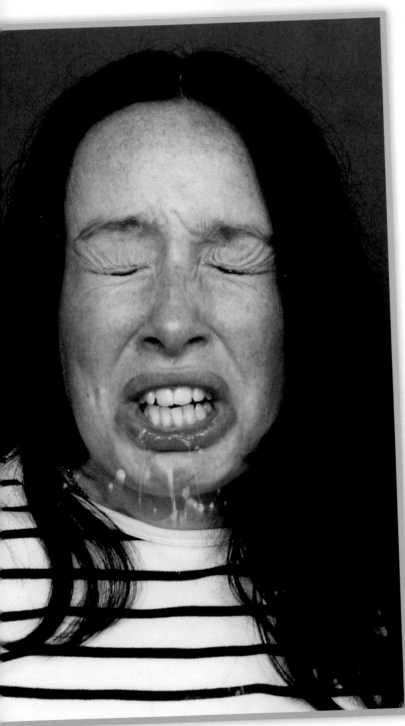

GUM METROPOLIS

Inspired by houses of cards and matchstick constructions, artist Jeremy Laffon from Marseille, France, took nearly three months to build a 6.6-ft-tall (2-m), 10-ft-long (3-m) city skyline from 4,000 pieces of chewing gum. The sticks of gum were stacked, carefully balanced and assembled into towers, held upright initially with just his saliva before he eventually had to use glue. Finally, he melted a few pieces of gum so that the skyline would gradually crumble to the ground, replicating a city that had turned to rubble.

BIDDING FRENZY

British artist Francis Bacon's studies of his friend Lucian Freud sold for $142.4 million at auction in New York City in 2013—after just six minutes of bidding, with the price going up $395,500 every second.

PETROLEUM PORTRAITS

Belarusian artist Ludmila Zhizhenko paints with petroleum. She needs only ⅓ oz (10 g) of petroleum for one of her typical oil paintings, which resemble vintage, yellowed photos. However, because of the dangerous fumes, she usually has to paint outdoors and has to keep the finished paintings away from fire.

GENETIC LIKENESS

New York City student Heather Dewey-Hagborg creates portrait sculptures from DNA she finds on discarded chewing gum, hairs and cigarette butts. She extracts the genetic material in a laboratory and then uses a computer program to build up an idea of the person's physical features before turning the information into sculptures for her Stranger Visions project.

SPOOKY SCULPTURES

Sculptor Brandon Vickerd from Toronto, Ontario, created a series of taxidermy statues—human bodies dressed in hooded tops but with stuffed animal heads in place of their faces. He put his sculptures, which featured the heads of raccoons, skunks, squirrels and a bunch of ducklings, in busy areas of major cities to observe public reaction.

WOODEN PUZZLE

Dave Evans of Dorset, England, spent 35 days hand-cutting a 40,000-piece wooden jigsaw puzzle featuring 33 images of Queen Elizabeth II's Diamond Jubilee. However, as he was making final adjustments to the 21 x 8 ft (6.45 x 2.41 m) jigsaw on its sloped board mounting, the whole thing collapsed and it took him another four days to reassemble.

BODY SOAP

Performance artist Orestes de la Paz, who is based in Miami, Florida, made 20 bars of soap from his own body fat after undergoing liposuction in December 2012. Each bar of human soap went on sale for $1,000.

CLIP ART

Every year for the past decade, Mike Drake from New York has collected hundreds of nail clippings and made a paperweight from them.

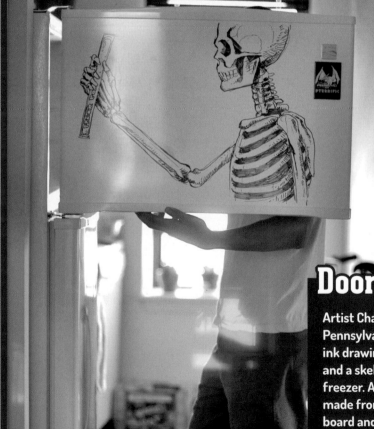

Door Drawings

Artist Charlie Layton from Philadelphia, Pennsylvania, has created a series of pen and ink drawings—including Darth Vader, Godzilla and a skeleton—on the door of his fridge freezer. After discovering that the door was made from the same material as a dry-erase board and could therefore work as an artistic surface, he did a new drawing every Friday, each one taking him about half an hour.

Playing with Fire

San Francisco, California, photographer Rob Prideaux literally plays with fire to achieve these pictures. Using a propane torch and a spray bottle, he sets fire to tiny amounts of gasoline in the loading bay of his studio and, with a wave sensor that reacts to the sound of the explosion to trigger the camera, he is able to capture that split second when flame erupts. He also creates patterns from smoke by burning incense in the dark and photographing it as it drifts through the air.

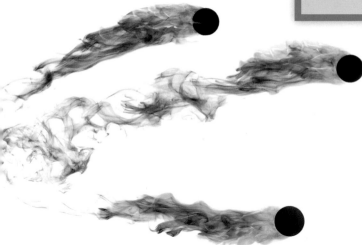

BACKYARD LANDMARK

Ken Larry Richardson from Mulvane, Kansas, spent 11 years and nearly $5,000 building a 150-ft-long (46-m) replica of San Francisco's Golden Gate Bridge to cross a small creek on his farm. He built it using 98 tons of concrete and lots of recycled materials, including cables from an oil rig and suspender cables salvaged from an old Boeing aircraft.

FINGERNAIL SCENES

Photographer and artist Alice Bartlett from London, England, creates miniature park scenes on her own fingernails. She coats her nails in textured green flocking to look like grass and then places tiny figures on them so that they appear to be enjoying a picnic or going for a stroll.

COMPLEX CORKSCREW

Mechanical sculptor Rob Higgs from Cornwall, England, has built the world's biggest and most complex corkscrew—a 5-ft-3-in-tall (1.6-m) brass contraption that weighs more than three-quarters of a ton and has 382 moving parts, including gears, pulleys, levers and springs.

RADIOACTIVE CHANDELIERS

Ken and Julia Yonetani from Sydney, Australia, produce vintage chandeliers made from radioactive uranium glass. They replace the crystals with uranium glass beads and add ultraviolet light to make them glow a beautiful green. They use a Geiger counter to check that their chandeliers emit safe levels of radiation.

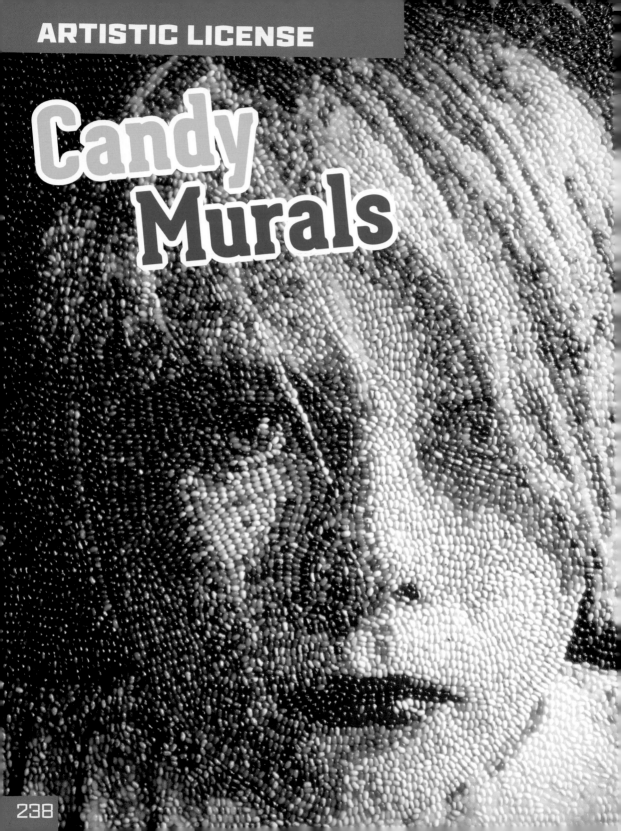

Candy Murals

Artist Kristen Cumings from Martinez, California, makes amazing pictures from thousands of colorful jelly beans.

As well as recreating iconic artworks, such as Van Gogh's *Starry Night*, Kristen has immortalized her son (left) and her young neighbor (below) in Jelly Belly Bean Art portraits. Starting from a photo of the subject, she paints an acrylic version onto a blank canvas. When it has dried, she applies the beans, matching the colors to the original as closely as possible and using spray adhesive to make sure the beans stick.

BOXED IN

Artist Tyler Ramsey, based in Los Angeles, California, spent a week living in a storefront window of a shoe store in Venice Beach. Between eating, sleeping and chatting to passersby, he customized newly bought shoes at the store by painting them with his fingers.

ARTISTIC FIELD

Dario Gambarin used a plow as his paintbrush to create a 328-ft (100-m) portrait of Pope Francis in a field on his parents' farm near Verona, Italy. The scale of his tractor pictures, which have also included Barack Obama and Edvard Munch's *The Scream*, means they can be viewed only from the air. He always removes them after a few days so that the field can be cultivated.

EVEREST DEBRIS

A group of 15 Nepalese artists collected several tons of garbage that had been left behind on Mount Everest and turned it into more than 70 different sculptures. The artworks incorporated discarded oxygen cylinders, cans, bottles and climbing tools, and even the remains of a helicopter that had crashed into the mountain in the 1970s.

Arty Booths

To deter graffiti sprayers and vandals, 100 artists transformed 100 street-side public phone booths in São Paulo, Brazil, into creative and colorful works of art. For *Call Parade*, a project sponsored by telecommunications firm Vivo, one booth creepily took on the appearance of a human brain, while another became a workman's helmet with a pencil through it.

UNDERWATER WHEELCHAIR

At a swimming pool in Weymouth, England, disabled artist Sue Austin performed an exhibition of acrobatics in the world's first self-propelled underwater wheelchair. Her art project *Creating the Spectacle!* featured a series of stunning underwater scuba routines in her modified wheelchair that is fitted with swimming floats, fins and two foot-controlled propulsion drives.

MIRROR WRITING

Leonardo da Vinci's personal notes were always written starting from the right side of the page and moving to the left, a technique known as "mirror writing," because anyone who wanted to read his private notebooks had to use a mirror. He wrote in the standard manner from left to right only if he intended for others to read what he had written down.

DOT MOSAICS

Lacy Knudson from San Diego, California, creates beautiful mosaics from thousands of tiny balls of Play-Doh. She paints the image first and then arranges the Play-Doh balls on the canvas over the corresponding colors. One piece took her six months to make and used 152 jars of Play-Doh rolled into 12,000 individual dots.

Toilet Tubes

Whereas most people simply throw old toilet paper tubes away, French artist Anastassia Elias has transformed more than 75 of them into imaginative miniature scenes. Using a scalpel and manicure scissors and the same paper color as the tubes, she spends hours patiently cutting out tiny shapes of everything from construction workers and circus performers to dinosaurs and ballerinas before carefully fitting them inside the used toilet rolls with a pair of tweezers.

Body Writing

For her photograph titled *Index*, Ariana wrote a description of one of her dreams on her legs with a knitting needle and then photographed the resulting text.

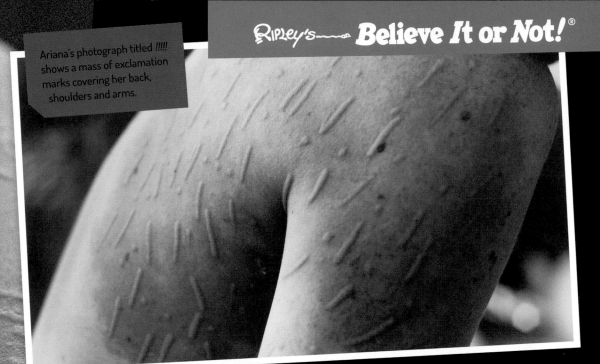

Ariana's photograph titled !!!!! shows a mass of exclamation marks covering her back, shoulders and arms.

Beauty really is skin deep for Ariana Page Russell. She has a medical condition called dermatographia, meaning that when she lightly scratches her skin it quickly puffs up into a red imprint. Yet, instead of trying to hide her condition, she embraces it by transforming her body into a magical canvas, using a blunt knitting needle to write elegant text or to create intricate patterns on her legs, arms and torso.

When the 34-year-old artist, based in Brooklyn, New York, scratches her hypersensitive flesh, the welts that appear usually last for about 30 minutes before fading. This allows her enough time to photograph the results. Sometimes she incorporates the freckles on her body into her designs. Although the marks look painful, she says they don't hurt and produce only a "warm" sensation.

Ariana's amazing "body art" photographs have been exhibited all over the U.S.A. and as far afield as Ireland, Bolivia and Australia. She also makes wallpaper, collage and temporary tattoos using the pictures of her skin cut into decorative designs.

Ariana only learned a decade ago that she had dermatographia (which literally means "writing on the skin"), but by then, she had already become interested in using her skin as art.

To help others with the condition become similarly empowered, she has started a blog, Skin Tome, where people can celebrate their exceptional skin. Ariana says that even if there was a cure, she wouldn't want one. She says, "I think it's fun to be able to draw on myself. I like it."

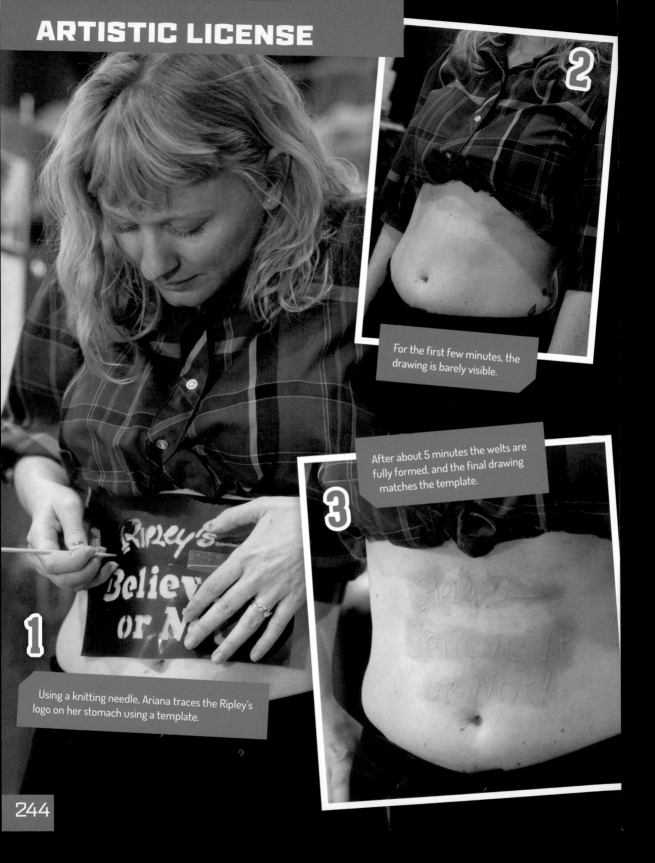

2

For the first few minutes, the drawing is barely visible.

After about 5 minutes the welts are fully formed, and the final drawing matches the template.

3

1

Using a knitting needle, Ariana traces the Ripley's logo on her stomach using a template.

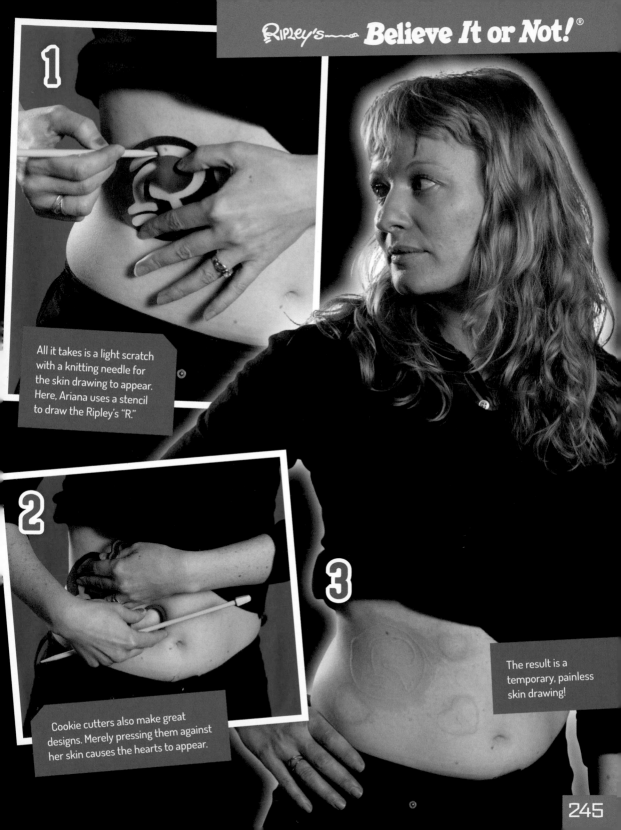

1

All it takes is a light scratch with a knitting needle for the skin drawing to appear. Here, Ariana uses a stencil to draw the Ripley's "R."

2

Cookie cutters also make great designs. Merely pressing them against her skin causes the hearts to appear.

3

The result is a temporary, painless skin drawing!

Chirpy Chip Chip

These beautiful life-size sculptures may look like fluffy animals and birds, but instead of fur and feather, they are really made of small slivers and chips of wood. Russian artist Sergey Bobkov uses 3-in-long (7.5-cm) sticks from Siberian cedar trees, which he cuts into around 150 thin slices. He prevents the strips from falling apart by soaking them in water for several days before carving them into shape with great precision.

GNOME INVASION

More than 2,300 paintings of gnomes—with little red hats, white beards and brown shoes—suddenly started appearing on telephone poles all over Oakland, California, in 2012. The hand-painted portraits on 6-in (15-cm) blocks of wood proved so popular that the Pacific Gas & Electric Co. decided to leave them in place.

PASSPORT PICTURE

Instead of a photograph on his passport, Swedish artist Fredrik Säker has a painted self-portrait. As government regulations stipulated that he had to submit a photo, he decided to photograph the brilliantly lifelike self-portrait that he had taken 100 hours to paint—and it was accepted without question.

AUTO ROBOT

French artist Guillaume Reymond created an art installation called *Transformers* from more than a dozen real vehicles—cars, vans and trucks. He carefully positioned each vehicle so that when viewed from above, the arrangement looked like a giant Transformer robot.

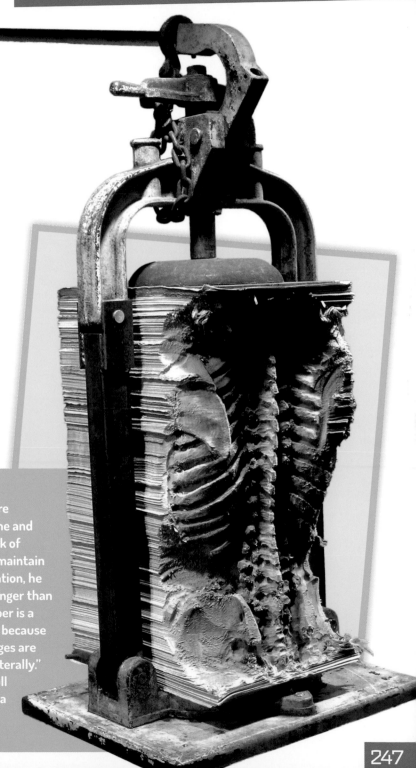

SINGLE HAIR
Mukesh Thapa from Himachal Pradesh, India, painted a self-portrait in oils using a single hair from his own beard. It took him a year to finish the picture with his unique, ultra-thin brush.

MILK MAGIC
French artist Vivi Mac creates celebrity portraits from foodstuffs, including crème brûlée and milk. She uses a straw to guide the liquid carefully around the plastic trays that serve as her canvases.

LEATHER ETCHINGS
Welsh artist Mark Evans uses leather as his canvas and a knife as his brush. He carefully cuts through the surface of animal hides to create amazing etchings that sell for up to £450,000 ($700,000) each.

Paper Bones

Canadian artist Maskull Lasserre intricately carved a human spine and ribcage into a compressed stack of ordinary daily newspapers. To maintain the required level of concentration, he worked in short bursts of no longer than an hour at a time. He says, "Paper is a very difficult medium to carve because of its grain and the fact the pages are not connected to each other laterally." Aside from newspapers, Maskull also works with different media such as books, tree branches and coat hangers.

Toy Soldiers

Artist Joe Black from London, England, made this incredible portrait of former Chinese leader Mao Tse-tung from more than 15,000 hand-painted, plastic toy soldiers.

Joe, who specializes in mosaics using everyday objects such as ball bearings and button pins, has also created a portrait of President Obama using 11,000 black-and-white toy soldiers, a sculpture of former Soviet dictator Joseph Stalin from 10,000 chess pawn pieces and one of former British Prime Minister Margaret Thatcher from iron bolts.

BOXING CLEVER

Giles Oldershaw from Oxford, England, takes old pieces of corrugated cardboard and, using nothing more than tweezers, scalpels and scissors, turns them into stunning portraits of movie stars such as Marilyn Monroe, Marlon Brando and Bette Davis. He does not incorporate any ink, paint or charcoal in his works, using only the cardboard's layers to highlight the subject's facial features.

COLORFUL CORDS

Founded by Keith and Stephanie Duffy from Salt Lake City, Utah, Little Cord Art creates custom-made artworks from newborn babies' umbilical cords. The customer sends a sample of the baby's cord to the artists, who put it on a microscope slide and cut it so that its cellular details become visible. The cross-section is then stained, magnified 400 times, photographed and framed to create a colorful digital picture of the baby's unique cord cells.

TEA-BAG COLLAGE

Armenian artist Armén Rotch arranges hundreds of used tea bags into intricate patterns to create huge pixelated collages. By selecting bags that have been left to steep for different lengths of time, he is able to use different shades of gold and brown.

BEAVER BOWLS

Artist Butch Anthony's Museum of Wonder in Seale, Alabama, includes such oddities as a chandelier made from cow bones and a range of bowls woven from sticks chewed by beavers. Even the bathroom windows in his house are made from gnawed beaver sticks.

PAINTING BY JET

Instead of traditional brushes, artist Princess Tarinan von Anhalt from Aventura, Florida, paints with $10-million airplane jet engines. She creates abstract artworks by hurling paints into the airflow of a Learjet engine, which splatters the colors onto a large 8 x 8 ft (2.4 x 2.4 m) canvas about 30 ft (9 m) away with a force many times stronger than a hurricane. The technique was pioneered by her late husband, Prinz Jurgen von Anhalt, 30 years ago and became so popular that her clients will pay $50,000 just to watch her work!

PAPER TOWELS

To give his artworks extra depth, artist Ken Delmar from Stamford, Connecticut, uses absorbent kitchen paper towels as his canvas—and sells his oil paintings on them for up to $10,000. He discovered his unlikely medium by accident. One evening he was cleaning his paintbrushes with paper towels and noticed that the colors on the towels were more vibrant than on the actual painting.

MATCHSTICK MODELS

Djordje Balac from Gospic, Croatia, has made a fully functional model of the world's largest crane—a Liebherr LTM 11200—from 175,518 matchsticks, 44 lb (20 kg) of glue and 17.6 lb (8 kg) of varnish. Working every day from 8 a.m. till midnight, it took him three months to make the crane, which, just like the real thing, has an extending arm. He has also made detailed matchstick models of trucks, complete with detachable cabins.

Scrap Sculptures

French artist Edouard Martinet creates delicate metal sculptures of insects, fish, mammals and birds from old pieces of scrap, including bicycle parts, kitchen utensils and typewriter keys. As with this wasp, the individual pieces are screwed rather than welded together, and each artwork can take him anything from a month to 17 years to complete as he scours flea markets and garage sales for the perfect parts.

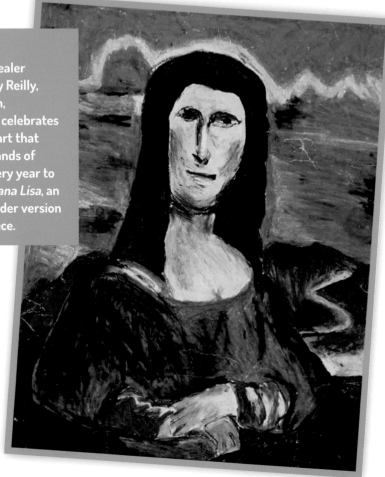

Mana Lisa

Established in 1994 by antique dealer Scott Wilson and his friend Jerry Reilly, the Museum of Bad Art in Boston, Massachusetts, proudly collects, celebrates and exhibits over 600 pieces of art that are so bad they are good! Thousands of visitors flock to the museum every year to see original works such as the *Mana Lisa*, an anonymously painted, cross-gender version of Leonardo da Vinci's masterpiece.

UNFINISHED PICTURE

U.S. President Franklin D. Roosevelt was posing for a portrait when he collapsed and died in 1945. The painting was never completed.

REFLECTED BEAUTY

Simon Hennessey from Birmingham, England, creates stunningly realistic paintings of famous world landmarks—including Tower Bridge, the Eiffel Tower and the New York City skyline—reflected in the lenses of tourists' sunglasses. Each picture can take him several months and will cost a buyer over £22,000 ($36,000).

EGG SHELL

Manjit Kumar Shah from Assam, India, used a black gel pen to draw 1,615 portraits of Mahatma Gandhi onto a single eggshell.

STYROFOAM SHIP

In Jeddah, Saudi Arabia, a group of artists built a giant Styrofoam ship that measured 45 ft (13.6 m) high, 60 ft (18.4 m) long and 15 ft (4.5 m) wide.

HEAVY PAINTING

The Rose, a 1966 painting by San Francisco artist Jay DeFeo, used so much oil paint that it took eight years to complete and weighs more than 2,000 lb (908 kg).

HEALTHY PROFIT

A 1,000-year-old Chinese bowl, bought for $3 at a yard sale, sold for $2.2 million at auction in 2013.

GARGOYLE HONOR

Nora Sly, a worshiper at St. Mary's church in the village of Cowley in Gloucester, England, for more than 60 years, has had her smiling face carved into a stone gargoyle mounted on the church roof.

Jody Steel, a student from Boston, Massachusetts, draws incredible portraits of people and animals on her thighs—and they are so striking that people mistake them for tattoos.

Thigh Doodles

Jody first used her flesh as a canvas because there was no paper handy, but in any case she says her skin is so pale it offers the same qualities as paper, as can be seen in this lifelike drawing of an elephant.

She began doodling on her legs during lectures, but when her lecturer reprimanded her for not paying attention, he was so impressed by her drawings that he offered her a job illustrating a novel.

It looks as if Jody's leg has been ripped open to expose the muscle, but happily it is just one of her imaginative doodles.

STRAW DALEK

To mark the 50th anniversary of *Doctor Who*, staff at an ice-cream parlor in Cheshire, England, built a 35-ft-tall (10.6-m) Dalek (the Doctor's arch enemy) from 6 tons of straw and 5 tons of steel.

IVORY SHIPS

A fifth-generation carver, David Warther II of Sugarcreek, Ohio, has painstakingly carved more than 80 ships from antique ivory, depicting the history of the ship from 3000 BC to the present day. He started carving ships when he was just six years old, and his work is so precise that the vessels' ivory rigging is handworked to a diameter of 0.007 in (0.18 mm).

BREAD CITY

Food artist Lennie Payne from London, England, sculpted models of the city's landmarks—including Tower Bridge, St. Paul's Cathedral and Big Ben—out of bread. He also used muffins, crumpets and sandwiches to form a complete 3-D city skyline.

WOODEN BIKE

Istvan Puskas from Tizaors, Hungary, spent two years crafting a fully working motorbike from wood. He built the machine from weather-resistant black locust wood, embellishing it with deer antler decorations and adding handlebars and exhaust pipes made from cow horns. Even the gas tank is a small wooden barrel and fuels a small Fiat car engine, enabling the bike to reach a top speed of 17.5 mph (28 km/h).

MINI MARXES

To celebrate the 195th anniversary of Karl Marx's birth, artist Ottmar Hörl placed 500 miniature statues of him throughout the philosopher's hometown of Trier, Germany. The little Marx men were all the same size and shape but were cast in different shades of red.

TINY SHIP

Micro-artist Willard Wigan from Birmingham, England, has created a luxury watch featuring a model of a ship that is half the size of the period at the end of this sentence. He spent 672 hours crafting the watch, which is valued at $1.5 million because the ship and sails are made from 24-carat gold.

Tree Trunk

Chinese artist Zheng Chunhui spent four years carving an intricate 40-ft-long (12-m) artwork from a single tree trunk.

The carving, which is 10 ft (3 m) tall at its highest point and 7¾ ft (2.4 m) wide, is a copy of a famous 12th-century Chinese painting and features boats, bridges, animals, buildings and 550 individually crafted people.

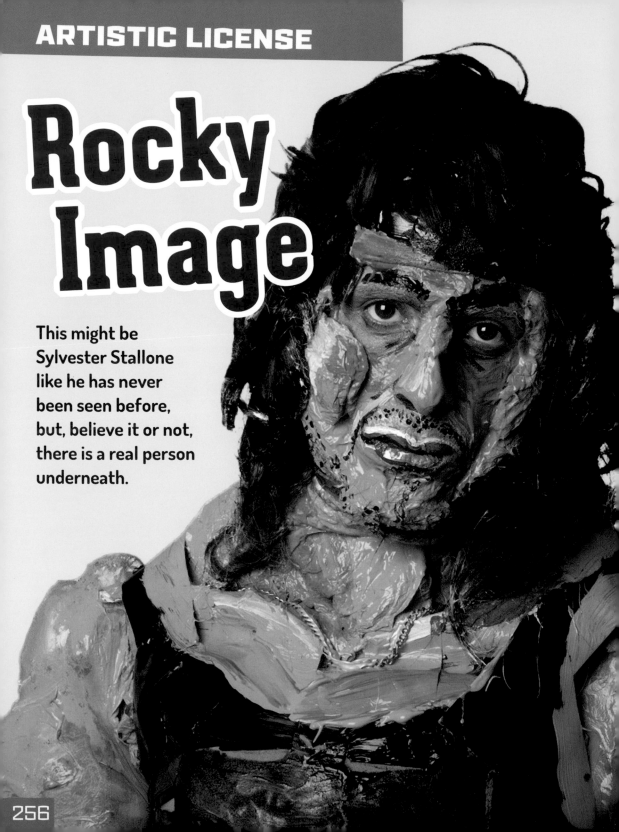

Rocky Image

This might be Sylvester Stallone like he has never been seen before, but, believe it or not, there is a real person underneath.

It is the work of artist Marie-Lou Desmeules from Quebec, who uses layers of paint, hair and plastic to turn her human models into exaggerated sculptures of iconic figures such as Michael Jackson, Pamela Anderson, Barbie and Sly.

What gave you the idea for your human sculptures?

Sitting in my workshop in Berlin in 2008, I decided to mold my boyfriend so that he blended into the wall behind him. I evolved the techniques I used that day to the more aesthetic techniques I use for my sculptures now. I began making the celebrity sculptures in 2012.

Why did you choose celebrities as your subjects?

I wanted to challenge stereotypes—the judgments we make without knowing the person. The series Celebrities was inspired by society's obsession with plastic surgery—with image, identity and consumerism.

Why did you choose Rambo as one of your subjects?

Rambo is a very complex and controversial character. I think his muscular body represents a shell that actually hides a sad interior. My next subject is going to be David Bowie.

How long does each sculpture take?

I research each subject, then collect ideas and materials. This process may take one day—or one lifetime! The creation (or "surgery" as I call it) takes three hours including the time for the transformation, the lighting and the photographing. The model wears the sculpture for about 15 minutes before we take the photograph.

What materials do you use?

I use mostly acrylic paint, sheets of plastic, lengths of hair, duct tape, clothes, paper and anything else useful that comes my way.

Finally, if you were a human sculpture, who would you be?

I would like to sculpt myself into the Invisible Man.

EGG CARTONS

Charlotte Austen and Jack Munro used 6,500 egg cartons to create a life-size, World War II Spitfire fighter plane at Duxford Imperial War Museum in Cambridgeshire, England. The egg cartons were attached to a timber and steel frame, which had to be broken down into 12 sections so that the replica could be transported by truck.

MEDICAL JARS

Artist Tamsin van Essen of London, England, has created a series of ceramic jars containing deliberate faults and blemishes to represent various illnesses and diseases. Inspired by apothecary jars of the 17th and 18th centuries, her "Medical Heirlooms" range includes acne, osteoporosis, psoriasis and scars, and, as family heirlooms, her jars can be passed down through generations like hereditary medical conditions.

DRIFTWOOD SCULPTURES

Sculptor Jeffro Uitto from Tokeland, Washington, combs the coastline for abandoned driftwood and turns it into items of furniture and giant wooden creatures such as a rearing horse or a swooping eagle. His pieces can take years to create while he searches for the right pieces of driftwood.

ARTISTIC LICENSE

Screw Heads

Believe it or not, this lifelike crumpled shirt was created from around 6,500 metal screw heads. It is the work of Andrew Myers from Laguna Beach, California, who draws his outlines on wood before drilling in thousands of screws at various depths to create an amazing 3-D art piece. He then paints each screw individually by hand to form a finished piece that is a drawing, sculpture and painting all in one.

Book Folding

Through painstaking hand cutting and origami folding, Isaac G. Salazar from Artesia, New Mexico, gives new life to old books by turning their paper pages into works of art that spell out words such as "Read," "Dream," "Faith" and "Love." A full-time accountant who has never been to art class, Isaac works on art in his spare time. Each piece can take him anything from two days to two weeks.

DOMINO TOWER

Tom Holmes, a graduate engineer from Bristol, England, spent a staggering 7½ hours and used 2,688 dominos to build a freestanding tower that was more than 17 ft (5.2 m) tall.

BIG BLOW

Tim Thurmond from Brighton, Michigan, inflated more than 8,000 balloons in 24 hours, averaging nearly six balloons a minute, and turned them into sculptures.

MINI MONET

By the age of ten, talented landscape artist Kieron Williamson from Norfolk, England, had made more than £1.4 million ($2.2 million) from the sales of his paintings. His artworks are so sought-after that a 2013 sale of 23 of his paintings raised more than £230,000 ($360,000) in just 20 minutes.

TITANIC MODEL

Working 12 hours a day for ten days, Vivek Kumar of Uttar Pradesh, India, made a 6-ft-long (1.8-m), 3-ft-tall (0.9-m) model of the *Titanic* from 8,000 ice cream sticks.

MOUSE STUFFING

Taxidermist Shannon Marie Harmon from London, England, runs a class teaching people how to stuff dead mice and to dress and pose them in unusual positions, all in the name of art. Each student leaves the four-hour session with their own stuffed and embalmed mouse.

WOODEN WONDERS

Arizona State professor Tom Eckert produces sculptures that look as if they are made of silk, glass, paper, stone, plastic, metal or fruit—even though they are really made entirely of wood. Working mainly with basswood, linden and limewood, he carves, turns, whittles, bends and laminates the wood. Then he applies fine layers of waterborne lacquer paint with spray guns and brushes to incorporate subtle wrinkles and reflections into his pieces, making them almost impossible to distinguish from the real thing.

Graffiti Block

For just one month before it was demolished in early 2014, an unremarkable derelict Paris apartment block was transformed into an incredible ten-story art installation by 100 of the world's finest street artists.

The artists were invited by gallery owner Mehdi Ben Cheikh to create whatever they wanted on every available surface of Tour 13, which stands close to the River Seine in the French capital's 13th district. The result was a rich mosaic of faces, animals, mythical creatures, patterns and scriptures—some warm and welcoming, others more serious and thought-provoking—that decorated all 36 apartments as well as the stairwells and the exterior brickwork.

Some artists brought their own props to extend the fantasy, while others created clever optical illusions featuring boxes that appeared to float and walls that seemed to bend.

ARTISTIC LICENSE

Artist Nebay from France creates raw and colorful graffiti, carrying messages of anger and hope.

Azooz, Deyaa, Maryam and Maz are some of the first Saudi Arabian graffiti artists, producing murals influenced by comics and traditional calligraphy.

NUTTY CELEBS

Steve Casino from Fort Thomas, Kentucky, turns peanut shells into $500 mini statues of celebrities including Elton John, Sean Connery and Joey Ramone. Having found a shell the right shape for his subject, he removes the nuts, glues the shell back together and sands down the surface. Using a tiny brush, he then applies acrylic paint before creating arms, legs and any props from wood, bamboo or dense foam.

PERFECT PICTURES

Using just pencils, oil paints and charcoal, Zimbabwe-born artist Craig Wylie creates huge portraits that are so accurate they are often mistaken for photographs. Working from images on his laptop screen, which enables him to zoom in on the tiniest facial detail, he spends up to three months on each piece, his largest to date measuring 6½ x 9¾ ft (2 x 3 m).

GIANT DRAWING

Working five hours a day for eight days, Singapore's Edmund Chen single-handedly created a drawing of koi fish and lotus flowers on a giant roll of paper that measured over 1,968 ft (600 m) long—that's six times the length of a soccer field.

Colored Clouds

Irby Pace from Denton, Texas, traveled the U.S.A. releasing canisters of colored smoke in rural and urban locations and then photographed the results for his beautiful series called *Pop!* He placed the canisters in different settings using helium balloons and string and created clouds of different shapes, colors and intensity, although laws restricted where his canisters could actually be discharged.

Crushed Man

It looks like this homeless man has been crushed under the corner of a falling apartment block in Prague, Czech Republic—but it is really a wacky urban artwork by Italian artist Fra Biancoshock whose "pop up" installations have been appearing unannounced in streets all over Europe.

SOAPY PICTURES

Amateur photographer Jane Thomas from Kilmarnock, Scotland, takes close-up pictures of soapy water and turns them into works of art that look like psychedelic paintings from the 1960s. She was inspired by seeing "the strange and fantastic patterns in soap" while she was washing dishes.

PAPER WINDOWS

Eric Standley, an associate art professor at Virginia Tech, creates 3-D images of Gothic stained-glass windows from hundreds of pieces of colored paper. With mathematical precision, he spends up to 80 hours laser-cutting the paper, and he then stacks the cut pieces together into layers, often more than 100 deep, before binding the sheets together.

GRAFFITI REVENGE

A worker was sent to remove graffiti from a wall in London, England, just eight hours after stencil artist DS had finished creating it. Frustrated, DS secretly photographed the man as he worked and painted an image of him on the same wall a few hours later!

CROCHET TIMELORDS

For a unique Christmas gift, Allison Hoffman from Austin, Texas, made mini crocheted dolls of the first 11 Doctors from the popular TV series, *Doctor Who*.

HEAVY WORK
Beth Johnson of LaRue, Ohio, built an enormous wooden yo-yo that measured 12 ft (3.6 m) in diameter and weighed 4,620 lb (2,096 kg)—and bounced it up and down using a crane.

MISSING ISLAND
Is Land, a $13,000, 23-ft-wide (7-m), helium-filled sculpture of a desert island, floated away from a 2011 music festival in Cambridgeshire, England, after vandals cut its tether ropes. Although its creators, Sarah Cockings and Laurence Symonds, launched a worldwide search for the giant inflatable and sightings were reported in Canada and Switzerland, the island has never been found.

EGG-STRAORDINARY
Vietnamese Ben Tre uses a tiny electrical dentist's drill to carve detailed portraits and landscapes onto eggshells. Each artwork takes a day, and because the shells are not chemically hardened, they are extremely fragile, so he offers customers the option of having them encased in a glass globe for protection.

WATER COLORS
Wearing full diving gear, Ukrainian artist Alexander Belozor paints underwater landscapes—at depths of up to 85 ft (26 m). His canvases are covered in a waterproof coating to prevent the colors running.

EXPLOSIVE PICTURES
Chemist and photographer Jon Smith from Fishers, Indiana, creates explosive artwork by taking pictures of lightbulbs, filled with brightly colored materials, shattering. He fills the glass bulbs with objects such as candies, sprinkles, chalk dust and beer caps, then fires at them with a pellet gun and captures the moment of impact on camera.

ROYAL TOAST
Nathan Wyburn from Cardiff, Wales, created an image of the Duchess of Cambridge from 35 slices of toasted white bread and a pot of Marmite yeast extract.

Feather Art

Chris Maynard from Olympia, Washington, creates beautiful images of flocks of birds by cutting into real feathers. He sources the feathers from private aviaries and zoos, waiting patiently for the right shape and coloration to become available. The feathers he uses come from a range of birds, including parrots, pigeons, crows, pheasants and turkeys. He strengthens the feathers with backing to stop them curling, and then working with magnifying glasses, tiny surgery scissors, scalpels and forceps, he carefully cuts and carves them before mounting them onto frames known as shadowboxes to create a 3-D effect.

Human Frog

Body-painter Johannes Stoetter from South Tyrol, Italy, produced this amazing image of a tropical tree frog resting on a leaf by using five cunningly camouflaged painted women to re-create the creature's torso, legs, arms and head.

He takes up to five months to plan each project, working out the coloring and the precise positioning of his human models. He then spends eight hours applying special breathable paint to their bodies to turn them into animals, fruit and landscapes that play unbelievable tricks on the viewer's eye.

He started body-painting in 2000 and has become so successful that in 2012 he became the world champion. He says, "Body-painting is special because the artwork is alive and can move. While a canvas painting lasts forever, a body-painting exists only for a few hours."

DA VINCI SKILL

Leonardo da Vinci could write with one hand and paint with the other simultaneously.

CORK RHINO

Californians Jim and Mary Lambert from Carmichael, and Bob and Di Nelson from Fair Oaks, spent three years making a life-size, 12-ft-long (3.6-m) rhinoceros sculpture out of plywood, foam and 12,000 wine-bottle corks. Jim has been collecting corks for 20 years and named the sculpture *Rhinocirrhosis* after the liver disease often caused by heavy drinking.

RUBBER DUCK

Since 2007, several giant yellow PVC rubber ducks created by Dutch artist Florentijn Hofman have made a big splash in cities all over the world, appearing in harbors in Japan, Australia, New Zealand, Brazil, the Netherlands and China.

RICE STATUE

New York City-based artist Saeri Kiritani created a 5-ft-tall (1.5-m), life-size sculpture of herself by gluing together one million grains of rice. Even the statue's hair was made from rice noodles.

HUMAN BONES

During the Napoleonic Wars, French prisoners-of-war built model warships out of human bones.

Acquired Taste

Death Row Dinners

Since 2000, Oregon artist Julie Green has painted images of the final meals of almost 700 death row inmates onto plates.

Her project, *The Last Supper*, began after she moved to Norman, Oklahoma. The state has the highest number of executions per capita in the U.S.A. and each week the local newspaper printed several notices of execution, which included the inmate's last food request. These ranged from ice cream to cigarettes but mostly consisted of burgers and KFC.

Indiana, March 14, 2001 A dish of German ravioli and chicken dumplings was prepared as an inmate's final meal by his mother and prison dietary staff.

Texas, September 21, 2011 An inmate requested two chicken-fried steaks, a triple-patty bacon cheeseburger, 1 lb (450 g) of barbecued meat, a meat-lover's pizza, three fajitas, an omelet, a bowl of okra, a pint of Blue Bell ice cream, some peanut butter fudge and three root beers—but ate none of it. As a result, Texas banned the option of allowing prisoners to request final meals.

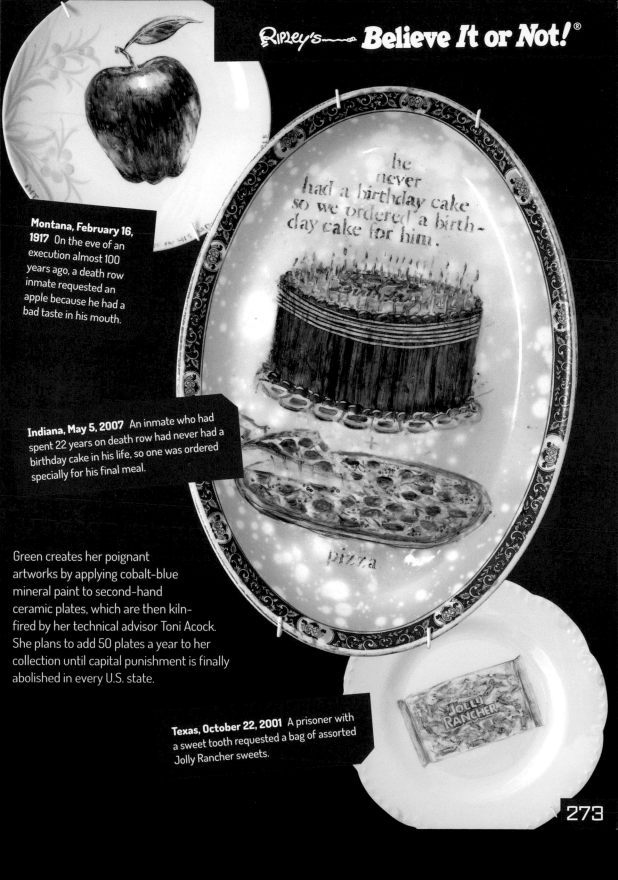

Montana, February 16, 1917 On the eve of an execution almost 100 years ago, a death row inmate requested an apple because he had a bad taste in his mouth.

he never had a birthday cake so we ordered a birthday cake for him.

pizza

Indiana, May 5, 2007 An inmate who had spent 22 years on death row had never had a birthday cake in his life, so one was ordered specially for his final meal.

Green creates her poignant artworks by applying cobalt-blue mineral paint to second-hand ceramic plates, which are then kiln-fired by her technical advisor Toni Acock. She plans to add 50 plates a year to her collection until capital punishment is finally abolished in every U.S. state.

Texas, October 22, 2001 A prisoner with a sweet tooth requested a bag of assorted Jolly Rancher sweets.

JOLLY RANCHER

273

Larvae Cupcakes

British baker Twisted Fondant has created this gross cupcake, which looks to have been infected with botfly larvae. The cake is served with tweezers and a surgical glove. You use the tweezers to extract the edible "maggot" and with gloved fingers you then carefully squeeze out the creamy, mango-flavored "pus."

RADIOACTIVE RUM

As an alternative to the lengthy process of maturing cachaça—a rum-like spirit—in barrels, Brazilian researchers have tried zapping the drink with gamma radiation for a few minutes. They say not only is it much quicker than the barrel method; it is also safe to drink immediately after being irradiated.

PUMPKIN WORSHIP

Residents of Bokaro, India, began worshiping and leaving offerings to a huge oval 190-lb (86-kg) pumpkin in March 2013, believing it to be a reincarnation of the Hindu god Shiva. The pumpkin bore a resemblance to a shivalinga—a symbolic object used for worship in Hindu temples.

BAKER'S ERROR

When 22-year-old Laura Gambrel from Zionsville, Indiana, graduated from college, her proud mother Carol ordered a graduation cake with a cap drawn on it. However, the baker misheard her instruction, and when the cake was delivered it had a drawing of a cat perched on top of her daughter's head instead!

FRIED CAT

At the controversial Gastronomical Festival of the Cat in La Quebrada, Peru, townsfolk feast on hundreds of specially bred domestic cats for two days. They believe that eating cat burgers, fried cat legs and fried cat tails can cure bronchial disease.

MILK VODKA

Farmer Jason Barber from Dorset, England, produces vodka from pure cows' milk. He ferments the whey using a specialist yeast that turns milk sugar into alcohol. It took him three years to perfect the recipe for his Black Cow vodka.

GARLIC SHRINE

The Stinking Rose restaurant in San Francisco, California, serves more than 3,000 lb (1,360 kg) of garlic every month and is home to dozens of items of garlic-related memorabilia, including a braid composed of 2,635 garlic bulbs.

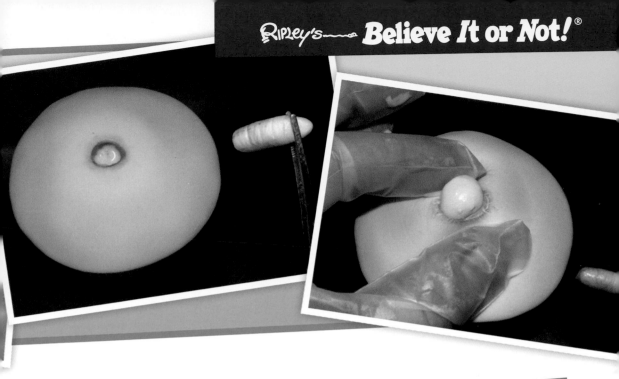

RESIGNATION CAKE

When Chris Holmes, a part-time baker from Cambridgeshire, England, decided to quit his day job as an immigration officer at Stansted Airport, he baked a cake for his bosses and wrote his resignation on it piped in frosting.

MONTHLY BILL

U.S. presidents must pay for all of their food in the White House. They receive a food bill every month.

LOST IN TRANSLATION

When restaurant owner Fred Bennett of Nelson, New Zealand, began serving Thai food, he added a sign printed in Thai and discovered only months later that it translated to "Go Away and Don't Come Back!"

Bloodsucker

The creations of Chris Verraes look disgusting yet taste great. From his base in London, England, he specializes in candies that confuse the taste buds. He created this leech feasting on a wound by sculpting a clay shape to make a silicone mold for the chocolate. Colored cocoa butter completes the illusion.

Sausage Ice Cream

Matthias Muenz, "The Crazy Ice Cream Maker" from Munich, Germany, serves a range of unusual ice cream flavors, including beer, sausage, bacon and eggs, grilled chicken, and goose with red cabbage. His white-sausage ice cream is served with a pretzel and mustard.

FLY BURGERS

Villagers living near Lake Victoria in East Africa coat saucepans with honey to catch the trillions of flies that swarm around the area. Then they make the trapped insects into nutritious flyburgers, which they fry before eating.

LORD OF THE RINGS

At the first Riders 4 Relief National Onion Ring Eating Championship, held in Coshocton, Ohio, in May 2013, Jamie "The Bear" McDonald of Granby, Connecticut, ate 6.73 lb (3.1 kg) of onion rings in only eight minutes.

SCHNITZEL CHOICE

Micha Hentschel, owner of the Haus Falkenstein Restaurant in Lougheed, Alberta, has 347 different varieties of pan-fried schnitzel on his menu—that's nearly twice as many as any restaurant in Germany. Hentschel's favorite fare from his extensive menu is the green peppercorn cream schnitzel.

SILENT SUPPER

Eat restaurant in Brooklyn, New York City, runs special events where customers have to eat their meals in complete silence. The idea of head chef Nicholas Nauman, if customers make so much as a sound, they have to finish their food outside on a bench.

DREAM DIET

To celebrate the German beer festival Oktoberfest, Evo Terro from Arizona drinks up to six beers a day and eats only sausages for the whole of October—a total of about 15,000 calories a week. Amazingly, his diet results in him losing up to 14 lb (6 kg) in weight and his cholesterol dropping by a third.

CHINESE FAN

Since 1955, Los Angeles attorney David Chan has eaten at more than 6,300 Chinese restaurants—and he has kept a spreadsheet documenting his experiences at every single one.

ELEPHANT DUNG

Coffee made from beans plucked from elephant dung sells for $50 a cup at the Anantara Hotel in Golden Triangle, Thailand.

HORNET VODKA

A rare type of Japanese vodka is made from fermented giant hornets—venomous insects with ¼-in (6.4-mm) stingers that cause over 40 human deaths every year. The hornets are left to ferment in alcohol for three years, producing a muddy-brown liquor that smells like rotting flesh and has a salty aftertaste from the insects' poison.

STEEL CUBES

To cater to people who like their drinks on the rocks but do not want extra water from melting ice, Dave Laituri from Wayland, Massachusetts, has designed ice cubes made from stainless steel. He was inspired by 20th-century French designer Raymond Loewy, who used to drink scotch chilled with ball bearings.

[YOUR / UPLOADS]

Apples to Apples

This picture of an apple with a perfect natural apple imprint on its skin was sent in to Ripley's by Angela Feo-Gilberti from New Jersey. Angela's daughter, Isabella, found the fruit with its unusual marking in a box of apples at a local food store when out shopping with her mother.

Zombie Cake

We've all seen cakes that look too beautiful to eat . . . well, this zombie cake looks too terrifying to eat.

The zombie's brain was made from strawberry jello.

It was made by Elizabeth Marek from Portland, Oregon, who began her monstrous creation by layering cake over an internal structure that was used to keep the torso, head and arm upright. She then used Rice Krispie Treats to build up the rib cage and hideous facial features. She made the single eye and ripped shirt from fondant before painting the eyeball with food coloring. She also added melted marshmallows to make it look as if the face had simply rotted away. The entire zombie cake took three days to make.

The spine and skin were textured using a sculpting tool and then colored with oil-based food coloring, modeling chocolate and petal dust.

BITING WINE

A woman from Shuangcheng in northern China was rushed to a hospital after she was bitten by a venomous snake that had been pickled in wine—a popular Chinese medicine—for three months. Liu had been given the snake wine to treat her rheumatism. She drank a glass of the wine every day, but when she went to refill the jar and used chopsticks to adjust the seemingly dead snake's position, the creature sprang to life and bit her. A snake expert suggested that the creature may have been able to survive in the jar for three months because it was hibernating.

GLOBAL FEAST

Carrie Hollis and Simon Day from Surrey, England, ate a 24-hour meal in 2013, during which they sampled 193 bite-sized courses from around the world, including grasshoppers from the Congo, meat gutab (stuffed flatbread) from Azerbaijan and birds' milk from Romania.

CANNED BUGS

Sold online, the Edible Bug Gift Pack features seven cans of flavored and cooked bugs—barbecue bamboo worms, bacon and cheese grasshoppers, nori seaweed armor-tailed scorpions, salted queen weaver ants, sour cream and onion dung beetles, wasabi house crickets and giant waterbug chili paste.

Gourmet Gator

Chicago restaurant Frontier, which serves whole smoked animals, has one creature on the menu that might not appeal to everybody. Smoked alligator, served whole and big enough to feed 12 hungry people, is available for around $600. The gators are sourced from Louisiana and then prepared by stuffing them with whole chickens and smoking them for six hours. Chef Brian Jupiter describes the meat as having a "delicious, tender taste, similar to that of frog legs" and recommends beer to wash down the snappy supper.

BACON SANDWICH

Paul Philips, a café owner from Cheltenham, England, has created a £150 ($237) bacon sandwich made from seven slices of bacon from a rare breed of pig, truffle spread, a free-range egg, sliced truffles, saffron and edible gold dust. It is cooked in truffle oil.

PRINCELY PIZZA

Restaurant owner Domenico Crolla from Glasgow, Scotland, created a pizza decorated to show the Duke and Duchess of Cambridge holding their newborn baby, Prince George. He used a scalpel to sculpt the cheese and tomato and coated the finished artwork in resin to preserve it. He has also made pizza portraits of Barack Obama, Marilyn Monroe and Marlon Brando.

FISH SUPPER

Five chefs cooked a giant portion of fish and chips at Poole, England, comprising 65 lb (30 kg) of halibut and 130 lb (59 kg) of fries—making enough to feed 180 people.

SPICY SAUCES

Vic Clinco from Phoenix, Arizona, has a collection of more than 6,000 bottles of hot chili sauces. He has been collecting for nearly 20 years, and his most expensive bottle is worth around $1,500.

WEDDING RECEPTION

After a string of burger-joint dates, Steven and Emily Asher held their wedding reception at a McDonald's in Bristol, England. They arrived by stretch limo and paid £150 ($225) to feed 33 guests with milkshakes and McNuggets.

MILK BOOST

Dairy cows fitted with dentures can chew for longer than cows with regular teeth, enabling them to produce more milk.

CHAMPION CHOPPER

Using just a sharp knife, Orlando, Florida, grocery store manager Matt Jones can slice and dice an entire watermelon in 21 seconds.

CANNED MEAL

British student Chris Godfrey has created a 12-course meal in a can. With 12 different layers of food, the "All In One" includes French onion soup, ravioli, halibut, shiitake mushroom, pork belly, rib-eye steak, crack pie and ice cream, and pastry and coffee.

SWEATING MUSHROOM

The "sweating mushroom" of Europe and North America causes uncontrollable sweating and crying if ingested.

DUMPSTER DIET

To raise awareness about the amount of food wasted in the U.S.A., Rob Greenfield from San Diego, California, ate only out of dumpsters for a week—and managed to fill his fridge with fresh fruit, vegetables and bagels, worth $200.

Lizard Lunch

The Uromastyx lizard is a popular meal in the Arabian Peninsula. Also known as "fish of the desert," the reptile can grow to 3 ft (0.9 m) in length. It may be grilled as part of a traditional kabsa rice dish or eaten raw, as some believe its blood can treat diseases. The lizards, which live in sand burrows, are caught in the spring by hunters using sniffer dogs.

FROG SASHIMI

The Japanese dish frog sashimi is often served alongside a freshly killed dead frog while the creature's heart is still beating.

RECYCLED PEE

NASA scientists have designed special bags for astronauts to urinate in, which then turns their urine into a safe, pleasant-tasting, sugary drink.

EXTRA DRY

Pakistan's 153-year-old Murree Brewery produces millions of barrels of beer a year—in a country in which it is illegal for 97 percent of the population to drink it.

MONSTER CHEESECAKE

At the 9th Annual Cream Cheese Festival in Lowville, New York, Philadelphia Cream Cheese unveiled a 6,900-lb (3,130-kg) cheesecake that was big enough to serve 24,533 people! It was prepared in a pan that measured 90 in (2.25 m) in diameter and was 30 in (0.75 m) deep.

CHICKEN FEET

Packets of fried chicken feet are sold in Chinese supermarkets as a snack, often seasoned with rice vinegar and chili.

David and Natalie were watching a horror movie when she came up with the idea for a severed head wedding cake.

Scary Cake

For her marriage to a horror movie fan, cake artist Natalie Sideserf designed a gruesome wedding cake in the shape of their severed heads.

Topped with buttercream frosting and modeling chocolate, the cake showed Natalie and husband David with blank eyes, matted hair and blood seeping out of their necks. After their Halloween season wedding in Austin, Texas, Natalie admitted that her grandma was not too keen on the gory cake but had appreciated the detail and realism of the heads.

Till Death Do Us Part

HOT PIZZA

Using ghost chili enhanced with a special chili paste, Paul Brayshaw of East Sussex, England, has created the Saltdean Sizzler, a pizza that is three times hotter than police pepper spray.

LAB BURGER

At a cost of $325,000, Dr. Mark Post of Maastricht University in the Netherlands has grown a beef burger in a laboratory from the stem cells of a cow.

SUN BAKED

People in Villaseca, Chile, use only the sun to cook their food—and have found that their solar-powered ovens can generate temperatures of 356°F (180°C). The region has over 300 days of sunshine a year and turned to solar-powered cooking after wood, which had previously fueled ovens, became scarce.

FRUIT CAKE

Three hundred children in Managua, Nicaragua, baked a giant fruitcake that stretched 1,640 ft (500 m)—the length of four city blocks—and weighed 31,865 lb (14,454 kg). The cake included more than 60,000 eggs.

HEAVY CUP

In 2012, in London, England, kitchen appliance manufacturer De'Longhi made a coffee cup that was 9½ ft (2.9 m) high and 8½ ft (2.6 m) wide and held 3,434 gal (13,000 l) of coffee. When full, it weighed nearly 14 tons—the same as a double-decker bus laden with passengers.

ARMPIT CHEESE

U.S. scientist Christina Agapakis and Norwegian scent expert Sissel Tolaas have made a range of 11 cheeses from skin bacteria found in human feet, belly buttons and armpits. Each cheese was created from starter cultures sampled from human skin and taken from volunteers by means of sterile cotton swabs.

CHOCOLATE SAUSAGE

Chefs in Cavalese, Italy, used chocolate, eggs, butter and cookies to make a 250-ft-long (76-m) chocolate sausage on a row of tables that stretched through the town center.

Insect Cupcakes

Guests attending the launch party for *The Insect Cookbook* in Wageningen, the Netherlands, were served cupcakes topped with maggots or glazed grasshoppers. Henk van Gurp, who co-authored the book, which promotes the eating of protein-rich insects, also cooked a giant pie containing more than 100 dead grasshoppers.

Snake Snack

A dead snake is dried on a slab in the Chinese "Snake Village" of Zisiqiao, where three million serpents are raised each year for food or medicine.

The most common snakes reared there are sharp-nosed vipers, and after the venom has been extracted, the snakes are either chopped up and their meat put in soup or they are preserved in alcohol and sold for medicinal purposes. The village also breeds the notorious pit viper or "five-step killer," so called because its victims are said to die within five paces of being bitten.

OLDEST DINER

Frank's Diner in Kenosha, Wisconsin, claims to be the oldest continuously operating lunch car in the U.S.A. Old-timers recall it being pulled to its 58th Street location in 1926 by six horses.

EXPLODING CHUTNEY

A jar of exploding rhubarb chutney blew the door off the fridge in Margaret Goodwin's retirement apartment in Oxfordshire, England, flinging it across the kitchen and causing widespread damage to the walls and ceiling. The chutney, a gift from a friend, exploded after gas had fermented and built up inside the jar.

RICH HONEY

Elvish honey is extracted from caves, not hives, and at $6,800 per kilo it is as expensive as a small car. The mineral-rich, natural honey is prized because it can only be found lining the walls of a 5,900-ft-deep (1,800-m) cave in Turkey's Saricayir Valley.

LONG FRY

Kim Medford of Waynesville, North Carolina, was eating a meal in an Arby's fast-food restaurant when she found a curly fry that measured 38 in (95 cm) long.

Spider Hunters

This young Cambodian boy is fearlessly holding what is soon to be his lunch—a venomous (and still alive) tarantula spider. Children as young as five hunt tarantulas by using a stick to tickle the spider's web and lure it from its underground den. When the spider emerges—and a full-grown tarantula can be the size of an adult's palm—the children grab it just in front of its abdomen, taking care to avoid its toxic bite. They then put the spider in a water bottle, drown it and clean it before it is cooked in hot butter or oil. From catching the tarantula to eating it takes just ten minutes—the ultimate in fast food.

285

Pumpkin Art

For its month-long 2013 Halloween Fest, Ocean Park theme park in Hong Kong exhibited the world's largest collection of pickled pumpkin sculptures—more than 400 spooky designs created by master carvers Ray Villafane and Andy Bergholtz.

The centerpiece was a grotesque gremlin carved from a giant pumpkin (right) weighing more than 1,000 lb (454 kg), which had been specially handpicked by Ray in the U.S.A. Using just spoons and scalpels, Ray and his team spent hours on each sculpture before the finished pumpkins were immersed in vinegar to preserve them for visitors to enjoy.

ACQUIRED TASTE

Andy cuts away the skin of the pumpkin before getting to work, using just a scalpel and a spoon.

When looking for a good pumpkin to carve, Ray selects the meatiest. "I also like a pumpkin with character—one with knobbly ridges is good so that I can utilize that in the carving process, like sculpting noses."

However, because the process is unpredictable, he can never be sure whether the texture or flesh color will be ideal for sculpting until he actually starts carving.

Ray uses the natural textures in the pumpkin flesh to work on his design's features.

ACQUIRED TASTE

Ray's previous lifelike pumpkin sculptures have included gorillas, clowns, birds and actor Johnny Depp. He began carving pumpkins one day to entertain his art students at a school when he lived in Bellaire, Michigan. "Sculpting has always been my passion," he says, "but most importantly the kids at school absolutely loved them. For days after that there would be a dozen pumpkins sitting on my desk waiting for me to carve them."

The finished designs are dipped in vinegar to preserve them.

CARING ROBOT

Scientists at Cornell University, New York, have built a robot that knows when to pour its owner a beer. They have fitted the robot with a camera and a database of 3-D videos outlining basic human actions so that it can respond appropriately to each one. Powered by 16 laptop batteries, the robot can also make breakfast, put food in the refrigerator and tidy up.

INSECT DIET

David Gracer, an English teacher from Providence, Rhode Island, is so addicted to eating insects that in 11 years he has devoured 5,000 species—including cockroaches and scorpions. He has eaten insects sautéed, baked and roasted, and he always keeps a ready supply of more than 12,000 bugs in his basement freezer.

Rotten Egg

Century egg is a Chinese dish where an egg is preserved for several months in a mixture of clay, ash and lime. This turns the egg yolk dark green and gives it a putrid stench of sulfur.

ASPARAGUS SURPRISE

Ann and Jim McFarlane found a live tree frog nestled in a packet of Peruvian asparagus tips they had bought from a supermarket in Portsmouth, England. The frog, who was given the name Maurice, went on to live in a local aquarium, where the McFarlanes' daughter was working.

SQUID BOTTLES

In Japan's Fukui Prefecture, the dried bodies of whole squid are traditionally used as liquor bottles.

EYES OF TERROR

Eyes of Terrors are gruesome, blood-shot human eyeball candies complete with red veins and spots to make them look lifelike.

DRIED GRUB

A 22-year-old man who flew from Burkina Faso to England in 2013 and was stopped at London's Gatwick Airport with 207 lb (94 kg) of dried caterpillars in his luggage told customs officers that the insects were intended as food for his personal consumption.

SAUSAGE CHARGE

Bradley Davidson of Perth, Scotland, was cleared in 2012 on a charge of behaving aggressively with a blood sausage.

COCONUT CURSE

Police seized an inscribed coconut from a polling station on Guraidhoo—an island in the Maldives—for fear that it had black magic powers and was being used to influence voters in the country's 2013 presidential election.

RAW BLOOD

Tiet Canh, a soup made with raw ducks' blood, infused with herbs and nuts and served cold, is a popular dish in Vietnam.

SPECIAL MELONS

The Japanese Yubari melon is the most expensive fruit in the world. In 2008, one pair sold for more than $30,000.

SUPER NUGGET

To celebrate the company's 75th anniversary, Empire Kosher Poultry made a giant chicken nugget weighing 51.1 lb (23 kg) and measuring 3.25 ft (1 m) long and 2 ft (0.6 m) wide at Secaucus, New Jersey. The gigantic nugget was coated in more than 2¼ lb (1 kg) of breadcrumbs. It took six people more than three hours to make the nugget, which was larger than 720 regular-sized nuggets combined.

Shell Chicken

Designer Kyle Bean, based in London, England, made this ingenious chicken sculpture titled *What Came First?* by patiently gluing together dozens of eggshells of varying colors that he had collected from his local bakery.

SILVER CARROTS

German food company The Deli Garage has invented a tasteless edible spray paint called Food Finish to give meals an exciting splash of color—it comes in shades of gold, silver, red and blue.

SURPRISE STUFFING

When Linda Hebditch from Dorset, England, opened a packet of supermarket-bought dried sage leaves from Israel, a 3-in-long (7.6-cm) exotic praying mantis leapt out at her.

HOT EGG

India Dining, a restaurant in Surrey, England, has created a spicy chocolate Easter egg that is as hot as 400 bottles of Tabasco sauce. The "Not for Bunnies" egg, made from fiery ghost chili, Scotch bonnet and habanero chilies and Belgian chocolate, is so hot that it can only be served to patrons over 18—and even then they must sign a disclaimer and wear protective gloves before they take a bite.

CHOCOLATE STAMPS

The Belgian Post Office released a grand total of 538,000 chocolate-flavored stamps for Easter 2013. The stamps had pictures of chocolate on the front and essence of cacao oil impregnated in the glue on the back to give them a chocolate taste when licked. The ink with which they were printed was also infused with cacao oil so that the stamps smelled of chocolate.

Testicle Beer

A key ingredient of Rocky Mountain Oyster Stout, made by the Wynkoop Brewing Company of Denver, Colorado, is freshly sliced and roasted bull testicles! The dark brew is said to have a deep flavor of chocolate and nuts. The idea was originally a 2012 April Fool's Day spoof video, but it received such a great response that Wynkoop decided to manufacture the beer for real.

BEHEMOTH BROWNIE

Something Sweet Bake Shop in Daphne, Alabama, made a 234-lb (106-kg) brownie, which measured 11 x 6 ft (3.3 x 1.8 m). The giant brownie had to be cooked in a specially made, 262-lb (120-kg) pan and was big enough to cut into nearly 1,200 slices.

LARVETS

Larvets are real larva snacks dried and coated with different flavors, including barbecue sauce, cheddar cheese and Mexican spices.

MONSTER PIZZA

A team of chefs baked a pizza in Rome, Italy, that measured 131 ft (40 m) in diameter and had a circumference of more than the length of a football field. Covering nearly a third of an acre (a tenth of a hectare) and weighing more than 25 tons—four times the weight of an adult African elephant—the giant pizza was made using 10 tons of flour, 5 tons of tomato sauce, almost 4½ tons of mozzarella cheese, 1,488 lb (675 kg) of margarine, 551 lb (250 kg) of rock salt and 220 lb (100 kg) of lettuce. It took 48 hours to bake.

[YOUR / UPLOADS]

Chocolate Onions

For a real sweet-and-sour taste, Chocolate by Mueller sells onions covered in white or milk chocolate at its store in Reading Terminal Market, Philadelphia, Pennsylvania. The idea originated back in 1981 when a TV comedy show asked Mueller to make something crazy for Valentine's Day. As well as the $5 chocolate onions, Mueller sells chocolates in the form of life-size, anatomically correct hearts, lungs, kidneys, ears and teeth.

CHILI CHAMP

Tim "Eater X" Janus of New York City ate 2 gal (8 l) of chili in just six minutes to win Ben's Chili Bowl's World Chili Eating Championship in October 2012.

EXOTIC ICES

Snow King, an ice cream shop in Taipei, Taiwan, sells more than 70 exotic flavors of ice cream, including sesame-oil chicken, pig knuckle, beer and curry.

TURNED GREEN

A 24-year-old man was hospitalized in Guizhou Province, China, after turning green because he ate too many snails. The man had been feasting daily on river snails. However, parasitic worms that live in the snails had entered his body and caused an infection in his liver, which made his skin go green.

MASSIVE MOUSSE

At the 2013 Chocolate Festival, the Aventura Mall in Florida invited chefs to create a gigantic chocolate mousse weighing 496 lb (225 kg)—2½ times the weight of an average man. It included 108 lb (49 kg) of chocolate, 66 lb (30 kg) of butter, 24 lb (11 kg) of egg yolk, 20 lb (9 kg) of sugar, 50 quarts (47 l) of heavy cream and 5 gal (19 l) of milk and took five hours to make.

BIG STEAK

The Duck Inn in Redditch, England, has a £110 ($177), 150-oz (4.2-kg) steak on the menu that is free to anyone who finishes it in under an hour. Heavier than most newborn babies, the steak is typically 12 in (30 cm) long, by 12 in (30 cm) wide and 4 in (10 cm) thick, and it needs two hours to cook it medium rare.

Robot Dancers

A restaurant in Tokyo, Japan, has its own troupe of dancing-girl robots. Each dancer at the Robot Restaurant consists of an upper torso and legs mounted on a metal, motor-driven base. With the help of human operators, the robots can move their arms, head, fingers, mouth and legs in time to the music as part of a colorful floorshow that also features flashing lights, giant LED screens and animatronic pterodactyl dinosaurs.

CAREER SWITCH

Ben Cohen and Jerry Greenfield, the founders of Ben & Jerry's, originally intended to make and sell bagels, but when the equipment proved too expensive, they instead paid $5 for a correspondence course at Penn State University on how to make ice cream.

CHRISTMAS COOKIE

Leslie Canady, of Wichita, Kansas, keeps a 28-year-old Christmas cookie in a blue velvet jewelry box. The cookie, which still looks as good as new, was made for her by her mother when Leslie was five months old.

NO TOMATOES

Although ketchup is an iconic American product, the sauce actually originated in 17th-century China, where it was made with pickled fish and spices and did not contain tomatoes.

COCKTAIL KING

Erik Mora, a bartender in Las Vegas, Nevada, can make and pour 1,559 different cocktails in one hour.

Blood Lust

For Halloween, young people in China get the chance to act like vampires by drinking blood. It is not real blood, however, but a red beverage served in plastic bags that look just like hospital blood packs.

Moon Cakes

These cheeky butt-shaped moon cakes—complete with confectionery thong and hand—were baked by a Hong Kong firm for the Singapore Full Moon Festival in reference to the eighth lunar month, which in Cantonese is a slang word for "buttocks."

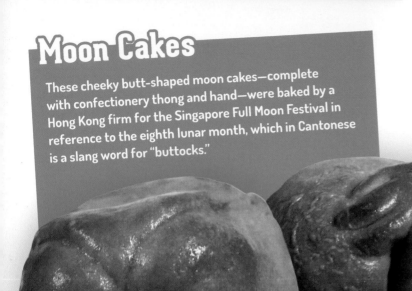

TURTLE BURGER

A man in China tried to smuggle his pet turtle through airport security by stashing it in a KFC burger before boarding a flight from Guangzhou to Beijing. However, when X-rays detected "odd protrusions" sticking out of the burger inside his bag, the deception was uncovered and he was forced to leave his turtle behind with a friend.

FRUIT TREE

Fruit sculptor Shawn Feeney helped build a 10-ft-tall (3-m) fruit tree, made up of more than 1,200 pieces of pineapple, orange, strawberry, peach and mango, on a street corner in Calgary, Alberta, Canada.

BUSY RESTAURANT

The Varsity in Atlanta, Georgia, is the largest drive-in restaurant in the world, serving up to 40,000 people every day.

POPPADOM PILE

Tipu Rahman, a chef from an Indian restaurant in Northampton, England, spent two hours creating a 5-ft-8-in (1.7-m) stack of 1,280 poppadoms.

SHORT STAY

The 1,500-seater McDonald's restaurant, the largest in the world, at the London 2012 Olympic Park was open for only six weeks.

LIME PIE

At Key West, Florida, in July 2013, bakers prepared an 8¼-ft-wide (2.5-m) key lime pie. Containing 5,760 key limes, 200 lb (91 kg) of graham crackers and 55 gal (208 l) of condensed milk, the pie was big enough to feed 1,000 people.

WORM SOUP

Earthworm soup is a popular dish in the Guandong Province of China and is thought to cure fevers.

BEER ROOM

Market research company PAR Research has an 11,000-sq-ft (1,020-sq-m) test room at its headquarters in Evansville, Indiana, which is full of more than 17,300 unique beer bottles and nearly 12,000 different brands of beer from around the world.

Live Octopus

This man at a food festival in Seoul, South Korea, is eating an octopus that is still very much alive.

Festival-goers can pull the wriggling creatures out of a bucket and then force the tentacles into their mouth—no mean feat when the suction pads on the eight arms automatically cling on to fingers, lips, cheeks and even the inside of the mouth. Novices are strongly advised to chew thoroughly before swallowing because they might choke to death if the octopus tries to climb back up their throat.

Odd
Enterprises

Into the Death Zone

Towering 20 times the height of the Empire State Building, Mount Everest, the highest point on the planet, is home to one of the most unpredictable environments on Earth, experiencing hurricane force winds and temperatures plunging to –70°F (–57°C).

More than 5,000 climbers are believed to have scaled the 29,029-ft (8,848-m) summit, yet despite modern techniques and hi-tech equipment, the mountain is still a lethal place for humans, posing terrible threats of avalanches, falling ice and frostbite. Since the first recorded attempt on the mountain in 1922, hundreds of climbers have lost their lives trying to climb Everest. A 2006 study found that for every ten climbers that reach the top, one dies.

Despite the risks, climbing Everest is more popular than ever, and when there is a window of good weather there can be hundreds of mountaineers making the climb at the same time. There are worries that the numbers are making the trip even more dangerous—causing bottlenecks, lines, tangled ropes, and even arguments between climbers. Any time wasted on the mountain uses up vital oxygen and energy and increases the risk of being caught out by the weather—climbers are advised to turn around if they haven't reached the summit by 2 p.m. on their final day, as deadly storms can close in suddenly in the afternoon.

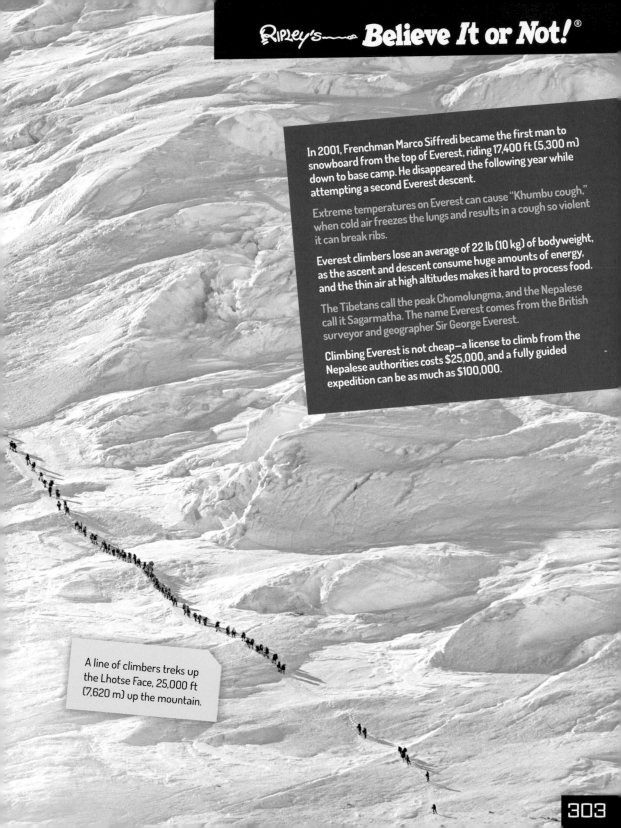

In 2001, Frenchman Marco Siffredi became the first man to snowboard from the top of Everest, riding 17,400 ft (5,300 m) down to base camp. He disappeared the following year while attempting a second Everest descent.

Extreme temperatures on Everest can cause "Khumbu cough," when cold air freezes the lungs and results in a cough so violent it can break ribs.

Everest climbers lose an average of 22 lb (10 kg) of bodyweight, as the ascent and descent consume huge amounts of energy, and the thin air at high altitudes makes it hard to process food.

The Tibetans call the peak Chomolungma, and the Nepalese call it Sagarmatha. The name Everest comes from the British surveyor and geographer Sir George Everest.

Climbing Everest is not cheap—a license to climb from the Nepalese authorities costs $25,000, and a fully guided expedition can be as much as $100,000.

A line of climbers treks up the Lhotse Face, 25,000 ft (7,620 m) up the mountain.

The Death Zone

When climbing Everest, any time wasted in the "death zone"—over 26,250 ft (8,000 m)—can be life-threatening. At this altitude the air contains only 30 percent as much oxygen as at sea level, and the lack of oxygen makes breathing hard and leads to lethargy, loss of appetite and mental confusion. Those suffering from this severe altitude sickness have been described as having no idea where they are or how they got there. In extreme cases, the brain can swell and induce a coma. If a climber encounters difficulties in the death zone and cannot continue, then it is extremely risky for others to attempt a rescue. Congestion in the death zone was blamed for the deaths of six climbers in one weekend in 2012.

Early Pioneers

When George Mallory was asked why he wanted to climb Mount Everest, the British mountaineer replied, "Because it's there." Mallory wanted to be the first to conquer Everest, and he made three attempts. The first, in 1922, was without oxygen tanks; then, in 1924, he made his final ascent, with Andrew Irvine. They climbed in clothing that offered little protection against the cold, but this time they took oxygen. A member of their team spotted them less than 2,000 ft (610 m) from the summit, but Mallory and Irvine never returned to camp. In 1999, Mallory's frozen remains were discovered at 26,760 ft (8,157 m), leaving the question of whether or not he and Irvine reached the summit unanswered.

A traffic jam at 29,000 ft (8,839 m). Climbers wait to ascend the Hillary Step in 2012, just 30 feet (9 m) from the summit. Four climbers died on this day in 2012. Mountaineers have suggested fixing a ladder to the step to accommodate the increasing numbers of climbers.

Lincoln Hall

In May 2006, the experienced Australian mountaineer Lincoln Hall was descending from the summit when he was struck down with altitude sickness. His brain began to swell and his climbing companions were forced to leave him for dead at 28,200 ft (8,600 m). He spent the night alone, hallucinating, but incredibly he survived until the morning, when a group of ascending climbers found him sitting in the snow, suffering from severe frostbite. They abandoned their ascent in order to save his life. Had he not been found, he would have been the 12th climber to die on Everest that year.

First to the Top

At 11:30 a.m. on May 29, 1953, Edmund Hillary and the Sherpa Tenzing Norgay became the first men to step foot on the top of Mount Everest. Their ascent took seven weeks, but after spending 15 minutes at the summit, they returned to base camp in three days. Just over 50 years later, in 2004, Sherpa Pemba Dorje climbed the mountain in 8 hours 10 minutes. Hillary's son Peter has climbed Everest five times.

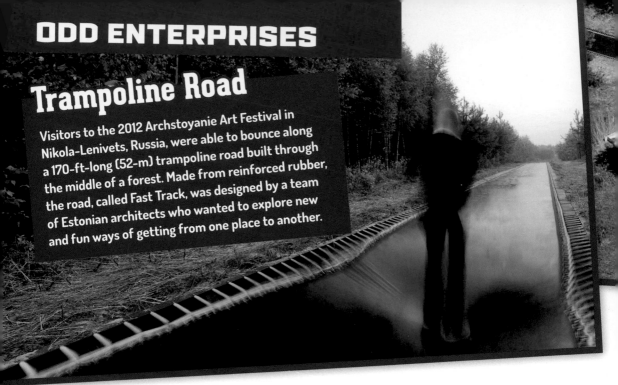

Trampoline Road

Visitors to the 2012 Archstoyanie Art Festival in Nikola-Lenivets, Russia, were able to bounce along a 170-ft-long (52-m) trampoline road built through the middle of a forest. Made from reinforced rubber, the road, called Fast Track, was designed by a team of Estonian architects who wanted to explore new and fun ways of getting from one place to another.

TEARS FOR HIRE

In the Indian state of Rajasthan, professional female mourners called rudaali are hired to cry in public on behalf of the family members of a dead man.

DEAD DIALECTS

The world's first Akkadian-language dictionary was completed in 2011 at the University of Chicago, Illinois, although the language's dialects of Assyrian and Babylonian haven't been spoken in around 2,000 years.

BIG SCHOOL

The City Montessori School in Lucknow, India, is populated with 47,000 pupils, 2,500 teachers, 3,700 computers and—to house them all—1,000 classrooms.

RAT BATTLE

At the Festival of Dead Rats, held annually in El Puig, Spain, revelers hit a cucaña—a type of decorated container—that is filled with frozen rat corpses. When it breaks open, they hurl the dead rodents at each other. The mock battle dates back to when the cucañas were filled with fruit, and rats that had infiltrated them were bludgeoned to death by festival-goers and thrown about the square.

CAFFEINE POLLUTION

Water tested by scientists off the coast of Oregon has been found to contain high levels of caffeine. High rainfall can cause sewage pipes to overflow so that human waste is flushed out into the ocean—and the region is noted for its population's love of coffee.

INFLATABLE ROOM

Architect Alex Schweder created an inflatable hotel room in Denver, Colorado, that rises a staggering 22 ft (6.7 m) in the air courtesy of a scissor lift on top of the van on which it is perched. The 5 x 7 ft (1.5 x 2.1 m) aluminum and vinyl room has a chemical toilet, a shower, a sink, curtains and an inflatable bed and couch.

CEMETERY BONES

Heavy rain in January 2013 caused human bones from the cemetery at St. Mary's Church, Whitby, England, to be washed down the cliff into the town. The scattered bones were gathered up and reburied in the 900-year-old cemetery, which was used by author Bram Stoker as the setting for his novel *Dracula*.

WALL OF DUST

A towering wall of dust a mile high engulfed Phoenix, Arizona, on August 26, 2013, leaving the city blanketed in grit. Arizona's storm season produces massive dust storms called haboobs, which can stretch over 100 mi (160 km).

BLIND FAITH

Every weekday, Chris Smith of Dedham, Massachusetts, rides his bicycle to and from work—a round trip of 24 mi (38 km)—even though he is legally blind.

YOUNG PILOT

At age 21, James Anthony Tan from Kajang, Malaysia, flew a single-engine Cessna aircraft 23,628 mi (38,025 km) around the world in 48 days.

Wine Fight

Every year on June 29, thousands of people climb a mountain near Haro, Spain, to take part in a three-hour mass wine fight. For the La Batalla de Vino de Haro event, which dates back 300 years, trucks are filled with thousands of gallons of red wine. With around a gallon (4 l) of wine allocated per person, the combatants proceed to soak each other using water pistols, buckets, hollowed-out gourds and even old boots. All participants start out wearing white shirts, but by the end of the evening, the whole town is a lighter shade of grape.

REMOTE LOCATION

The Zanskar region in India's states of Jammu and Kashmir is located high in the Himalayan mountain range and is cut off by snow from the rest of the world for more than half of the year.

VAMPIRE ALERT

In November 2012, the mayor of Zarožje, Serbia, warned that a vampire was on the loose and that local residents should put garlic on their doors. Legendary vampire Sava Savanović reputedly lived in an old wooden mill where he sucked the blood of millers, but when the mill recently collapsed, local villagers believed that the vampire was roaming the mountains looking for a new home.

LAST SPEAKER

Gyani Maiya Sen, 76, from Nepal is the last fluent speaker of the Kusunda language, which is uniquely unrelated to any of the world's major language groups. Academics are trying to document Kusundu so that when Gyani dies, the language will not die with her.

STORE STORM

Lakeisha Brooks was struck by lightning while standing inside a store in Houma, Louisiana. The lightning bolt hit the roof, traveled through the sprinkler system and up through a metal plate on the floor. Lakeisha had gone into the store only to escape the storm.

Iron Beetle

Three Croatian craftsmen have created a wrought-iron Volkswagen Beetle.

Over a period of four months, they removed the car's original sheet metal bodywork and replaced it with wrought-iron sections that had been designed to fit perfectly onto the existing VW frame. As a finishing touch, they added 24-carat gold-leaf embellishments to the car's exterior.

ODD ENTERPRISES

SNORING MUSEUM

In the German town of Alfeld, there is a museum dedicated to snoring. Doctor Josef Alexander Wirth has collected more than 400 devices and medications used to cure snoring, including nosepins, electroshock machines, leather chinstraps with attached mouth coverings, and heavy cannonballs that were sewn into the insides of snoring soldiers' uniforms during the American Revolutionary War to prevent the snoring soldiers turning onto their backs and disturbing the rest of the men with their noise.

MELTING CARS

During the summer of 2013, the Sun caused such a bright glare reflected from a new 37-story skyscraper in London, England, that the metal roofs of vehicles parked in the street below began to melt.

FROST FLOWERS

When temperatures plunge to around –8°F (–22°C), small cracks or imperfections in young sea ice can result in beautiful ice crystals—or frost flowers—sprouting up from the surface. These Arctic blooms grow several inches tall and contain high levels of salt and marine bacteria. In fact, there is more bacterial life in the frost flowers than in the frozen water beneath them.

STICKY STRUCTURE

Measuring a huge 490 x 230 ft (150 x 70 m) and standing 85 ft (26 m) tall, the Metropol Parasol in Seville, Spain, is the world's largest wooden building—and is held together entirely by glue.

NO SWEAT!

A customary farewell among the Kanum-Irebe people of New Guinea is to stick a finger in a person's armpit, sniff the finger and rub the scent on themselves.

Algae Sea

Visitors to a beach in Qingdao, China, in 2013 romped in thousands of tons of thick green algae. Luckily the algae—*Enteromorpha prolifera*, or sea lettuce—is harmless, edible and rich in nutrients that are said to improve skin and lower blood pressure. Even so, 20,000 tons of the algae were removed in just a few days because if left to decompose and rot, it could produce large amounts of highly toxic hydrogen sulfide gas. It is not the first time the beach has suffered a green invasion. In 2008, the area was swamped by 20 sq mi (52 sq km) of algae, but 10,000 volunteers cleared it so that Qingdao could host the Beijing Olympics sailing events.

Fat Contest

For six months, young men from the Bodi tribe, who live in southern Ethiopia's Omo Valley, gorge on only a stomach-churning drink made from cow's blood and milk in order to get fat and almost double their weight.

The area's scorching heat means that the men must drink the half-gallon (2-l) bowls quickly before the mixture coagulates. At the end of the six months, the men show off their bloated stomachs in a New Year's competition, where the fattest is declared the winner and is feted as a hero for life by the rest of the tribe. The cows, which are sacred to the Bodi, are not killed to provide the blood for the ritual. Instead it is taken by making a hole in a vein with a spear or an axe; then the wound is sealed with clay.

Clean Sweep

This man tried to clean the streets of Mohe, China, with his own ingenious, homemade road sweeper—a tractor with 12 large rotating brooms attached. However, people complained that, far from tidying the streets, his whirlwind contraption made them dustier than they had been before.

TREE PROTEST

Australian environmental campaigner Miranda Gibson spent 449 days living at the top of a 200-ft-high (60-m) eucalyptus tree in Tasmania in a protest against logging. She climbed the tree in December 2011 and stayed there until March 2013 when smoke from a bushfire forced her to come down.

OLDEST WATER

Water found pouring out of boreholes 1½ mi (2.4 km) below ground at a remote copper and zinc mine in Timmins, Ontario, has been trapped there for as much as 2.64 billion years, making it the oldest free-flowing water discovered anywhere in the world.

DRESS CODE

Under crime prevention laws, convicted robbers in Manchester, England, can be banned from wearing hoods within 160 ft (50 m) of shops, banks and cash delivery vans and from wearing false mustaches and beards in public.

GREAT SURVIVOR

A spiderwort plant has been growing inside a bottle without air or water for more than 40 years. David Latimer of Surrey, England, planted it inside a large globular bottle in 1960 to find out whether it could flourish in a self-contained environment. It had its second and last drink in 1972, after which he sealed the bottle neck with a bung that has not been removed since.

OVAL OFFICE

Presidential memorabilia collector Ron Wade has installed an exact replica of the Oval Office in his Longview, Texas, home at a cost of $250,000. Some 250 workers labored on the project, which took 2½ years to design and eight months to build. Ron's collection also includes 10,000 political buttons and a rocking chair that once belonged to J.F.K.

VETERAN DRIVER

Margaret Dunning of Plymouth, Michigan, drives a 1930 Packard Roadster that she has owned since 1949. The 103-year-old learned to drive on the family farm at age eight and has been driving ever since—for more than 90 years.

AMBULANCE ARTISTS

Writers Ernest Hemingway and Somerset Maugham, and composers Maurice Ravel and Ralph Vaughan Williams, all drove military ambulances for the Allies.

Play-Doh Car

To mark the U.K. launch of the Chevrolet Orlando, eight model makers spent two weeks handcrafting a life-size replica car from Play-Doh modeling clay. Positioned on a London street, the 15-ft-long (4.6-m) vehicle was made from 1.6 tons—10,000 pots—of the children's putty at a cost of around $10,000.

LITTLE PLANE

"Bumble Bee II," built in 1988 by Robert H. Starr of Phoenix, Arizona, was the world's smallest piloted airplane—with a wingspan of only 5 ft 6 in (1.7 m).

MINI MOTOR

Austin Coulson from Phoenix, Arizona, has built a roadworthy car that is just 25 in (63.5 cm) tall, 25¾ in (65 cm) wide and 49¾ in (126 cm) long. It has a tiny windshield, headlights, taillights, turn signals, rear-view mirror, seat belt and functional horn.

HOME FRONT

During World War I, American women donated their corsets to the war effort, contributing 28,000 tons of steel—enough metal to build two battleships!

WAR WRITERS

English fantasy authors and friends C.S. Lewis and J.R.R. Tolkien both survived the Battle of the Somme in World War I.

GOOD HEARING

The British Navy's Astute Class nuclear submarine can detect a ship leaving port from more than 3,000 mi (4,800 km) away.

Freezing Fire

When a huge vacant warehouse on Chicago's South Side went up in flames on the night of January 22, 2013, freezing temperatures meant that the water spray from the firefighters' hoses encased everything in ice—including the building itself, trucks and even the crews.

Attended by more than 200 firefighters, the fire was the city's biggest blaze in seven years and was still smoldering 19 hours after it started, by which time the firefighters had inadvertently created an eerie winter wonderland.

An ice-encrusted truck. The fire at the site was so intense that its heat and smoke even showed up on weather radar systems.

FROZEN COMBAT

Austrian and Italian troops fought battles in the mountains and glaciers of the Alps. In recent years, melting glaciers have revealed the frozen remains of soldiers who have been on the mountains for almost a century.

MUSICAL BRIDGE

Officials brightened up a drab bridge in Shijiazhuang, China, by painting huge piano keys and musical notes all over it.

ATLANTIC CROSSING

In March 2013, 50-year-old Charlie Pitcher from Essex, England, finished rowing 2,700 mi (4,320 km) across the Atlantic Ocean from the Canary Islands to Barbados in just 35 days.

PLANE ENTHUSIASM

Volunteers at the San Diego Air and Space Museum, California, spent 12 years and 100,000 man-hours building a 1932 Boeing P-26 fighter airplane from scratch.

NERVES OF STEEL

The Stairway to Nothingness, a new Austrian tourist attraction, allows visitors with a head for heights to walk down 14 steps to a glass-bottomed platform perched 1,300 ft (400 m) directly above the Dachstein glacier.

SHIP SHED

A wooden shed, 30-ft-long (9-m), 15-ft-high (4.5-m), in the shape of the H.M.S. *Victory*, Admiral Nelson's flagship at the Battle of Trafalgar in 1805, was built in Clare Kapma-Saunders's garden in Southampton, England.

BRITISH INVASION

There are only 22 countries in the world that Britain has not invaded—Guatemala, Bolivia, Paraguay, Sweden, Liechtenstein, Luxembourg, Belarus, Andorra, Monaco, Vatican City, São Tomé and Príncipe, Uzbekistan, Mongolia, Kyrgyzstan, Tajikistan, Mali, Ivory Coast, Chad, Central African Republic, Burundi, Republic of Congo, and the Marshall Islands.

GREEN HOUSE

Agricultural lecturer Sheng Xiugi has turned the exterior of his house in Yiwu, China, into a five-story orchard. The walls of his huge house are covered entirely in crops such as grapes, eggplants and plums so that if he wants fruit or vegetables all he has to do is open a window and pick some.

Off the Rails

Jason Shron built a full-size replica of a 1980 VIA Rail Canada train coach in the basement of his home in Vaughan, Ontario. It took him more than 2,500 hours and $10,000 to fulfill his dream, and everything is accurate down to the last detail, including seat numbers, timetable racks, coat hooks and period carpet. He also installed a photographic mural at the end of the coach to make it appear part of an entire train.

COW STAMPEDE
At the centuries-old Ekadashi religious festival in Madhya Pradesh, India, dozens of male villagers volunteer to lie on the ground and wait to be trampled upon by a herd of rampaging cows.

WILD RIDE
The Texas SkyScreamer swing ride, which opened at the Six Flags Over Texas theme park in San Antonio on May 26, 2013, towers 400 ft (120 m) above ground and swings riders in a 124-ft (38-m) circle at speeds of 35 mph (56 km/h).

TWISTED TOWER
The 75-story Cayan Tower in Dubai has a twist of 90 degrees from top to bottom so that residents in the lower part have views of Dubai Marina while those on the upper floors face the Persian Gulf. The concrete structure's columns rotate by just over a degree as they ascend from floor to floor.

Whale Boat

Part speedboat and part submarine, Innespace's *Seabreacher Y* not only looks like a killer whale, but also can leap out of the water like one, too. With its 260-horsepower engine, the hi-tech two-seater can be launched 16 ft (5 m) into the air when it breaches and is capable of speeds up to 55 mph (88 km/h) on the surface and up to 20 mph (32 km/h) underwater.

Underwater Park

Summer divers at Grüner See (Green Lake) in Styria, Austria, find things they would not expect at the bottom of most lakes, such as grassy meadows, flowerbeds, paved paths, benches and a bridge.

In winter, the lake is only 6½ ft (2 m) deep and the surrounding area is a country park, but in spring the snow on the surrounding mountains melts, causing the whole area to fill with melt water. By summer, the lake is 40 ft (12 m) deep and the park is submerged. The underwater grass and foliage make the water appear a beautiful emerald green, giving the lake its name.

Bright Idea

This mother and son are taking no chances while riding their mobility scooters in Wassenaar, the Netherlands. Both wear high-visibility clothing and have fitted their scooters with an array of bells, sirens, horns and fluorescent stickers. The pair are well known locally. Well, it would be completely impossible to miss them.

DRY ISLAND

There are no rivers, streams or lakes on the 122-sq-mi (316-sq-km) Mediterranean island of Malta.

SURRENDER FLAG

The final truce flag of World War I was actually a tablecloth!

GREEN POLICY

To make people feel more positive and convince them that spring was just around the corner, officials in Chengdu, China, gave nature a helping hand by painting the city's grass green in February 2013. Locals spotted the trick when they walked on the grass and paint came off on their shoes.

SCHOOL SITE

There has been a public school on the site where Shishi High School in Chengdu, China, now stands—for more than 2,100 years.

FAT BLOCKAGE

A 16-ton lump of festering food fat was found blocking an underground sewer in London, England, in 2013. The "fatberg," which was the weight of a double-decker bus, was so big it reduced the sewer to just 5 percent of its normal capacity, and it took workers using a high-pressure jet hose three weeks to blast it away. The congealed mass was first discovered when residents complained that their toilets would not flush.

INSTANT FREEZE

Temperatures fell to −58°F (−50°C) in Siberia in December 2012. It was so cold that when a man in Novosibirsk threw a pot of boiling water from his balcony on one of the top floors of an apartment block, the water turned into a shower of frozen droplets.

FALSE ECONOMY

Liechtenstein, which is the sixth smallest country in the world, is in fact the world's largest producer of sausage casings and of false teeth.

Rocket Bike

French cyclist François Gissy hit 163 mph (263 km/h) while riding a self-built mountain bike along an abandoned runway in northeastern France in May 2013. He achieved the astonishing speed by attaching a hydrogen peroxide-powered rocket to the frame of the machine, creating temperatures of 650°F (343°C) and a gas-flow velocity of more than 1,000 meters per second to give the bike its powerful thrust.

Rainbow Mountains

It looks like a fairy tale landscape created by an animation studio, but these beautiful striped mountains in all the colors of the rainbow are a natural phenomenon that can be found at the Zhangye Danxia Landform Geological Park in China. The dazzling spectacle has been created by layers of different colored sandstones and minerals that have been pressed together and shaped over a period of 24 million years, by a combination of water erosion and tectonic movement. At different times of day, and in different seasons, the colors change, making the "Seven-Color Mountain," as it is known locally, more magical than ever.

PARIS GUN

Germany's Paris Gun, a World-War-I artillery cannon, could bombard the French capital from 70 mi (112 km) away and could be fired so high that the Earth's rotation affected its trajectory.

EXTREME RIDE

The Giant Canyon Swing at Steve Beckley's Glenwood Caverns Adventure Park, Colorado, swings riders at super-speeds of 50 mph (80 km/h) out over a 1,300-ft (400-m) sheer drop to the Colorado River below.

SWALLOWED GEMS

A 25-year-old man, arrested as he waited to board a plane from Johannesburg, South Africa, to Dubai, had swallowed 220 diamonds worth $2.3 million in an attempt to smuggle them out of the country.

Rainbow Waterfall

Photographer Justin Lee from British Columbia captured the brief moment when the late-afternoon sunlight caught fine water spray to form a spectacular rainbow at the bottom of Bridalveil Fall in Yosemite National Park, California. The 620-ft-high (189-m) waterfall takes its name from the mist that sometimes drifts off it in a breeze and resembles a bride's flowing veil.

No-Fly Zone

In 1,426 days, just under four years, Graham Hughes from Liverpool, England, visited all 201 nations of the world–without once flying! Instead, he used trains, buses, taxis and cargo ships—and did it all on a budget of $100 a week.

Traveling a total of 155,000 mi (250,000 km), Graham said that his most hazardous journey was a four-day ocean crossing in a leaky wooden canoe from Senegal to Cape Verde. He was imprisoned for a week in the Congo and ate live octopus in South Korea. He literally had to cross a minefield to reach the border in Western Sahara, only to be told he needed a visa from a town 1,250 mi (2,000 km) away—and he was arrested trying to sneak across the border into Russia!

Graham's trip in numbers

201 nations visited • **67** of them visited more than once • **193** of them were U.N. members • **59** of them were islands • Average money spent: **$100** a week • **18** bonus territories (for good measure) • Traveled: over **155,000** mi **(250,000** km) • **736** blog entries • **352** hours of video footage • **196** days spent at sea • **157** ships sailed • **12** days spent in jail

Image labels: CHINA, EGYPT, ICELAND, ISRAEL, AUSTRALIA, AFGHANISTAN, BAHAMAS, BENIN, SUDAN, REUNION, CANADA, INDON, MICRONESIA, SRI LANKA, GABON, SOLOMON ISLANDS, RUSSIA, SOUTH SUDAN, U.S.A., CAMERO

Believe It or Not!®

The Rules

- ✈ I cannot fly
- I may not drive
- 🚌 I must use scheduled ground transport
- I must step foot on dry land

CENTRAL AFRICAN REPUBLIC

EQUATORIAL GUINEA

THAILAND

TIBET

KENYA

ITALY

TOGO

CHAD

SWAZILAND

PALAU

TONGA

WEST PAPUA

VANUATU

OMAN

MEXICO

PAPUA NEW GUINEA

SERBIA

FIJI

TANZANIA

NIGER

IRAN

ESTONIA

NEPAL

WESTERN SAHARA

ENGLAND

PACIFIC OCEAN

NORTH KOREA

KIRIBATI

VENEZUELA

MARSHALL ISLANDS

BACK HOME!

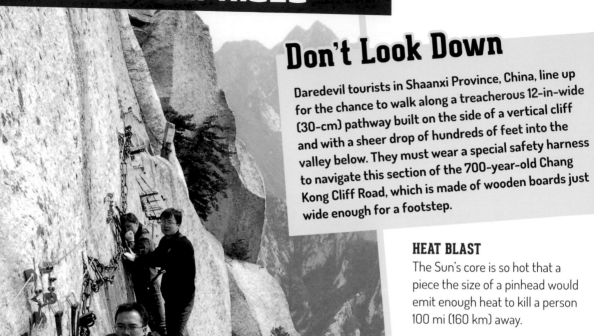

Don't Look Down

Daredevil tourists in Shaanxi Province, China, line up for the chance to walk along a treacherous 12-in-wide (30-cm) pathway built on the side of a vertical cliff and with a sheer drop of hundreds of feet into the valley below. They must wear a special safety harness to navigate this section of the 700-year-old Chang Kong Cliff Road, which is made of wooden boards just wide enough for a footstep.

HEAT BLAST

The Sun's core is so hot that a piece the size of a pinhead would emit enough heat to kill a person 100 mi (160 km) away.

LIVING CEMETERY

Owing to a shortage of housing, more than 6,000 people live among the dead as squatters in the North Cemetery of the Philippines capital, Manila. Wooden and corrugated iron shacks are perched on top of hundreds of stacked tombs, and the 133-acre (54-ha) site has sprouted fast-food stalls, karaoke parlors and Internet cafés, while still staging up to 80 funerals a day.

OFFICE TREE

The office building of Cove Auto Towing and Recovery in Astoria, New York, was built around a living tree, which now grows right through the roof to a height of 50 ft (15 m).

TOO OLD

Mzee Julius Wanyondu Gatonga was told in 2012 that he could not receive Kenyan medical insurance coverage because his I.D. showed that he was 128 years old and the computer system only recognizes birthdates after 1890, six years after he was apparently born. If his date of birth is genuine, it would make him the oldest person to have ever lived.

DEER GOGGLES

The Inuit people of the Arctic traditionally made snow goggles from carved caribou bones and sinew.

KITTY KINDERGARTEN

The Kindergarten Wolfartsweier building in Karlsruhe, Germany, is constructed in the shape of a cat. Children enter by the mouth and exit by the cat's tail, which takes the form of a slide. The classrooms and dining room are in the cat's belly.

PUMICE ISLAND

An island of floating pumice measuring 300 mi (482 km) long and 30 mi (48 km) wide—larger than the area of Israel—was spotted off the coast of New Zealand in 2012. The island was probably spewed to the surface by an underwater volcano, as pumice forms when volcanic lava cools rapidly.

NICE VIEW

A restroom on the 18th floor of New York City's Standard Hotel has 10-ft (3-m), floor-to-ceiling windows, which gives users amazing views of the Manhattan skyline but also enables them to be seen on the toilet by people in other blocks or on the street below!

Solitary Life

Maxime Qavtaradze, a 60-year-old monk, has lived in solitude at the top of the 131-ft-high (40-m) Katskhi Pillar in Georgia for more than 20 years—and has to have food winched up to him by his followers. He leaves the limestone pillar only twice a week to pray, a precarious ladder descent that takes him 20 minutes. Luckily, as a former crane driver, he has a head for heights. When he first moved in, the accommodation was so basic that he had to sleep in an old fridge.

Snow Art

British map designer and artist Simon Beck is making his mark on the landscape of the French Alps by creating art in the snow simply by using his feet!

Using geometric designs created by working with an orienteering compass, Simon can spend from ten hours to two days on each piece, braving the icy climate and "drawing" his picture with snowshoes. Some of his pieces are as large as six football fields, but they are short lived, usually only lasting a day or two until the wind blows or the next snowfall.

Using designs inspired by mathematical patterns or even crop circles, Simon starts by plotting his art on graph paper. He then spends a couple of hours surveying and carefully measuring his site with a compass before starting to walk. He can walk up to 25 mi (40 km) when creating a piece and often listens to Beethoven to keep himself going.

Ripley's Believe It or Not!®

Simon says that designs created in powdery snow, ideally around 9 in (23 cm) deep, make the best pictures. He likes to work on a level site with an even amount of snow.

WORLDS APART

Windsor, Ontario, was just about the safest city in Canada in 2011, while Detroit, Michigan—only half a mile away—was branded the most dangerous city in the U.S.A. Windsor recorded just one murder while near-neighbor Detroit had more than 340.

HANGING PARTS

The Igreja Nosso Senhor do Bonfim—a church in Salvador, Brazil—has a Room of Miracles where wax or plastic replicas of body parts, including arms, feet, heads, hearts, spines and breasts, which represent people who have been cured over the centuries, hang from the ceiling.

MINI TAJ

As a monument to his late wife, 77-year-old retired mailman Faizul Hasan Kadari set about building a miniature 5,000-sq-ft (465-sq-m) replica of the Taj Mahal in the garden of his home in Bulandshahr, Uttar Pradesh, India.

ALGAE POWER

For six months, an apartment complex in Hamburg, Germany, was powered entirely by algae. Fed via a water circuit, the algae was grown in a series of panels mounted onto the sun-facing sides of the building. When ready to be harvested, it was turned into a pulp that was processed at a biogas plant to create renewable energy.

A Dyeing Tradition

Ohaguro is an ancient Vietnamese and Japanese tradition in which married women, and some men, dye their teeth black for protection against evil spirits.

The tradition was widely practiced from prehistoric times up until the mid-19th century, and some women still perform Ohaguro today.

The lacquer used in teeth-blackening prevented tooth decay, much like a modern-day dental sealant, and by using it, women could keep a full set of teeth all their lives. Ancient human remains reveal skeletons with all their teeth—albeit dyed black—proving the practice to be more medically beneficial than you might expect.

Dyeing teeth black was a way not only to ward off evil spirits, but also to ensure you yourself were not mistaken for an evil spirit—who were said to have sharp, white teeth. This distinctive blackened look, which was seen as beautiful, became part of Vietnamese women's identity and a way for them to distinguish themselves from the Chinese, who kept their teeth white.

Antarctic Hero

In the era of heroic polar exploration, Sir Ernest Shackleton (1874–1922) spent 18 months leading the crew of his ship, the *Endurance*, to safety after a disastrous journey to Antarctica.

Their survival, in the most extreme conditions on Earth, was a feat of unbelievable endurance, celebrated for Shackleton's leadership and the fact that every single member of his crew survived.

Over 100 years ago, in August 1914, Shackleton and his crew left British waters to embark on the most ambitious polar expedition of all time—the Imperial Trans-Antarctic Expedition to cross Antarctica from one side to the other via the South Pole. He took 27 men and 70 dogs onboard, but unfortunately for his crew, their safe return was far from assured, and it would take them over two years to get home.

Although polar expeditions were incredibly tough, there was never a shortage of men willing to risk everything for glory. More than 5,000 men applied to join Shackleton's Imperial Trans-Antarctic Expedition in 1914.

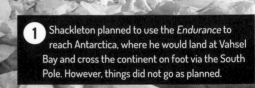

1 Shackleton planned to use the *Endurance* to reach Antarctica, where he would land at Vahsel Bay and cross the continent on foot via the South Pole. However, things did not go as planned.

5 The crew left the *Endurance* with just three lifeboats and lived for five months on the constantly changing, precarious ice. On April 9, the ice floe they were camping on broke in two, and Shackleton ordered them into the lifeboats. Five days later, and five months after abandoning ship, the boats landed at Elephant Island—346 mi (557 km) from the sunken vessel, and the first time they had set foot on solid ground in 16 months.

2 In December 1914, the *Endurance* left the remote South Atlantic island of South Georgia and soon entered pack ice in the Weddell Sea. Six weeks later, she became stuck in the ice. Shackleton decided they would spend the winter onboard the ship, hoping that she would eventually be released from the ice to continue her voyage in the spring. To make more space in their "winter station," the crew made igloos on the ice for the dogs.

4 Unfortunately, as the ice started to break up and move in the September springtime, it put tremendous pressure on the ship's hull, and on October 24, the *Endurance* was crushed and water poured in. Shackleton ordered everything to be removed from the wrecked ship and the weakest animals to be shot—three weeks later, the *Endurance* finally sank.

3 For nine long months over the winter, the crew continued to live onboard the ship in the inhospitable environment of the Antarctic, slowly moving north as the *Endurance* traveled with the ice floe. The men's spirits remained high, despite the fact that they had to eat, sleep and live in very close and cramped quarters.

6 Shackleton realized there was no hope of rescue on this small spit of land, so he started to plan the 920-mi (1,500-km) journey back to a whaling station on South Georgia. Two weeks after reaching Elephant Island, he set off with five men on the Southern Ocean—one of the most dangerous oceans in the world—in the *James Caird*, a lifeboat just 22 ft (6.7 m) long.

7 After 17 days of strong gales, freezing cold, and giant waves, the *James Caird* reached South Georgia. However, the ordeal was not over yet—Shackleton had been forced to land on the uninhabited side of the island, and the whaling station was an arduous 32-mi (51-km) away, over icy slopes, snowfields and unpredictable glaciers.

8 It took four attempts and a further three months for a rescue ship to reach the rest of the crew on Elephant Island, on August 30, 1916. Amazingly, all of the 22 men left behind had survived, although a number were missing toes from frostbite. Shackleton's courage, ingenuity and determination had prevailed, and as a result, he has always been remembered as a hero and as one of the great leaders of the 20th century.

Alien Island

Described as "the most alien place on Earth" on account of its sci-fi landscape, the remote island of Socotra in the Indian Ocean has examples of a plant species that is 20 million years old. The island, which was separated from mainland Africa some seven million years ago, is home to 800 rare species of flora and fauna, a third of which cannot be seen anywhere else on the planet. The trees and plants, including the dragon's blood tree, whose red resin was used in medieval magic, have evolved to adapt to the hot, dry climate. Although Socotra has some 40,000 inhabitants, its first roads were built just a few years ago.

SLIDING BUILDING
When a historic building in Anda, China, had to be moved to make way for a railway line in the winter of 2013, engineers transported it to its new location 790 ft (240 m) down the road by sliding it on ice. They sprayed water underneath the structure and along its route until they created an ice bed that was strong enough to support the building. Then they inserted large rollers and gently slid it down the road—an operation that took more than two weeks.

PROFESSIONAL SLEEPER
The Hotel Finn in Helsinki, Finland, advertised in 2013 for a "professional sleeper" to stay as a guest for 35 days, testing the hotel's rooms and writing an Internet blog about the experience.

MIGHTY MISSISSIPPI
An amazing 7,000 rivers feed into the Mississippi, giving it a vast catchment area of around 1.15 million sq mi (2.98 million sq km), roughly 37 percent of the land area of the continental U.S.A.

A Sufi holy man pokes his own eye with a sharp object during the annual Urs religious festival in Ajmer, India.

Each year, thousands of Sufi devotees from different parts of India take part in a procession to mark the death of Sufi saint Khwaja Moinuddin Chishti, and some show their devotion by performing eye-watering feats such as this, using pointed knives, sticks and spears to make their eyeballs protrude alarmingly.

Eye Popping

HARD HATS

When World War I began in 1914, none of the countries involved issued protective steel helmets to their troops.

FOAM STORM

On the morning of January 28, 2013, residents of Mooloolaba in Queensland, Australia, woke to find the beach town covered in up to 10 ft (3 m) of foam. Rough weather had whipped up the foam from the ocean and then carried it ashore.

MARTIAN TWINNING

The remote village of Glenelg in the Scottish Highlands has been twinned with a valley on Mars—a rocky plain 140 million mi (225 million km) away.

HIDDEN HOUSE

Following 60-mph (96-km/h) winds in the region, Josh Pitman of Midland, Texas, found his house almost completely obscured by hundreds of stacked tumbleweeds.

BATTLE MOVIES

Scenes in the French movie *J'Accuse* (1919) were filmed in the middle of the Battle of Saint-Mihiel. In 1917, filmmaker D.W. Griffith also went to the French front to film his movie, *Hearts of the World*.

LIGHTNING STRIKES

Alexander Mandón from Sampués, Colombia, was struck by lightning four times in six months and survived each strike. Believing he must be positively charged to attract lightning, local healers had him buried neck deep in the ground in an attempt to draw out the charge from his body.

FORGOTTEN LAND

Andorra declared war on Germany during World War I but wasn't included in the 1919 Treaty of Versailles that ended the war. It didn't sign a peace treaty with Germany until September 25, 1939.

BIGGEST VOLCANO

The world's largest volcano—roughly the size of New Mexico—has been discovered on the floor of the Pacific Ocean 1,000 mi (1,600 km) east of Japan. Believed to be inactive, the Tamu Massif covers 120,000 sq mi (310,000 sq km), rising over a mile above the ocean floor and boring 18 mi (30 km) into the Earth's crust. It is a staggering 60 times bigger than Hawaii's Mauna Loa, the world's largest active volcano.

Skull Pods

The *Antirrhinum* gets its common name of snapdragon from the flower's resemblance to a dragon's head—but when the flower dies, its seedpod looks even more macabre, just like a human skull. With such eerie pods, it's no wonder that in the Middle Ages people thought the plant possessed supernatural powers and could offer protection from witches.

Aquarium Wall

Turkish businessman Mehmet Ali Gökçeoğlu has replaced the metal fence around the front of his luxury, beachfront villa in Çeşme with a 160-ft-long (50-m) aquarium filled with hundreds of fish and octopuses. He acquires the marine creatures in his living aqua-fence from the nearby Aegean Sea, to which it is connected via a 1,300-ft-long (400-m) buried pipeline in order to ensure that the water is changed regularly and that the aquarium's occupants remain healthy.

STAG CALLS

Elvis Afanasenko won the 2012 World Bolving Championships, held in Exmoor, England, where competitors imitate the bellowing sounds made by rutting red deer stags. A four-time winner, his mimicry is so accurate that his mating calls are returned by jealous stags out in the wild.

MOUNTAIN MIRRORS

Located in the shadow of the Gaustatoppen Mountain, the Norwegian town of Rjukan never saw any sunlight in winter until, in 2013, three 183-sq-ft (17-sq-m) computer-controlled mirrors were placed on top of a nearby peak to redirect winter light and keep the town square bathed in sunlight during the day.

Near Misses

Sinking Feeling

Sixty-year-old school principal Pamela Knox was driving quietly along a street in Toledo, Ohio, when a 10-ft-deep (3-m) sinkhole suddenly opened up and swallowed her car. Plunged into darkness, she began to fear the worst when water from a burst pipe flooded into the car, but fire crews lowered a ladder into the hole to enable her to climb to safety.

Rubble Trouble

An entire parking lot in Taiyuan, China, was demolished around a parked solitary vehicle, leaving the car intact but surrounded by a sea of rubble. The builders had waited ten days for the driver to return to the car but then decided they could not delay the street-widening project any longer.

In the Balance

This Chevrolet Epica was left hanging over the edge of a parking lot 50 ft (15 m) above ground in Changsha, China, after the driver reversed too fast and too far and smashed through the guardrail. Luckily, he and his wife managed to climb out safely.

Tight Space

Passersby in Kiev, Ukraine, thought they were seeing things when they glanced up and saw a Toyota Yaris parked 60 ft (18 m) above ground on the balcony of a third-floor apartment! How and why the car got there remains a mystery.

341

SHOPPER CHOPPER

Cal VanSant of Lancaster, Pennsylvania, spent $15,000 building a 130-mph (208-km/h) oversized supermarket cart to promote his son-in-law's store. The Shopper Chopper is powered by a 5.8-liter V8 Chevrolet engine and can seat six people.

COIN CAR

Ali Hassan Gharib from Dubai has had his Range Rover covered in $16,000 worth of coins. The 57,412 dirhams amounted to half a ton of spare change. An artist spent weeks polishing the coins and then gluing each one to the vehicle individually by hand.

JAM BUSTER

Gridlocked motorists in Wuhan and Jinan, China, can hire someone to sit in the congestion for them. With one call a motorcycle will arrive to pick them up and leave a driver to take the car to its destination.

LEATHER CAR

A wealthy motorist from Moscow, Russia, has had the exterior bodywork of his car completely covered in Canadian wood-bison leather. Inside, the dashboard and seats are covered in leather and fur, while even the engine is draped in treated leather that can withstand high temperatures. The engine and trunk are also inlaid with Swarovski crystals, giving the car a cool price tag of $1,215,000.

GOLDEN BIKE

Turkish designer Tarhan Telli has built a golden motorcycle worth more than $1 million. It took him over a year to build the unique bike, which weighs a third of a ton and has a chassis and body shell made of white and yellow gold leaf.

PIPING HOT

Tim Burton from London, England, found an unusual way to cook his Christmas turkey—by roasting it in red-hot flames shooting from the exhaust of a £300,000 ($500,000) Lamborghini Aventador. He put the fresh turkey on the end of a pitchfork and stood behind the 700 bhp supercar while the owner revved the engine up to 9,000—and in just ten minutes, the bird was cooked to perfection.

MAIL SERVICE

In 2012, Graham Eccles from Cornwall, England, started his own local postal service delivering mail on a vintage penny farthing bicycle.

FIELD MEDICINE

Army doctors used to apply garlic to wounds to stop gangrene and septic poisoning.

Beetle Ball

Sculptor Ichwan Noor from Jakarta, Indonesia, transformed a 1953 Volkswagen Beetle car into a perfect sphere for a 2013 art exhibition in Hong Kong.

He actually used parts from five cars, combined with polyester and aluminum, to create the metallic orb that stands almost 6 ft (1.8 m) tall.

MUD DAY

The Westland suburb of Detroit, Michigan, hosts an annual Mud Day where hundreds of children wallow and play in a giant pit containing more than 200 tons of dirt mixed with 16,700 gal (76,000 l) of water. Events include mud limbo, wheelbarrow races and the contest to crown the King and Queen of Mud.

PIGEON CAMERA

During World War I, the German army experimented with pigeons fitted with cameras for aerial surveillance behind enemy lines.

CHURCH SKATERS

Every day between December 16 and 24, streets in Caracas, Venezuela, are closed to traffic until 8 a.m. so that people can rollerskate to church for a traditional early morning service called Misa de Aguinaldo. Before children go to bed during this period, they tie one end of a piece of string to their big toe and hang the other end out of the window of their house. The next morning, passing skaters tug on any string they see to remind the children to get up for church.

CHRISTMAS SOCCER

During the Christmas of 1914, soldiers on the Western Front in World War I crossed lines to exchange presents and play soccer.

PARKING PRICE

Lisa Blumenthal paid $560,000 for two parking spaces near her home in the Black Bay neighborhood of Boston, Massachusetts. When she bought the spaces, at an auction, each one cost almost as much as the price of an average family home in the state.

MOON TRACKS

Since the Moon has no atmosphere to erode them, tracks from astronauts and rovers at Moon landing sites are still visible and undisturbed after decades.

Rainbow Trunk

After shedding their bark, these rainbow eucalyptus trees on Kauai, Hawaii, resemble brilliantly colored works of art. The trees shed patches of bark at different times throughout the year to reveal a bright green layer beneath. This inner bark then darkens and matures into vivid shades of orange, blue and purple.

Methane Bubbles

Each winter, man-made Abraham Lake on Canada's North Saskatchewan River is host to a rare natural phenomenon—stacks of huge underwater ice bubbles composed of trapped methane gas.

Released by plants, the gas bubbles are frozen in time and place, and they keep stacking up for as long as the lake remains solid—until the spring thaw.

Where the gas is allowed to escape through a hole in the ice, the methane is highly flammable.

345

The Boneyard

The Boneyard is a huge aircraft cemetery in Arizona, home to more than 4,400 airplanes on a 2,600-acre (1,052-ha) area of desert on Davis-Monthan Air Force base. Here, $35 billion worth of old U.S. Air Force aircraft are kept as spare parts for current models.

The yard, officially named the 309th Aerospace Maintenance and Regeneration Group, was established after World War II as storage for bombers and transport planes, and it now includes 7,000 aircraft engines and even NASA spacecraft. The dry desert environment is ideal for keeping parts in good condition, and the hard soil means that planes can easily be maneuvered without roads and ramps being constructed.

The bizarre appearance of the yard has seen it featured in several Hollywood movies, and its planes have also appeared in films, such as *Top Gun*. However, not all the planes in the cemetery have seen any action. In 2013, a number of brand-new military cargo planes were consigned to the Boneyard for financial reasons, in the hope that they may find a home in the future.

SMOKED BODIES

Tribes in Papua New Guinea, Indonesia, preserve the bodies of respected relatives by smoking the corpses over a fire. The smoked corpses are then suspended in a bamboo frame, carried up a sacred mountain and placed on wooden poles so that they look out over the village hundreds of feet below.

ANCIENT CALENDAR

Archaeologists excavating a field in Aberdeenshire, Scotland, found a lunar calendar dating back 10,000 years. Twelve pits unearthed at Crathes Castle appear to represent the phases of the Moon and lunar months.

TREE TUGGERS

In 2012, residents of League City, Texas, decided to move a 100-year-old oak tree to a new location rather than cut it down. Using heavy machinery, it took ten hours to transplant the tree a quarter of a mile away to make way for a road-widening project.

TIME ZONES

The tiny island of Märket in the Baltic Sea is only 1,000 x 260 ft (300 x 80 m) in area—yet it has two time zones. Sweden and Finland each own half the island, so half keeps to Swedish time and the other to Finnish time.

BUS DRIVER KING

Barry Watson, a former bus driver from Chepstow, Wales, is revered as a king among the Yanadi tribe of Andhra Pradesh, India, and has over 130 subjects who faithfully walk ten paces behind him. He was given the title after helping the impoverished tribespeople to construct new homes, thereby fulfilling their ancient prophecy that one day a white man would come and build them a village.

Velvet Porsche

This Porsche Panamera is the smoothest car in town after being covered in velvet by British car-wrap company Raccoon. The £2,500 ($3,750) wrap contains special adhesives and durable fibers to withstand severe weather and comes in a range of colors, including orange and fuchsia pink. The material lasts for about three years and can be removed by professionals to restore the car to its original state. It can even be cleaned by hand or with a jet wash, but it should definitely not be put through a regular car wash.

ROBOT JELLYFISH

A 5-ft-long (1.5-m) robot jellyfish is used to patrol U.S. coasts with a view to mapping ocean floors, studying marine life and monitoring ocean currents. Developed by an engineering team from Virginia Tech, battery-powered Cyro has electric motors that enable it to swim underwater just like a real jellyfish.

NO ISLAND

Sandy Island—midway between Australia and New Caledonia—was charted on marine charts and world maps for more than a century, but when scientists from the University of Sydney went to check it out in November 2012, they found clear water and no sign of any island. Sandy Island was quickly removed from National Geographic Society maps and Google Maps.

SEAWEED RAIN

It rained seaweed over the village of Berkeley in Gloucestershire, England, in August 2012. Residents collected entire bucket loads of the green slime from their gardens after a freak twister had swept up the debris from a beach 20 mi (32 km) away and then deposited it on the village.

TOOTH CURRENCY

Dolphin teeth have been used as currency in the Solomon Islands for centuries. They are preferred to paper notes, and it is still common for a Solomon Islander to be able to purchase a bride using dolphin teeth.

Deadly Crossing

A group of Indonesian schoolchildren risked their lives by tiptoeing their way across a collapsed suspension bridge over a swollen river to reach their school in the village of Sanghiang Tanjung until a new bridge could be built. The 530-ft-long (162-m) bridge collapsed in January 2012 as a result of flooding, but the children still decided to take the dangerous route daily, as the alternative was a 3-mi (5-km) walk.

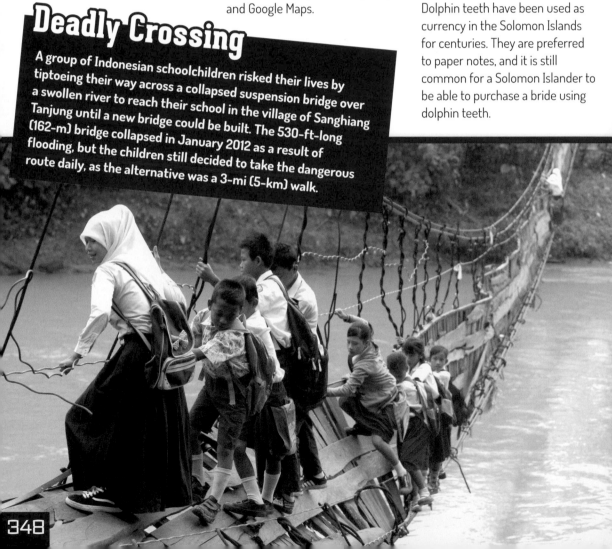

See-Through Path

You really need a head for heights to take on this new Chinese tourist attraction—a 200-ft-long (60-m), 3-ft-wide (0.9-m) glass path built high on the side of Tianmen Mountain. There is just 2½ in (6.4 cm) of glass between you and a sheer drop of 4,700 ft (1,433 m) to the ground below. Cleaners are obviously not keen to work on the path, so tourists are asked to put on shoe covers before setting off in order to help keep the walkway from getting dirty.

HIGH PRESSURE

At the bottom of the deepest point on Earth, the Mariana Trench in the Pacific Ocean, the water pressure is equivalent to an elephant wearing high heels and standing on your head.

FAT PIG

With a pineapple in its mouth, a sacrificed pig—the unlucky winner of a fattest pig festival—is paraded outside the Tsuhsih Temple in Sanxia, Taiwan. The temple holds an annual "Pigs of God" contest to raise the fattest pig, with the 2013 victor weighing 2,112 lb (960 kg).

RAT CATCHERS

Authorities in the South African township of Alexandra, Johannesburg, offer a free cell phone to any citizen who catches 60 rats.

ACID SOIL

Pollution from 19th-century factories has left Bleaklow Moor, east of Manchester, England, with peat soil that is more acidic than lemon juice.

CHRISTMAS BABIES

In 2012, Hamima Juma from Coventry, England, gave birth to her second Christmas Day baby in three years, defying odds of more than 130,000 to one. Both daughters had a due date of December 19.

THAWED MOSS

Catherine La Farge, a biologist at the University of Alberta, collected some frozen moss that had been buried under the ice in northern Canada for 400 years and brought it back to life in her laboratory.

LONG CABLES

The cables of the iconic Golden Gate Bridge in San Francisco, California, are made from more than 80,000 mi (129,000 km) of steel wire.

Jeweled Skeletons

Thousands of 400-year-old human skeletons, each adorned in gold, silver and precious gems, were hidden away in church vaults, storage units and containers all over Europe before being recently discovered by Paul Koudounaris, a Los Angeles historian dubbed "Indiana Bones."

The skeletons were dug up from Roman catacombs in the 16th century and, on the orders of the Vatican, were given fictitious names and certificates identifying them as early Christian martyrs. They were then sent to Catholic churches in Germany, Austria and Switzerland to replace religious relics that had been destroyed in the wake of the Protestant Reformation.

There, the skeletons were dressed in ornate costumes and lavishly decorated, mostly by nuns because such was their supposed status they could be handled only by someone who had taken a sacred vow to the church. Some corpses took five years to decorate with hundreds of sparkling jewels and several pounds of gold and silver. The jewels alone are worth thousands of dollars.

Many were true works of art. To construct the relic of St. Deodatus in Rheinau, Switzerland, a wax face was molded over the upper half of the skull, and a fabric wrap was used to create a mouth in order to make the corpse look more lifelike.

Known as the Catacomb Saints, they became holy shrines even though none of them had actually been canonized. In fact, few of the skeletons are thought to have belonged to anyone of religious significance.

By the 19th century, the fake saints had been exposed and were considered an embarrassment to the Catholic Church. Most of them were removed from display, stripped of their honors and locked away in containers for safe keeping. There they remained, largely forgotten, until Paul Koudounaris found their secret hideaways during his three-year trawl of European churches and ossuaries. He hunted down and photographed dozens of the skeletons to tell the amazing story of the jewel-encrusted skeletons of the Catholic Church.

The jewel-encrusted relic skeleton of St. Benedictus was found in the church of St. Michael in Munich, Germany.

The skull of "St. Deodatus" was covered with wax and given fake eyes and a veil to make it appear more lifelike.

The skeletal gold-encrusted hand of St. Valentin, or St. Valentine, was found in Bad Schussenreid, Germany. There have been 11 St. Valentines recognized by the Catholic Church, but the one that the Church believes to be the real St. Valentine resides in Terni, Italy.

Paul found this carefree skeleton of St. Freidrich in the world-renowned Benedictine Abbey in Melk, Austria.

INDEX

3-D paintings from resin, 58–59

13 Black Cats barnstormers, 220–221

24-hour meal, 279

999 Eyes Freakshow, 131

2001: A Space Odyssey, 189

accidents
- arrow shot through neck, 132
- baseball bat impales chest, 152
- chest impaled by pen, 152
- child impaled on fence spike, 152
- eye socket impaled by pruning shears, 146
- French accent after head injury, 132
- harpoon into brain, 147
- javelin impales long jumper, 152
- man pulled into cement mixer, 125
- man revived by friend falling on him, 125
- man severs arm and drives to hospital, 124
- parachute failure, 132
- pencil lodged in head, 152
- screwdriver wedged in nose, 145
- sisters lift tractor, 152
- spear gun misses spine, 145
- toothbrush impales roof of mouth, 146

Acock, Toni (U.S.), 273

acupuncturist leaves patient alone in office, 136

Afanasenko, Elvis (U.K.), 339

Agapakis, Christina (Norway), 283

Agrawal, Pavan and Amit (India), 137

Air Jordan shoe collection, 174

airplanes
- Barnstormers, 218–221
- Boneyard cemetery, 346
- cardiologists save woman, 35
- circumnavigates the world, 309
- group wedding ceremony, 56
- highway landing, 19
- jet engines for art, 250

P-26 fighter built from scratch, 318

parachute suit, 25

permanent airsickness, 127

smallest, 315

stowaway in luggage compartment, 38

airsickness, permanent, 127

AKB48 group too large for stage, 175

Akkadian-language dictionary, 308

Al Fard, Amnah (UAE), 26

algae grown for renewable energy, 332

algae invasion, 312

alligators
- attempts to eat turtle, 76
- California Alligator Farm, 20–23
- in O'Hare International Airport, 82

Allwine, Wayne (U.S.), 165

Alps frozen soldiers, 318

ambulance drivers for Allies, 315

amnesia in specific brain parts, 146

amphibians
- frogs eaten for desert survival, 140
- frogs in elephant dung, 108
- frozen wood frog, 105
- Indian bullfrog color, 95
- southern gastric-brooding frog, 81
- toads move before earthquake, 96
- tree frog in asparagus package, 292

Amriding, Martin (Scotland), 125

anchovies to protect voice, 173

Andersen, Hans Christian (Denmark), 167

Anderson, Beth (U.K.), 145

Anderson, Jordan (U.S.), 35

Andorra declaration of war, 338

animals
- animal print clothing banned at safari park, 170
- anteater with panda-like markings, 100
- babirusa pig tusks, 91

beaver causes Internet and phone outage, 80

bird imitates meerkats, 106

bird suicides in India, 27

burning goat manure, 29

California Alligator Farm, 20–23

capybara pet, 105

cat beards, 180

chimpanzee painter, 93

cow beauty contest, 80

cow nose prints, 106

cow resembling bulldog, 104

cow with prosthetic legs, 100

cows fed magnets, 106

cows with dentures, 281

cows with fluffy hair, 75

deer following monkeys for food, 81

dog stays at owner's church, 109

dog with two noses, 38

drunk pig, 69

ducks get police escort, 57

elephants listen to girl, 82

European stoat in dead rabbit carcass, 69

ferrets disguised as poodles, 74

frozen donkeys, 100

goats arrested for vandalism, 74

goats as lawn mowers, 108

gopher feet stolen, 17

gorilla eating habits, 77

grasshopper mouse eats scorpions, 105

guinea pig armor, 68

hippo living in sewage plant, 109

leopard pet of Josephine Baker, 181

lion in car, 95

man is wolf pack leader, 78–79

moles discover Roman artifacts, 104

panda video for mating, 73

porcupine falls on woman's head, 57

raccoon invasion, 83

INDEX

raccoon relatives in Colombia, 85

racehorse painter, 85

rat hunters in Manhattan, 93

reindeer change eye color, 104

sheep beauty contest TV show, 158

sheep invade ski shop, 103

shrews form caravan, 90

skateboarding goat, 68

skateboarding mouse, 32–33

sloth's grip strength, 91

squirrels damage lawn bowling club, 101

squirrels escape zoo, 71

squirrels knotted together, 24

tiger hairball, 11, 84

two-tone lamb, 104

vampire bat venom in stroke drug, 134

Zarafa the giraffe, 98–99

Antarctic Shackleton expedition, 334–335

Anthony, Butch (U.S.), 250

Anton's Syndrome, 119

ants

fire ants escape container, 81

nest in doorbell, 57

survive microwave, 107

apple with apple-shaped mark, 277

apps

Facebook app for detecting flu, 169

navigation causes drive in airport, 183

prosthetic hand controlled by, 125

for toilet paper, 174

aquarium as wall, 339

Arby's curly fry, 285

Archstoyanie Art Festival, 308

armadillo musical instrument, 168

armless woman in fitness competition, 214–215

armored guinea pig, 68

art. See also miniatures; portraits

3-D images of stained glass windows, 266

2,000-lb oil painting, 251

airplane jet engines, 250

birds carved into feathers, 267

body painting, 231

body painting tree frog, 268

body writing, 242–245

burning gasoline, 237

candy wrapper collage of Miss Piggy, 230–231

carved ships from ivory, 253

ceramic jars depicting illness and disease, 257

chandeliers from radioactive glass, 237

Chinese bowl sold at auction, 251

city skyline from gum, 235

doodles on leg, 252–253

driftwood, 257

Duchess of Cambridge portrait in jelly beans, 231

etchings in leather, 247

FDR died before portrait finish, 251

film done backwards, 180

finger-painted shoes, 239

food, 11

Gandhi portraits on eggshell, 251

gargoyle with woman's face, 251

giant painting of koi and lotus flowers, 264

giant yo-yo, 267

from gnawed beaver sticks, 250

gnome paintings, 246

Golden Gate Bridge replica on farm, 237

graffiti artist paints worker removing art, 266

houseflies paint from regurgitation, 231

human skin rug, 166

incense smoke, 237

invisible body sculptures, 233

landmarks in sunglasses' reflection, 251

Mao Tse-tung from toy soldiers, 248–249

Marx statues, 253

masterpiece bought at Goodwill, 232

McCartney, Paul, on VW hood, 11

Michelangelo found behind couch, 30

miniature display in ear, 27

Monroe, Marilyn, packing tape portrait, 11

mouse taxidermy, 259

murals from candy, 238–239

murals from corn, 231

Museum of Bad Art, 251

nail Olympics, 152

paintings of death row meals on plates, 272–273

on paper towels, 250

park scenes on fingernails, 237

petroleum, 235

phone booths, 240

photography under ice, 16

Play-Doh mosaics, 241

portrait plowed in field, 239

portraits from chewed gum, 231

portraits from food, 247

portraits from written words, 232

racehorse painter, 85

refrigerator door drawings, 236

sale from short bidding, 235

self-portrait passport, 246

sneeze photographs, 234–235

snow art, 330–331

spine carved from newspapers, 247

street artists paint condemned building, 260–263

Styrofoam ship, 251

tapestry depicts the Doctor's travels, 179

tea bags, 249

Tetris-like installations, 231

thread portrait on skin, 60

INDEX

toast and Marmite Duchess of Cambridge, 267

toilet paper tubes, 241

Transformers installation, 246

trash left on Everest, 239

tree holes, 232

tree trunk carving, 254–255

from umbilical cords, 249

underwater landscapes, 267

urban art installations, 266

young artist millionaire, 259

Arundale, Matthew (U.S.), 12

Asher, Steven and Emily (U.K.), 281

Asquith, Phoebe (U.K.), 226

astronauts recycle urine, 282

Astute Class nuclear submarine, 315

Atlas moth, 91

Austen, Charlotte (U.K.), 257

Austin, Sue (U.K.), 241

autographs, tattooed, 18

automobiles. *See* vehicles

Ayona, Mizuki (Japan), 28

Azooz street artist, 262–263

babirusa pig tusks, 91

Bacon, Francis (U.K.), 235

Bajracharya, Samita (Nepal), 62

Baker, Josephine (U.S.), 181

Balac, Djordje (Croatia), 250

Ball, Zora (U.S.), 189

ball built from tape, 222

ballet in car factory, 167

Barber, Jason (U.K.), 274

barber cuts with eyes closed, 135

Barbie
human look-alikes, 159, 182
large collection, 156–157

Barnard, Analise (U.S.), 182

Barnes, Demi (U.K.), 161

Barnstormers, 218–221

Barr, Brady (U.S.), 52

bartender tipped with lottery tickets, 40

Bartlett, Alice (U.K.), 237

BASE jump
off Everest, 204
in wheelchair, 197

baseball, scoreless games, 207

batfly, 93

bats, Mexican free-tailed bats, 80

battery recycling, 205

Battilana, Nichola (Canada), 233

batting for 24 hours straight, 225

Bayrak, Yasar (Turkey), 19

Bean, Kyle (U.K.), 293

Beard, Frank (U.S.), 164

bear, head trapped in jar, 77

Beaumier, Drew (U.S.), 183

Beck, Simon, 330–331

Beckley, Steve (U.S.), 324

Bednarek, Bryan (U.S.), 217

beer
alcohol free for dogs, 80
testing research, 298

bees
chase carjackers, 29
detect land mines, 93

Bell, Catharine (U.K.), 127

Bell, Karen (U.K.), 175

Bell, Matthew (N.Z.), 82

Belozor, Alexander (Ukraine), 267

Ben Cheikh, Mehdi (France), 260–263

Benjamin, Laura (U.S.), 230–231

Bennett, Cheryl (U.S.), 37

Bennett, Fred (New Zealand), 275

Bergholtz, Andy (U.S.), 11, 286–291

berry boarding, 212

Bertolozzi, Joseph (U.S.), 164

Bettin, Dennis (Germany), 27

Beverly Clock, 60

Biancoshock, Fra (Czech Rep.), 266

bicycles
blind man bikes to work, 309
dog rides, 102
file jumpers, 202
hearse, 42
tallest building in the world, 217

Bieber, Justin (Canada), 173

Bigras, Lydia (Canada), 69

Binard, Guillaume (France), 33

Bir Khalsa stunt group (India), 206

bird-dung spider, 94

birds
airport blasts Tina Turner, 157
camera recovery, 40
chicken receives CPR, 69
drongo bird imitates meerkats, 106
duck has hatched 24 ducklings, 101
geese down chimneys, 29
hawk overeats, 77
hummingbird metabolism, 69
Laysan albatross lays eggs at 62, 84
owl ring bearer, 83
parakeet at drunk driver, 70
parrot calms bipolar owner, 96
parrot rides motorcycle, 96
parrot warns of sleep apnea, 90
pet cockatiel house fire alert, 69
sea eagle steals camera, 91
stretchy spider webs in nest, 100
suicides in India, 27
swan thought to be spy, 99
woodpecker's third eyelid, 82

birth
$1 million hospital bill, 132
10 boys in one family, 152
12 boys in one family, 152
cesarean due to kidney tumor, 119
Christmas Day, 349

Bissonnette, Lonnie (Canada), 197

Bitzer, Billy (U.S.), 162–163

INDEX

Black, Jason (U.S.), 130–133

Black, Joe (U.K.), 248

black teeth, 332–333

Blair, Ryan (N.Z.), 90

blindness

    Anton's Syndrome, 119

    girl uses tongue and lips, 147

    man bicycles to work, 309

    pole vaulter, 212

    water skier, 196

Blixt, Claes (Sweden), 223

Blondin, Charles (France), 198–201

blood

    cocktails, 297

    donation, 223

    types, Rhesus disease, 119

Blue Ear superhero, 189

Blumenthal, Lisa (U.S.), 344

Blythe, June (U.K.), 152

bobbit worm, 81

body modification

    280 facial piercings, 138

    Barbie look-alikes, 159, 182

    beard mold, 153

    Blue Comma tattooed man, 135

    body writing, 242–245

    face piercings, 118

    horn implants, 118

    to look like Justin Bieber, 167

    to look like Nefertiti, 167

    Michael Jackson impersonator, 173

    Red Skull look-alike, 132

    scars to appear as crocodile skin, 127

    tightlacing, 148–151

    waist training, 148–151

body painting

    316 people, 231

    tree frog on models, 268

body parts

    1-lb bladder stone, 128

100-in hips, 140–141

999 Eyes Freakshow, 131

coat from chest hair, 146

eye drawn on mouth, 146

eye focusing muscles, 127

feet similar to apes, 146

folding ear, 35

hanging in Room of Miracles, 332

lobster claw syndrome, 130–133

long nails, 114–117

long tongue, 139

man severs arm and drives to hospital, 124

man with tail, 129

nose implant on forehead, 134

paralyzed boy walks on hands, 152

skin shedding each day, 135

tongue with double taste buds, 145

vampire-like teeth, 140

woman touches shoulders together, 152

writing with, 119

Bojorquez, Luis (Mexico), 81

Bolotowsky, Ilya (Russia), 232

bolving, 339

Boneyard aircraft cemetery, 346

books

    Captain Underpants signing, 190

    domino chain, 26

    microscopic, 190

Borbidge, Kelvin (U.S.), 19

border crossings

    in dashboard, 45

    inside car seat, 33

Bouchard, Emilie Marie (France), 151

Boulton, Claire and Nicola (U.K.), 27

bouncy office chair, 232

Boyes, Fred and Ron (U.K.), 56

Bozhyk, Oleksandr (Ukraine), 169

Bradbury, Ray (U.S.), 167

brain leaking fluid, 152

Brandt, Sherry (U.S.), 77

Brayshaw, Paul (U.K.), 283

breast milk jewelry, 168

Brewer, Flame (U.K.), 224

bridges

    painted with piano keys, 318

    suspension bridge collapse, 348

Brieschke, Lance (U.S.), 142–144

British invasion, 318

Britton, Andrew (U.K.), 145

Broberg, Skye (N.Z.), 213

Brockbank, Kevin (Scotland), 125

Brockman, Paul (U.S.), 190

Brooklyn Atlantics baseball card, 202

Brooks, Lakeisha (U.S.), 310

brothers, separated, living parallel lives, 56

Brown, Charlotte (U.S.), 212

Brown, Les and Helen (U.S.), 36

Brown, Louise (Scotland), 182

Brown, William (U.S.), 216

Brumotti, Vittorio (Italy), 217

bubble wrap popping competition, 202

Buddhist temple

    with cultural and movie figures, 170

    moonstone, 30

building moved by sliding on ice, 336

bungee jumping, 202

Burge, Sarah (U.K.), 182

burger grown in lab, 283

burial

    in car, 30

    St. Pancras train station, 47

    walrus in coffin with humans, 47

Burns, Colleen (U.S.), 140

Burton, E.N. (U.S.), 161

Burton, Tim (U.K.), 342

Bushar, Lauren (U.S.), 50

Buss, Ron (U.S.), 85

Button, Jenson, 223

Butts, Jerry (U.S.), 70

INDEX

Cabrera, Ryan (U.S.), 165

Cadman, Sonia (U.K.), 83

caffeine in ocean water, 308

California Alligator Farm, 20–23

Calment, Jeanne (France), 161

calorie burning in movies, 173

cameras
    around bird's neck, 40
    lost scuba diving, 63
    takes photos around corner, 169

Campbell, Alligator Joe (U.S.), 20–23

Canada's safest city, 332

Canady, Leslie (U.S.), 297

Canchola, Enrique Aguilar (Mexico), 33

candlefish, 103

Canik, Candan (Turkey), 183

Caninus band, 164

canyon swing, 324

Capezzuti, Cheryl (U.S.), 233

Captain Underpants book signing, 189

Captain Werner (U.S.), 186

capybara pet, 105

cardboard layer portraits, 249

caribou bone snow goggles, 329

Carr, Daniel (U.K.), 132

cars. See vehicles

Caruso, Enrico (Italy), 173

Casino, Steve (U.S.), 264

Cassidy, Michele (U.S.), 13

Castleberry, Patrick (U.S.), 76

Caswell, Joseph (U.S.), 164

Cata, David (Spain), 60

Catalano, Bruno (Italy), 233

cats
    camera mounted cyclist, 57
    cat beards, 180
    cleft palate, 97
    Colonel Meow's long hair, 109
    dog nursing kitten, 77
    eyebrow markings, 93
    fall from 11th floor, 95
    goes through carwash, 94
    Hank, Senate nominee, 72
    hidden in luggage, 57
    kitten lodged in bumper, 108
    lion hats, 74
    missing bones in front legs, 108
    returns after funeral, 101
    rides on owner's head, 77
    Snoopybabe, 94
    swallows TV antenna, 82
    tiger with hairball, 11, 84
    traveling with hitchhiker, 85
    travels 190 mi, 96

Cayenne Tower twisted building, 319

Celik, Cenigizhan (Turkey), 183

cell phones
    62 tweets in one minute, 164
    access, 60
    judge in contempt for own phone, 189
    prosthetic controlled by, 125

cemeteries
    bones wash into town, 308
    homeless man sleeping, 37
    squatters living in, 328

centipede in throat, 137

century eggs, 292

Cerniello, Anthony (U.S.), 171

Chambers, Bernard (U.K.), 217

Chambers, Cindy (U.S.), 97

chandeliers from radioactive glass, 237

Chang Kong Cliff Road, 328

Chapman, Ray (U.S.), 202

Chase, Linda (U.S.), 27

Chavannes, Marc (U.S.), 202

checks, oversized, 58

cheese made from skin bacteria, 283

Chen, Edmund (China), 264

chest hair coat, 146

Chevrolet Orlando modeled
    from Play-Doh, 315

Chicotsky, Brandon (U.S.), 125

Chief White Eagle (U.S.), 221

Chien, Nguyen Van (Vietnam), 128

children
    falls off balcony, 140
    four-year-olds search, 47
    toddler mayor, 30

chili eating championship

Chocolate by Mueller, 295

chocolate-flavored stamps, 294

Christmas tree throwing, 202

Chronic Lateness Syndrome, 146

Chung, Vang Seo (Vietnam), 129

Chunhui, Zheng (China), 254

circumnavigating the world, 205, 207, 216

city skyline from gum, 235

Ciuti, Mervat (Egypt), 57

Clayderman, Richard (U.K.), 106

Cleveland Browns pallbearers, 30

climber's chair, 45

Clinco, Vic (U.S.), 280

clocks, death watch, 61

clothing. See fashion/clothing
    ban on hoods, 314
    diamonds in jeans, 182
    dress from roses for proposal, 181
    husband chooses wife's dresses, 190
    ties with zipper, 190

Cobb family (U.S.), 102

Cockings, Sarah (U.K.), 267

cockroaches suffer depression, 107

coffins
    jet-powered, 18
    karaoke machine, 38
    stereo system, 190

Cohen, Ben (U.S.), 297

coin covered car, 342

colored smoke photography, 264–265

Colorite, Stanley (U.S.), 156–157

Colting, Fredrik (Sweden), 61

INDEX

Colvin, Tyler (U.S.), 152

coma patient shoots baskets, 137

comic books
  rare copy found in home, 174
  sculpture from classics, 160

comic strip tattoo, 43

competitions
  armless woman in fitness
    contests, 214–215
  ball built from tape, 222
  bubble wrap popping, 202
  chili eating championship, 295
  Christmas tree throwing, 202
  Frisbee dogs, 68
  gostra (Malta), 207
  ice pole-sitting, 222
  metro surfing, 50
  onion ring eating, 276
  running on all fours, 223
  sailing Yorkshire pudding, 202
  sheep carrying, 222
  sidewall surfing, 41

Conant, Chrissy (U.S.), 166

conjoined twins, Two-headed Nightingale
  (McKoy twins), 120–123

conkers as parking payment, 29

contortionists, 48–49

Cooke, Melody (U.S.), 68

cookie preserved for 28 years, 297

corkscrew, 237

Corliss, Jeb (U.S.), 53

Corn Palace, 231

Cornwell, Sam (U.K.), 181

corpses
  smoked over a fire, 347
  storage for frozen, 119

corsets donated for war metal, 315

Coulson, Austin (U.S.), 315

counterfeit money, 47

couples. See also weddings
  love song on Billboard charts, 158

matching clothing, 17
same birthday, 36
seeing-eye dogs introduced, 42

Coutinho, Bruno Barcellos de
  Souza (Brazil), 147

cows
  49 years old, 81
  beauty contest, 80
  with dentures produce more milk, 281
  drink from blood, 313
  dung air freshener, 76
  fed magnets, 106
  with fluffy hair, 75
  noseprints, 106
  prosthetic legs, 100
  resembling bulldog, 104
  trample festival goers, 319

Crabtree, Audrey (U.S.), 226

Crater of Diamonds State Park, 47

Cressman, Alex (U.S.), 24

Crick, Frances (U.K.), 180

Crigler-Najjar Syndrome, 119

crime, text to police about drug deal, 164

crocodiles
  20-year-old, killed 200 people, 100
  attacks elephant, 92
  escape during heavy rain, 106
  as guards, 109
  traps kayaker, 90

Crolla, Domenico (Scotland), 280

crops cover house, 318

Cueter, Thayer (U.S.), 202

Cumings, Kristen (U.S.), 238–239

Cummings, Kyle (Australia), 73

Cusack, Lesley (U.K.), 119

da Silva, Romildo (Brazil), 202

da Vinci, Leonardo, 241

Dachstein glacier viewing, 318

Damerow, Scott (U.S.), 216

Damon, Henry (Venezuela), 132

Danilovic, Bojana (Serbia), 147

Darling, Sarah (U.S.), 37

Darth Valley Challenge, 50

Davidson, Bradley (Scotland), 292

Davies, Danielle (U.K.), 128

Davis, Hiram and Barney (U.S.), 138

Day, Simon (U.K.), 279

de Bont, Jan (U.S.), 86

de la Paz, Orestes (U.S.), 236

De' Longhi giant coffee cup, 283

death
  heart-attacking virus, 145
  wakes up before transplant, 140

death row paintings on plates, 272–273

death watch/clock, 61

debt, six centuries old, 57

deer
  follow monkeys for food, 81
  sika deer in Japanese city, 101
  trapped on ice, 76

DeFeo, Jay (U.S.), 251

del Mar Arjona, Maria (Mexico), 30

Delmar, Ken (U.S.), 250

DeLong, Steven (U.S.), 37

Denniss, Tom (Australia), 205

deodorant eating, 35

dermatographia, 243–245

Dermul, Mark (Belgium), 56

desert survival
  ate raw frogs and roots, 140
  drank urine and contact solution, 145

Desmeules, Marie-Lou (Canada), 256–257

Dettlaff, Michael (U.S.), 47

Dewey-Hagborg, Heather (U.S.), 236

Dey, Tapan (India), 119

Deyaa street artist, 262–263

Deyuan, Liu (China), 136

diamonds. See also gemstones
  bikini, 167
  jeans, 182
  swallowed for smuggling, 324

INDEX

Dickson, Krystal (U.S.), 152

Dillon, Jonathan (U.S.), 53

dinosaur noises in *Jurassic Park*, 183

Disneyland visited every day, 222

diving, every two minutes, 27

DNA used for sculpture, 236

Doctor Who, 176–179

    Dalek sculpture, 253

    mini crocheted dolls, 266

Dodds, Peter (U.K.), 40

dog tags returned, 44

dogs

    bank worker, 106

    barks at 113.1 decibels, 102

    beer, alcohol free, 80

    bicycle riding, 102

    blind dogs survive snowstorm, 95

    Caninus rock band, 164

    deaf dog knows sign language, 95

    eating money, 77

    ferrets sold as poodles, 74

    Frisbee, 68

    German police dogs in shoes, 83

    hair extensions, 83

    holiday resort, 102

    hydrotherapy weight loss, 100

    jumping tricks, 69

    loose skin removed after weight loss, 94

    marathon runner, 70

    nursing kitten, 77

    replica house, 83

    saves people from falling tree, 69

    service dog sniffs peanuts, 72

    skateboarding, 105

    stays at owner's church, 109

    tracks owner to hospital, 99

    two noses, 38

    on wrong flight, 84

Dolan, John (U.S.), 99

dolls

    paper, three-dimensional, 26

    village of life-size dolls, 28

dolphin

    gives family dinner, 104

    with octopus riding on stomach, 107

    teeth as currency, 348

Doman, Steve Nighteagle (U.S.), 172

domino tower, 259

donut-stealing police impersonator, 42

Dorje, Pemba (Nepal), 307

Dortmund, Borussia (Germany), 223

Drake, Mike (U.S.), 236

dress from thesaurus, 164

Dreyer, Jim "The Shark" (U.S.), 224

driftwood art, 257

drinks. *See* food and drink

driver's license for dead man, 40

driving test fail video, 168

drum kit of 900 pieces, 164

drumming, extreme, 169

dryer lint sculpture, 233

DS street artist, 266

Ducharme, Eric (U.S.), 51

Duchess of Cambridge portrait in jelly beans, 231

Duffy, Keith and Stephanie (U.S.), 249

Duhaime, Dana (U.S.), 72

Duke, Charles (U.S.), 27

Dunbar, Jim (Scotland), 146

Dunne, Liam (N.Z.), 147

Dunning, Margaret (U.S.), 314

dust storms, 309

Duthie, Denis (N.Z.), 124

dwarfism

    Captain Werner, "smallest man in the world," 184–186

    Human Doll, Margaret Ann Robinson, 184–187

    Laron syndrome, 146

ear print ID of robber, 45

Earl, Henry (U.S.), 35

Earnest, Frances (U.S.), 20–23

ears

    folding, 35

    music type of tinnitus, 145

earthquakes

    elephants fleeing before, 99

    toads move before, 96

earthworms

    flooding and, 68

    soup, 298

Eccles, Graham (U.K.)

Eckert, Tom (U.S.), 259

edible spray paint, 294

Edwards, Jamie (U.K.), 58

Edwards, Jeff (U.S.), 72

Eggers, Jim (U.S.), 96

Egües, Roberto Viza (Cuba), 52

electric bill sent to lamppost, 58

electric corsets, 151

electric eel shock, 73

elephant seal stops traffic, 71

elephants, girl talks to them, 82

Elias, Anastassia (France), 241

Elliot, Athena (U.S.), 117

Elliott, Dennis (U.S.), 18

Elliott, Lucy (U.K.), 52

Elvish honey, 285

Emelife, Uche (Nigeria), 37

Emperor of the U.S.A., 46

Entsminger, Scott (U.S.), 30

environmental protest, 314

escape artists, 33

Evans, Dave (U.K.), 236

Evans, Mark (U.K.), 247

Evans, Rachel (Australia), 132

Everest. *See* Mount Everest

exam taking by mother, 52

extreme mountain unicycling, 212

INDEX

eyes
- candy, 292
- different colored, 137
- drawn on mouth, 146
- eye socket impaled by pruning shears, 146
- globe luxation, 128
- larger in people from Arctic circle, 125
- lazy eye trained by playing Tetris, 170
- popping out, 128
- prosthetic pops out in court, 145
- shaving, 136
- Sufi devotees, 337
- tattooed, 139
- woman sees upside down, 147

face slapping skin treatment, 138

Facebook
- flu detection app, 169
- man uploads 115,000 photos, 181

Fairbanks International Airport drivers, 183

Fan, Xiao (China), 181

Fahrenheit 451 original title, 167

Farrell, David (Canada), 76

Fart By Mail, 50

fashion/clothing
- Air Jordan collection, 174
- animal print clothing banned at safari park, 170
- chest hair coat, 146
- diamond bikini, 167
- dress from thesaurus, 164
- gem encrusted bra, 174
- glasses frames from human hair, 174
- gold belt, 167
- Herzog eats shoe after bet, 170
- license to wear high heels, 159
- matching couples, 17
- odor-resistant shirt, 173
- Ripley's Trashy Fashion Show, 182

shoes with GPS, 165
skirts in place of shorts, 18
solid gold shirt, 165
toad skins as fashion accessory, 170
wedding dresses from roadkill, 175
wedding dresses soccer jerseys, 175
White, Vanna, 159

fat contest, 313

fatberg in sewer, 323

Featherstone, Nancy and Don (U.S.), 17

feats
- 84-year-old NASCAR driver, 202
- 99-year-old rappels down building, 216
- 142 eggs cracked on forehead, 216
- 181 people in bubble, 216
- 255 marathons completed, 217
- 800 drinking straws in mouth, 204
- armless woman in fitness contests, 214–215
- ball built from tape, 222
- Barnstormers, 218–221
- BASE jump in wheelchair, 197
- BASE jump off of Everest, 204
- batting for 24 hours straight, 225
- bicycles fire jumpers, 202
- Bir Khalsa stunt group (India), 206
- blood donation, 223
- bouncing on Hippity Hop, 226
- bungee jumping, 202
- cartwheels with sword in throat, 205
- catching baseball from helicopter, 217
- Christmas tree throwing, 202
- circumnavigating the world, 205, 207, 216
- claps per minute, 217
- cracks coconuts open, 196
- Disneyland visits every day, 222
- Everest summit at 80 years old, 223
- fire-eaters, 223
- flowers replicate soccer jersey, 223

giant butter knife, 223
Giants stadium replica, 223
gostra (Malta), 207
high school diploma at age 99, 226
holding 51 wine glasses, 225
jigsaw puzzle, 223
letter opener collection, 216
living image of Russian flag, 207
man run over by car while on broken glass, 206
man walked 10,000 mi in U.S., 202
Mighty Atom, 208–211
oldest winning pitcher, 217
one million push-ups, 216
paddling down drainage ditch, 225
pulling cars with teeth, 217
pulling truck with mustache, 224
race car tire changes, 223
racing pigeon flies from France to Canada, 217
Rubik's Cube solving, 226
running in costume, 226
skateboarding on highway, 217
ski park from abandoned buildings, 213
skywalkers, 226–227
smashing coconuts on forehead, 206
snowball measuring 12 ft, 212
spinning basketball on toothbrush, 207
stuffed body in box, 213
surfboard balanced on chin, 217
swimming around Isle of Wight, 205
swimming while in bag, 216
therapy for facing fears, 196
tightrope walking, 196, 198–201
toddler identifies countries, 224
touchdown pass to self, 204
visiting seaside piers, 226
wing walking, 224
writing on matchsticks, 226

INDEX

Yoshida Castle tower, 216

Feeback, Beth (U.S.), 232

Feeney, Shawn (Canada), 298

feet, flexible, apelike feet, 146

Feraren, Marvic (Philippines), 45

Fernando, Ravi (U.S.), 226

ferrets disguised as poodles, 74

Ferris wheel powered by humans, 50

Fielding, Al, 202

fig wasp eggs, 93

Filippone, Mike (U.S.), 225

film

    captures son's first year, 181

    done backward then played
      forward, 180

    time-lapse of age 19 to 31, 188–189

    total footage for *2001: A
      Space Odyssey*, 189

fingernails

    Doctor Who themed, 177

    extra long, 114–117

    man saves clippings, 124

    nail Olympics, 152

    painted park scenes, 237

    paperweight, 236

finger-painted shoes, 239

fire

    tea towel combustion, 27

    water spray freezes area, 316–317

fire salamander, two-headed, 80

fire-breathing shrimp, 72

fire-eaters, 223

fireplace TV show, 157

fish

    candlefish, 103

    Cookie Monster fish, 84

    European catfish jump
      out of water, 72

    goldfish distinguish music, 103

    goldfish with swim bladder disease, 81

    hagfish slime, 103

    merman, 51

    oarfish, 82

    shark skeleton, 69

    shark walks on ocean floor, 99

    sharks leave before hurricane, 95

    smuggled in pants, 24

    striped beakfish found in
      Washington State, 84

    venomous, 68

flag of truce tablecloth, 322

flatworm head regrowth, 72

Fletcher, Dorothy (U.K.), 35

Fletcher, Gemma and Ava (U.K.), 119

floods, earthworms and, 68

Flowers, Ramona (Mexico), 81

flowers replicate soccer jersey, 223

flu-detecting Facebook app, 169

fly burgers, 276

foam from ocean covers town, 338

food and drink

    12-course meal in a can, 281

    24-hour meal, 279

    38-in-long Arby's curly fry, 285

    131-ft-long pizza, 295

    150-oz steak, 296

    3,434-gal coffee cup, 283

    apple with apple-shaped mark, 277

    arrest for behaving aggressively
      with blood sausage, 292

    art, 11

    astronauts recycle urine, 282

    bacon sandwich from rare breed, 280

    banana piano, 44

    beef burger grown in lab, 283

    beer research, 298

    Ben and Jerry's bagels, 297

    bird's milk, 279

    blood cocktail, 297

    brewery in country where
      it's illegal, 282

    butt-shaped moon cakes, 298

cake as resignation, 275

cake with cat instead of cap, 274

candy leech, 275

century eggs, 292

cheese from skin bacteria, 283

chicken sculpture from eggshells, 293

chili eating championship, 295

chocolate mousse weighs 496 lb, 296

chocolate-covered onions, 295

chocolate-flavored stamps, 294

coconut suspected of
    black magic, 292

conkers as parking payment, 29

cow's blood and milk mixture, 313

Cream Cheese Festival, 282

crops cover house, 318

deodorant eating, 35

dishes made from cats, 274

donut-stealing police
    impersonator, 42

dried squid as liquor bottle, 292

drinks in an hour, 297

earthworm soup, 298

Edible Bug Gift Pack, 279

edible spray paint, 294

Elvish honey, 285

exploding chutney, 285

Eyes of Terrors candy, 292

fish and chips to feed 180, 280

fly burgers, 276

food bill for U.S. presidents, 275

Frank's Diner, 285

fried chicken feet as a snack, 282

frog sashimi, 281

fruit tree, 298

garlic specialty restaurant, 274

giant brownie, 295

giant chicken nugget, 293

giant chocolate sausage, 283

giant fruit cake, 283

giant key-lime pie, 298

gingerbread house, 36

grasshoppers, 279

hot dog and bun sold at Expos game, 207

hot sauce collection, 280

ice cream flavors, 295

insect cupcakes, 283

insect-eating teacher, 292

ketchup origins, 297

larvae cupcakes, 274–275

larvets, 295

live octopus, 299

man eats from dumpsters for a week, 281

man turns green from snail parasite, 296

meat gutab, 279

onion ring eating contest, 276

paintings of death row meals on plates, 272–273

pickled pumpkin sculptures, 286–291

pizza with ghost chilies, 283

pizza with portraits, 280

poppadoms, 298

praying mantis in sage packet, 294

preserved cookie, 297

pumpkin, worshipped, 274

pumpkin carved into gremlin, 11

radioactive rum, 274

robot pours beer, 292

Rocky Mountain Oyster Stout beer, 294

schnitzel flavors, 276

severed head wedding cake, 282

smuggled 207 lb of caterpillars, 292

snake in pickled wine bites woman, 279

Snake Village in China, 284

solar-powered ovens, 283

spicy chocolate Easter egg, 294

stainless steel ice cubes, 277

sweating mushrooms, 281

tarantulas as a snack, 285

TARDIS cake, 179

Thai food sign, 275

tie-dye cheesecake, 29

Tiet Canh, soup with raw duck's blood, 293

tree frog in asparagus package, 292

turkey roasted in car exhaust, 342

turtle smuggle attempt, 298

unusual ice cream flavors, 276

Uromastyx lizard, 281

vodka from cows' milk, 274

vodka from fermented hornets, 277

watermelon sliced in 21 seconds, 281

whole smoked animals, 280

Yubari melon, 293

zombie cake, 278–279

footgolf, 202

footprints on the Moon, 344

Foreign Accent Syndrome, 132

Foreman, Jay (U.K.), 191

Fostvedt, Karl (U.S.), 213

Fox, Jamie (U.K.), 167

Frank's Diner, 285

Frati, Norma (U.S.), 26

French, Jacob (Australia), 226

Freud, Lucian (U.K.), 235

Freund, Werner (Germany), 78–79

Friedberg, Zach (U.S.), 50

Frisbee dogs, 68

Frog Lady (U.S.), 202

frog memorabilia collection, 202

frost flowers, 312

frozen wood frog, 105

fruit tree sculpture, 298

Fuller, Sherry (U.K.), 127

funerals

bicycle hearse, 42

burial in car, 30

cremation won at baseball game, 56

JCB driver in bucket, 44

karaoke machine in coffin, 38

professional mourners, 308

Furrh, Michael (U.S.), 35

Gaffey, Mark (U.S.), 42

Gambarin, Dario (Italy), 239

Gambrel, Laura (U.S.), 274

Gandhi portraits on eggshell, 251

Gang, Jiali (China), 145

Ganjavian, Ali (U.K.), 171

garlic for wounds, 342

garlic specialty restaurant, 274

gas mask with man's name on it, 19

Gatonga, Mzee Julius Wanyondu (Kenya), 329

geese down chimneys as sweeps, 29

Geller, Jordan Michael (U.S.), 174

gemstones. See also diamonds

Crater of Diamonds State Park, 47

encrusted skeletons, 350–353

Gharib, Ali Hassan (Dubai), 342

ghost moth caterpillar, 63

Giants stadium replica, 223

Gibbons, Billy (U.S.), 164

Gibson, Miranda (Australia), 314

Gibson, Richard M. (U.S.), 124

Gibson, Walter (U.S.), 161

gingerbread house, 36

Gissy, François (France), 323

glass walkway on mountain, 349

glasses frames from human hair, 174

Glenelg village twinned on Mars, 338

gnome paintings, 246

goat skateboarder, 68

goats arrested for vandalism, 74

goats as lawn mowers, 108

Godfrey, Chris (U.K.), 281

Gökçeoglu, Mehmet Ali (Turkey), 339

gold shirt, 165

Gold Striker rollercoaster, 36

INDEX

Golden Gate Bridge
  cables, 349
  replica on farm, 237
goldfish with swim bladder disease, 81
golf
  14.2-ft-long driver, 35
  footgolf, 202
Gonzalez, David (U.S.), 174
Goodwin, Margaret (U.K.), 285
gopher feet stolen, 17
Gosling, Ryan (U.S.), 165
gostra (Malta), 207
government
  mayoral election coin toss, 45
  PM poses as taxi driver, 17
  toddler mayor, 30
GPS in shoes, 165
Grace, Kelly (Australia), 44
Gracer, David (U.S.), 292
Granger, Ethel (U.K.), 150–151
Grapengeter family (U.S.), 95
grass painted by city, 323
grasshopper exoskeleton, 70
grasshopper mouse eats scorpions, 105
Gravelet, Jean-François (France), 198–201
Green, Julie (U.S.), 272–273
Greenfield, Jerry (U.S.), 297
Greenfield, Rob (U.S.), 281
Greenslade, Christine (U.K.), 63
Greenstein, Joseph (Poland), 208–211
Greenstein, Mike (U.S.), 217
Griffith, D.W. (U.S.), 338
Griffith, Melanie (U.S.), 86–89
Grigg, Joy (U.K.), 119
Grigor, Ed (U.S.), 24
Grimshaw, Brendon (U.K.), 39
Grosset, Tom (Canada), 169
Groves, Alexander (U.K.), 174
Grüner See (Austria), 320–321
guinea pig armor, 68

guns, Paris Gun, 324
Gustafson, Stephanie (U.S.), 95
Gustavsson, Sonnie (Sweden), 173
Gwillim, Karen (Canada), 40

haboobs dust storms, 309
hair
  4-lb hairball in girl, 145
  13 ft long, 128
  barber cuts with eyes closed, 135
Hale, George C. (U.S.), 162–163
Hall, Jim (U.S.), 135
Hall, Lincoln (Australia), 306
Hample, Zack (U.S.), 217
Hao, Tian (China), 135
Harmon, Shannon Marie (U.K.), 259
Harris, Billy Ray (U.S.), 37
Harris, Rochelle (U.K.), 137
Harrison, Jake (U.K.), 225
Harrison, James (Australia), 119
heart-attacking virus, 145
Hebditch, Linda (U.K.), 294
Hedren, Tippi (U.S.), 86–89
height, Kulkarni family, 145
Helgen, Kristofer (U.S.), 85
helium-filled island sculpture, 267
helmets for troops, 338
Hemingway, Ernest, 315
Hemperly, Jason (U.S.), 158
Hendrix, Carissa (Canada), 223
Hennessey, Simon (U.K.), 251
Henry, Gordon (U.K.), 138
Hentschel, Micha (Canada), 276
Hercules beetle, 101
Hermann, Joe (U.S.), 133
Hernandez, Paige (U.S.), 43
Herzog, Werner (Germany), 170
Hickmott, Bronwen (U.K.), 30
Higgs, Rob (U.K.), 237
high school diploma at age 99, 226

Hill, Dusty (U.S.), 164
Hillary, Edmund (U.K.), 307
Hillary, Peter (U.K.), 307
Hindu goddess Kali, 62
hippo living in sewage plant, 109
hirsutism, drug induced, 119
Hitler's toilet, 24
Hjelmquist, Fredrik (Sweden), 190
H.M.S. *Victory* replica, 318
Hobbes, Katzen (U.S.), 54–55
Hoffman, Allison (U.S.), 266
Hogwarts model, 157
Hollis, Carrie (U.S.), 279
Holmborn, Sandra (Sweden), 146
Holmes, Chris (U.K.), 275
Holmes, Tom (U.K.), 259
Holt-Parks, Angi and Don (U.S.), 95
Hörl, Ottmar (Germany), 253
horsefly named for Beyoncé, 82
hot sauce collection, 280
hotels
  Hard Rock Hotel & Casino
    penthouse, 53
  inflatable, 308
  Palms Hotel, basketball court, 53
  professional sleeper, 336
house carried on back, 51
Hudson, Jasmine (U.K.), 47
Hughes, Graham (U.K.), 326–327
Hull, Rob (U.K.), 176
human scarecrow plays music, 167
human skin rug, 166
human-powered Ferris wheel, 50
hummingbird metabolism, 69
hurricanes
  butterflies leave area, 91
  sharks leave area, 95
Huttick, John (U.S.), 145
hypnosis weight loss, 128

INDEX

ice
building moved by sliding, 336
pole-sitting, 222
underwater bubbles of
methane gas, 345
underwater photography, 16
ice cream flavors, 295
Illis, Vittalii (Russia), 48–49
Innes, Sid (Scotland), 19
insects
ants' nest in doorbell, 57
ants survive microwave, 107
Atlas moth, 91
Australian horsefly named
for Beyoncé, 82
bees chase carjackers, 29
bees detect land mines, 93
beetle species names, 93
beetles remove whale flesh, 110–111
caterpillars smuggled to U.K., 292
cereal leaf beetle's poop guard, 47
cockroaches suffer depression, 107
cricket fights, 72
cupcakes, 283
Darwin's bark spider web, 71
Edible Bug Gift Pack, 279
Epomis ground beetle eats
frogs/toads, 108–109
fermented hornet vodka, 277
fig wasp eggs, 93
fire ants escape container, 81
flies paint from regurgitation, 231
fly species, smallest, 80
foliage spider young eat
the mother, 81
ghost moth caterpillar, 63
grasshopper exoskeleton, 70
Hercules beetle, 101
larvets snack, 295
locust on trial, 90
metal sculptures, 250

New Zealand batfly, 93
pink underwing moth caterpillar, 99
planthopper, 103
praying mantis in sage packet, 294
raft spider, 71
silkworm cocoons, 99
spider makes fake spiders, 84
spider web of thousands, 107
teacher addicted to eating, 292
termites eat cash, 29
trapdoor spider, 106
venomous centipede in throat, 137
walnut sphinx caterpillars, 77
wasp nest measured 22 ft, 107
woodlice drink from either end, 101
insurance money payback in coins, 36
invisible body sculptures, 233
iPad, high billing, 159
Irvine, Andrew (U.K.), 305
Isella, Francesco (Italy), 53
island has two time zones, 347
Ito, Kenichi (Japan), 223
Izzah, Dwi Nailul (Indonesia), 76

Jachacy, Mikey (Scotland), 217
Jackman, Hugh (Australia), 157
Jackson, Michael, 173
jails
escape, 19
escape in suitcase, 30
most arrested, 35
prisoner sneaks back in, 50
upgrades, 38
U.S. has highest prison population, 39
Jakus, Josh (U.S.), 190
Janssen, Scott (U.S.), 39
Janus, Tim "Eater X" (U.S.), 295
Japanese foliage spider, 81
Jarosz, Monika (France), 170
Jatinga bird suicides, 27

Jay, Mikki (U.K.), 173
Jayakar, Aanav (U.S.), 224
Jedlica, Justin (Ukraine), 159
jellyfish
lion's mane, 99
in nuclear plant, 90
Jesus face in floor tile, 40
jet-powered coffin, 18
jeweled skeletons, 350–353
jewelry
from breast milk, 168
homeless man returns ring, 37
jigsaw puzzles
24,000 pieces, 223
Queen Elizabeth II Diamond
Jubilee, 236
Johansson, Michael (Sweden), 231
Johnson, Al (U.S.), 220
Johnson, Beth (U.S.), 267
Johnson, Brad (U.S.), 204
Johnson, Claire (U.K.), 42
Johnson, Ray (U.S.), 127
Jones, Billy (U.K.), 44
Jones, Karen (U.K.), 101
Jones, Matt (U.S.), 281
Jones, Nicole (U.S.), 35
Joseph, Jean Jabril (U.S.), 139
Juma, Hamima (U.K.), 349
Jurassic Park dinosaur noises, 183
Juscamaita, Ivan (Peru), 105
Kadari, Faizul Hasan (India), 332
Kalina, Noah (U.S.), 188–189
Kanum-Irebe farewell custom, 312
Kapma-Saunders, Clare (U.K.), 318
Katseanes, Chelsea (U.S.), 45
Keeton, Daniel (U.S.), 80
Kelly Mill Elementary School
Odditorium, 12
Kenk, Kong (Vietnam), 181
Kephart, Aurora (U.S.), 40
Khumbu cough, 303

kidney transplants
    new wife match, 136
    old boyfriend match, 138
King, Michael (U.S.), 85
King Kong movie shown every day, 173
Kindergarten Wolfartsweiler, 329
Kisslack, Edward (U.S.), 223
Kitchen, Danny (U.K.), 159
Kite, Julian (U.K.), 83
kiteboarding, 205
Kitt, Camille and Kennerly, 190
Klingon Court street in Sacramento, 157
Klinkel, Wayne (U.S.), 77
knife buried in back, 119
knitting TV show, 174
Knox, Pamela (U.S.), 340
Knox-Hewson, Daniel (U.S.), 19
Knudson, Lacy (U.S.), 241
Knuth, John (U.S.), 231
Kober, Martin (U.S.), 30
Kohfeldt, Greg (U.S.), 24
Kohler, Maria (Germany), 140
Kopp, Messe (Israel), 180
Kopp, Michael (Germany), 207
Kositpipat, Chalermchai (Thailand), 170
Koudounaris, Paul (U.S.), 350–353
Krajewski, Ron (U.S.), 85
Kratoville, Matt (U.S.), 56
Kulkarni family (India), 145
Kumar, Amlesh (India), 128
Kumar, Vivek (India), 259
Kumaris, 62
Kusunda language, 310

La Farge, Catherine (Canada), 349
LaFever, William (U.S.), 140
Laffon, Jeremy (France), 235
Laituri, Dave (U.S.), 277
lake created by meltwater, 320–321
lamellar ichthyosis, 135

Lamichhane, Rabi (Nepal), 161
Landers, Yumiko (U.S.), 74
Lapps, Ben (U.S.), 174
Laron syndrome, 146
Larry da Leopard (U.S.), 142–144
larvae cupcakes, 274–275
larvets snack, 295
Lasserre, Maskull (Canada), 247
Latimer, David (U.K.), 314
laughter-induced syncope, 152
laundry-folding robot, 63
Lautner, Phil (U.S.), 75
Layton, Charlie (U.S.), 236
lazy eye trained by playing Tetris, 170
leaf jumping, 161
Leander, Dave (U.S.), 19
leather covered car, 342
leather etchings, 247
LeBlanc, Jason (U.S.), 202
Lee, Bill "Spaceman" (U.S.), 217
Lee, James (U.K.), 36
Lee, Justin (Canada), 325
left handedness, 138
Legacy, Gille (Canada), 37
Lennon, John, tooth, 134
leopard spot tattoo, 142–144
letter opener collection, 216
Lewis, C.S., 315
Li, Zhuoying (U.S.), 40
Liberty Head nickel, 30
libraries
    25,000 books borrowed, 182
    domino chain of books, 26
    fine for Keith Richards, 169
    smallest in the world, 181
Liechtenstein, 323
lightning
    man struck multiple times, 338
    woman struck inside store, 310
Lindburgh, Charles (U.S.), 219

Lingchao, Liu (China), 51
Link, George (U.S.), 23
lion hats for cats, 74
lion living with actors, 86–89
lion's mane jellyfish, 99
Livermanne, Matt "The Walker" (U.S.), 202
lizard squirts blood from eyes, 101
Lloyd, Caleb (U.S.), 217
lobster claw syndrome, 130–133
lobster with six claws, 104
loggerhead turtle with prosthetic fins, 71
Long, Doris (U.K.), 216
long-tailed tit bird nest, 100
lottery
    bartender tipped, 40
    man throws away $181
        million ticket, 170
    math problem requirement, 38
    Oksnes family, 44
    trashed ticket, 37
Lourenco, Decio (S. Africa), 217
Loveman, Richard (U.S.), 105
Lucero, Len (U.S.), 77
Luetscher, Leroy (U.S.), 146
Lukyanova, Valeria (Ukraine), 159
lunar calendar discovered, 347
Lundin, Ulf (Sweden), 234–235
Lye, Kent (Singapore), 58–59

Mac, Vivi (France), 247
MacDougall, Bon (U.S.), 220
Macon, Larry (U.S.), 217
Maddox, Robert (U.S.), 18
mail
    jail escape, 19
    postcard 55 years late, 32
Maiya, Gyani (Nepal), 310
make-up artists, special effects, 192–193
MaKey MaKey banana piano, 44
Mal de Debarquement Syndrome, 127
Mallory, George (U.K.), 305

INDEX

Malta lack of water features, 322

Mandela, Asha (U.S.), 12

Mandón, Alexander (Colombia), 338

Manx, Aerial (Australia), 205

marathons
  around the world, 50
  dog running half-marathon, 70

Marek, Elizabeth (U.S.), 278–279

Mariana Trench water pressure, 349

Marr, Ben (Canada), 225

Marshall, Noel (U.S.), 86–89

martial arts theme park, 165

Martin, Anthony (U.S.), 33

Martin, Brett (U.S.), 175

Martin, Janice (U.S.), 158

Martin, Rose (U.S.), 30

Martinet, Edouard (France), 250

Martinez, Hector "Tank" (U.S.), 43

Martini, Don (U.S.), 223

Maryam street artist, 262–263

mass hysteria in high school students, 146

Matagrano, Matthew (U.S.), 50

matchstick model crane, 250

Mathijsen, Tobias (Netherlands), 60

Matlock, "Spider" (U.S.), 220

Mattle, Andrew (U.K.), 83

Matveeva, Ann-Sofiya (Ukraine), 231

Maugham, Somerset, 315

Maxwell Grant novels, 161

May, Henrik (Germany), 217

Maynard, Chris (U.S.), 267

mayoral election coin toss, 45

Maz street artist, 262–263

McCoy, Sean (U.S.), 68

McDonald, Ann (Scotland), 137

McDonald, Jamie "The Bear" (U.S.), 276

McFarlane, Ann and Jim (U.K.), 292

McGriff, Hershel (U.S.), 202

McKevitt, Robert (U.S.), 38

McKoy, Millie and Christine (U.S.), 120–123

McManaman, Doug (Canada), 217

McMurry, Scott (U.S.), 32

McNeely, Billy (Canada), 119

Medford, Kim (U.S.), 285

Meier, Maggie (U.S.), 137

Melis family size (Sardinia), 207

Mellow Mushroom tie-dye
  cheesecake, 29

meltwater creates lake, 320–321

Melville's *Moby Dick* initially trashed, 171

merman, 51

message in a bottle
  97-years-old, 19
  England to Norway, 52
  England to South Australia, 47

methanol poisoning saved by whiskey, 124

metro surfing, 50

Metropol Parasol wooden building, 312

Meyer, Edward, 10

Mi, Yin (China), 181

Mickesh, Tonya (U.S.), 222

Mickey Mouse voice, 165

microphone 9-ft tall, 169

Midget City colony of little people, 184

Midgley, Richard (U.K.), 19

Mighty Atom strong man, 208–211

Miki, Rintya Apranti (Indonesia), 76

Miller, Donald Jr. (U.S.), 40

Miller, Randy (U.S.), 93

millionaire works as street sweeper, 38

miniatures
  crocheted dolls of The Doctor, 266
  landscapes in thimbles, 233
  paintings displayed in ear, 27
  watch with ship model, 253

Minnie Mouse voice, 165

mirror writing, 241

Miss Mena fire-eater, 124

Mississippi river, 336

Miura, Yuichiro (Japan), 223

mobility scooter decorations, 322

Mobutu, Joseph (Zaire), 33

Moby Dick initially trashed, 171

Modi, Shourabh (India), 226

Moeller, Preston (U.S.), 232

Mogavero, Allicia (U.S.), 168

money
  Canadian Mint, glow-in-the-
    dark dinosaur, 63
  computer key error, 63
  counterfeit money, 47
  dog eating, 77
  playing cards, 47
  termites eat cash, 29

monk lives on limestone pillar, 329

Monroe, Marilyn, 11

mood-sensing headphones, 168

Moon footprints, 344

Mora, Erik (U.S.), 297

Moreau, Sabine (Belgium), 38

mosaics from Play-Doh, 241

moss brought back to life, 349

motorbike from wood, 253

motorized shopping cart, 342

Mount Everest
  art from trash left behind, 239
  Chomolugma, 303
  cost of expedition, 303
  Death Zone, 302–307
  Hall, Lincoln, 306
  Hillary Step, 306
  Irvine, Andrew, 305
  Khumbu cough, 303
  Mallory, George, 305
  number of climbers, 306
  popularity, 302
  Sagarmatha, 303
  Siffredi, Marco, 303
  snowboarding, 303
  summit by 80-year-old, 223
  weight loss among climbers, 303

mountains, 324

INDEX

mourners, professional, 308

mouse taxidermy, 259

Mud Day festival, 344

Mudron, Bill (U.S.), 179

Mueller, Konrad (Switzerland), 57

Muhammad, Saddi (Pakistan), 224

mummies

    Civil War-era mummified arm, 119

    mailed home after 109 years, 32

    onions replace eyes, Ramesses IV, 127

    watches NASCAR with wife, 27

Munro, Jack (U.K.), 257

Murakami, Azuka (U.K.), 174

murals

    from candy, 238–239

    from corn, 231

Museum of Bad Art, 251

Museum of Wonder, 250

music

    AKB48 group too large, 175

    Caninus band, 164

    Eiffel Tower as drum kit, 164

    extreme drumming, 169

    human scarecrow plays, 167

    mood sensing headphones, 168

    outdoor concert in Siberia, 167

    Psy "Gentleman" video, 180

    rap album by 120-year-old, 161

    song names London Underground stations, 191

    type of tinnitus, 145

musical instruments

    900-piece drum kit, 164

    aerial violinist, 158

    from armadillos, 168

    banana piano, 44

    four violins at once, 169

    guitar playing while playing basketball, 174

    made from trash, 169

    man plays multiple guitars, 161

    from skateboards, 191

    twin harpists, 190

    violin strings from spiderweb silk, 167

Mustang Wanted (Ukraine), 226–227

Myakush, Konstantine (Russia), 132

Myers, Andrew (U.S.), 258

Mytting, Lars (Norway), 157

Nabucco, Sandra (Brazil), 57

Nageshwaran, Vignesh (India), 146

Nagy, Joe (U.S.), 152

nail clipping paperweight, 236

naked bike ride in protest, 44

name changes

    superhero names, 19

    website as last name, 167

Namita, Nileen (U.K.), 167

Nathip, Awirut (Thailand), 109

Navajo translation of *Star Wars*, 157

Naylor, Leighton (U.K.), 81

Nebay street artist, 262

Newton, Jimmy (U.K.), 26

Niagara Falls freeze, 61

Nichols, "Fronty," 220

Nogoy, Robert (Philippines), 38

Noor, Ichwan (Indonesia), 342

Norgay, Tenzing (Nepal), 307

Norton, Joshua (U.S.), 46

nose implant on forehead, 134

Nthambi, Irene (Kenya), 147

nuclear reactor built in class, 58

nut allergy service dog, 72

Nutella robbery, 58

Nyad, Diana (U.S.), 212

Nyrhinen, Juhana (Finland), 191

oarfish, 82

obese man removed from apartment, 126

O'Connor, Kayleigh (U.K.), 177

octopus eating, 299

Odditoriums, Kelly Mill Elementary School, 12

odor-resistant shirt, 173

Oksnes family lottery winners, 44

Oldershaw, Giles (U.K.), 249

O'Leary, Matthew (U.S.), 72

Oliveira, Shaukei (Canada), 125

Olsen, Jesper (Denmark), 50

orb spiderweb, catching birds, 73

Orton, Nerina (U.K.), 148–149

Osaki, Shigeyoshi (Japan), 167

Osberger, Kate (U.S.), 152

Osenton, Philip (U.K.), 225

Ostrich Pillow, 171

Oval Office replica, 314

Ovchinnikov, Yuri (Russia), 16

Oxley, Ron (U.S.), 86

Pace, Irby (U.S.), 264–265

paintings

    3-D from resin, 58–59

    chimpanzee uses tongue, 93

    death row meals on plates, 272–273

    duplicate carved in tree trunk, 254–255

    Michelangelo behind couch, 30

    miniature display in ear, 27

pajamas that read stories, 157

pandas view mating video, 73

paper towel as art canvas, 250

parachute suit, 25

parasites

    maggots in ear, 137

    named for Bob Marley, 103

    snails turn man green, 296

    tapeworm, 127

    worm grass, 63

Paris Gun, 324

parking paid with conkers, 29

parking space purchase, 344

INDEX

parrot

    calms bipolar owner, 96

    rides motorcycle, 96

    warns of sleep apnea, 90

Parton, Dolly, 159

passport is self-portrait, 246

Patterson, Chuck (U.S.), 40

Pauley, Jonason (U.S.), 159

Payne, Lennie (U.K.), 253

PayPal, -$92 quadrillion balance, 24

peanut shell sculpture, 264

Pearcy, Tom (U.K.), 179

peat soil acidity, 349

pen pals meet after 74 years, 26

pencil lodged in head, 152

Pendes, Luka (Australia), 58

Perito, Charlie (U.S.), 77

Perrotta, Jesse (U.S.), 159

Petkov, Jane (Macedonia), 216

petroleum paintings, 235

phantom train ride travelogues, 162–163

Philips, Paul (U.K.), 280

Phillips, Tori (Canada), 164

Phoenix, Jay (Australia), 202

Phoenix Sky Harbor Int'l Airport floor tile with Jesus, 40

phone booth art, 240

photography

    colored smoke, 264–265

    exploding light bulbs, 267

    under ice, 16

    left on the Moon, 27

    portraits mistaken for, 264

    sneeze capture, 234–235

    soapy water paintings, 266

Phuge, Datta (India), 165

piano keys painted on bridge, 318

Picken, Emma and Stacey (U.K.), 135

pigs

    drunk pig rampage, 69

    hypnotist, 70

K'Nex wheelchair, 77

looks like Yoda, 81

sacrifice in, 349

surfing, 82

Pilkey, Dav (U.S.), 189

pirate island on English estate, 161

Pitcher, Charlie (U.K.), 318

Pitman, Josh (U.S.), 338

planets mistaken for spy drones, 50

planthopper insect, 103

ploughshare tortoises endangered, 99

Plutano, Wild Man of Borneo, 138

police

    German dogs in shoes, 83

    impersonator steals donuts, 42

    men with same name arrested, 51

Porteous, Georgia (Scotland), 19

Portilla-Kawamura, Key (U.K.), 171

portraits

    cardboard layers, 249

    carved into eggshells, 267

    celebrities from food, 247

    from chewed gum, 231

    Duchess of Cambridge in jelly beans, 231

    FDR died before finish, 251

    Gandhi on eggshell, 251

    Mao Tse-tung from toy soldiers, 248–249

    mistaken for photographs, 264

    in pizza, 280

    plowed in field, 239

    self-portrait beard hair as brush, 247

    self-portrait passport, 246

    words pertaining to subject's life, 232

Post, Mark (Netherlands), 283

postal service on bicycle, 342

Powell, Rose (U.K.), 224

pranks, room at 90 degrees, 60

Pratl, Reinhold (Germany), 94

Preller, Jay and Hazel (U.K.), 226

presidents, Lincoln's pocket watch, 53

Pretorius, Isak (Seychelles), 73

Prickett, Elaine (U.K.), 106

Prideaux, Rob (U.S.), 237

prom suit from Mountain Dew labels, 158

proposals. *See also* weddings

    dress from roses, 181

    freeway, 43

prosthetics

    cow with prosthetic legs, 100

    eye pops out in court, 145

    hand controlled by phone app, 125

    loggerhead turtle with prosthetic fins, 71

Psy "Gentleman" video, 180

Pulsifer, Stacey (U.S.), 108

pumice island, 329

pumpkin carvers, 286–291

pumpkin worshipped, 274

Puskas, Istvan (Hungary), 253

Py, Boyet (Philippines), 45

python breaks into store, 91

Qavtaradze, Maxime (Georgia), 329

Queen Victoria, upside down printing on stamp, 56

raccoons

    hidden relatives in Colombia and Ecuador, 85

    invaded Germany, 83

racehorse painter, 85

radioactive rum, 274

raft spider, 71

Rahman, Tipu (U.K.), 298

rainbow eucalyptus trees, 344

rainbow waterfall, 325

Ramirez, Juan (Mexico), 30

Ramsey, Tyler (U.S.), 239

rap album by 120-year-old, 161

Rapid Realty employee tattoos, 158

Rapo, Roberta and Rayna (Australia), 69

INDEX

rat hunters in Manhattan, 93

rats

cell phone reward for catching, 349

dead rat festival, 308

Ready, Set, Mail contest, 13

Recht, Sruli (Iceland), 135

Redmayne, Eddie (U.K.), 159

Rees, Ben (U.K.), 69

Reichelt, Franz (France), 25

Reilly, Jerry (U.S.), 251

reindeer change eye color, 104

Reitz, Jeff (U.S.), 222

reptiles

20-year-old crocodile killed 200 people, 100

alligator in O'Hare Int'l Airport, 82

alligator tries to eat turtle, 76

Asian tortoise with two heads, 93

California Alligator Farm, 20–23

crocodile as guard, 109

crocodile attacks elephant, 92

crocodile traps kayaker, 90

crocodiles escape during heavy rain, 106

lizard squirts blood from eyes, 101

ploughshare tortoises, 99

tortoises get romantic music, 106

turtle pees from mouth, 103

turtle tears for butterflies, 85

two-headed salamander, 80

two-headed turtle, 108

undercover researcher, 52

restaurants

largest drive-in, 298

largest McDonald's, 298

people dressed as cows, 217

robot restaurant, 296

Reyes, Guillermo (Mexico), 70

Reymond, Guillaume (France), 246

Reynolds, Chris (U.S.), 24

Reynolds, Torz (U.K.), 32

Rice, Jonathan (U.S.), 50

Richard III skeletal remains, 24

Richards, Keith (U.K.), 169

Richardson, Ken Larry (U.S.), 237

Richman, Jesse (U.S.), 205

Richter, Jacob and Bonnie (U.S.), 96

Rigol, Fabio Beraldo (Brazil), 37

ring bearer robot, 24

Ripley, Robert

Believe It or Not! cartoon, 7

cannibal, 9

Hawaiian outrigger canoes, 7

headhunters, 9

letters received, 9

mustache measurements, 10

Nehi News, 8

Odditoriums, 7

radio program, 8

reporting career, 7

standards of collection, 10

tattoo on Christopher Sudduth, 13

robbery

arrest of slow robber, 56

bees chase carjackers, 29

cell phone left behind, 39

ear print identification, 45

man in cow costume steals milk, 29

metal bridge, 44

Nutella, 58

sheep stolen from village of Wool, 61

Roberts, Anthony (U.S.), 72

Robinson, Margaret Ann (U.S.), 184–187

robots

bomb-disposal ring bearer, 24

jellyfish marine life study, 348

laundry folding, 63

pouring beer, 292

restaurant dancers, 296

Transformer, human, 183

Rocky Mountain Oyster Stout beer, 294

rollerskate to church, 344

Roman artifacts discovered by moles, 104

Romano, Philip (U.S.), 139

Romulan Court street in Sacramento, 157

Roosevelt, Franklin D. (U.S.), 35, 251

Root, Susan (U.K.), 145

Rosa, Elisangela Borborema (Brazil), 145

Rosales, Axel (Argentina), 138

Rose, Jodi (Australia), 61

Rosen, Susan (U.S.), 167

Rotch, Armen (Armenia), 249

Rowe, Leanne (Australia), 132

Roy, Gladys (U.S.), 220

Rubik's Cube, 226

Ruffinelli, Mikel (U.S.), 134–135

running

on all fours, 223

in costume, 226

Russell, Ariana Page (U.S.), 242–245

Ryders Alley Trencher-Fed Society, 93

Sackett, John W. (U.S.), 44

Sadler, Jason (U.S.), 167

Säker, Fredrik (Sweden), 246

Salazar, Denise (U.S.), 128

Salazar, Isaac G. (U.S.), 259

Saldia, Rudi (U.S.), 57

sand skiing, 217

Sandy Island, 348

Sansweet, Steve (U.S.), 183

Santos, Eliel (Puerto Rico), 63

Sardari, Masha (U.S.), 182

Savanovic, Sava, 310

Scallan, Lindsay (U.S.), 63

Scheepens, Kees (Netherlands), 70

Scheeren, Ole (Germany), 157

Schilling, Curt (U.S.), 207

Schmitt family (U.S.), 42

schools

1,000 classrooms, 308

INDEX

on same site for 2,100 years, 323

Schroeder, Guenter (Germany), 53

Schwandt, Jay and Teri (U.S.), 152

Schweder, Alex (U.S.), 308

Schwend, Travis (U.S.), 189

screwdriver wedged in nose, 145

scuba diving, 213

sculpture
  animals from wood chips, 246
  carved books, 259
  of chicken from eggshells, 293
  from classic comic books, 160
  crumpled shirt from screw heads, 258
  Dalek, 253
  dryer lint, 233
  egg carton Spitfire fighter, 257
  extracted DNA, 236
  from flip-flops, 233
  fruit tree, 298
  helium-filled island, 267
  invisible bodies, 233
  landmarks from bread, 253
  Marx statues, 253
  metal insects, 250
  model crane from matchsticks, 250
  molded onto humans, 256–257
  peanut shells, 264
  pickled pumpkins, 286–291
  taxidermy, 236
  Titanic model from ice
    cream sticks, 259
  toast and Marmite Duchess
    of Cambridge, 267
  wood that looks like other
    material, 259

Sdiri, Salim (France), 152

sea creatures
  blanket octopus, 104
  bobbit worm eats fish, 81
  dolphin gives family dinner, 104
  dolphins caring for pod member, 81
  electric eel shock, 73
  elephant seal stops traffic, 71
  fire-breathing shrimp, 72
  jellyfish, lion's mane, 99
  jellyfish in nuclear plant, 90
  loggerhead turtle with
    prosthetic fins, 71
  six-clawed lobster, 104
  split-color lobster, 72
  sponges look like Cookie Monster, 84
  turtle shell repaired, 102

sea eagle steals camera, 91

sea lettuce, 312

Seabreacher Y speedboat, 319

seaweed rain, 348

Selfridges department store gold belt, 167

sepak bola api, 205

severed head wedding cake, 282

sewer holds fatberg, 323

Shackleton, Ernest (U.K.), 334–335

Shaeri, Khaled Mohsen (Saudi Arabia), 126

Shah, Manjit Kumar (India), 251

Shambala Preserve, 88

sharks
  hurricane warning, 95
  skeleton, 69

Shaw, Brian (U.S.), 60

Sheath, Peter (U.K.), 196

sheep invade ski shop, 103

Shehzad, Areesha (U.K.), 119

Sheldon, Toby (U.S.), 167

Shinn, Steve (U.S.), 77

shipping container entrapment, 39

shoes with GPS, 165

shopping cart with engine, 342

shrews form caravan, 90

Shron, Jason (Canada), 318

Sideserf, Natalie and David (U.S.), 282

sidewall surfing, 41

Sievwright, Zoe (Scotland), 132

Siffredi, Marco (France), 303

Sigfrids, Tif (U.S.), 27

Sikkel, Paul (U.S.), 103

Simpson, Charlie (U.K.), 167

Sims, Audrey (Australia), 26

Singer's Midgets, 187

Singh, Inderjeet (India), 206

Sinka, Zsolt (Hungary), 196

sinkholes, 340

Sinniger, Karin (Angola), 213

Sirchio, Keith (U.S.), 171

sitting without seat, 37

skateboarding
  goat, 68
  on highway, 217
  mouse, 32–33
  musical instruments from
    skateboards, 191

skeletons
  beetles remove whale flesh, 110–111
  grasshopper exoskeleton, 70
  jeweled, 350–353
  Richard III, 24
  sharks, 69

skiing
  on sand, 217
  ski park in derelict buildings, 213
  surf skiing, 40

skin
  Geisha Facial with bird poop, 137
  ring made from, 135
  sheds each day, 135
  slapping treatment, 138
  snail facials, 135

skydiving
  diver knocked out, 36
  flower shape formation, 37
  parachute fails twice, 147
  wingsuits, 53

skywalkers, 226–227

sleep driving, 32

INDEX

sleepwalking
- 6-mi journey, 119
- eating during, 119

sloth grip strength, 91

Sly, Nora (U.K.), 251

Smajic, Jamiro (Netherlands), 60

smell, restored after 40 years, 152

Smith, Anthony (U.S.), 189

Smith, Chris (U.S.), 309

Smith, Dallin (U.S.), 45

Smith, David (U.K.), 226

Smith, Haylee and Hannah (U.S.), 152

Smith, Jon (U.S.), 267

Smith, Joseph (U.S.), 120–121

Smith-Schafer, Barbara (U.K.), 90

snail facial, 135

snakes
- child keeps eggs, 73
- crocodile-swallowing, 103
- dead snake bites man, 72
- European grass snakes mating ball, 66–67
- hibernating baby adders, 95
- king cobras in car, 104
- pickled in wine, 279
- python breaks into store, 91
- python organs after eating, 102
- python swallowing ringtail possum, 51
- snake infestation Louisiana State Capital, 84
- Snake Village in China, 284

snapdragon seed pods, 338

sneeze photographs, 234–235

Snoopybabe, 94

snoring cures, 312

snow art, 330–331

snow goggles from caribou bones, 329

snowboarding
- back garden course, 217
- Everest, 303

soap from body fat, 236

soccer
- barefoot with fireball, 205
- junior league has 36 red cards, 202
- team masseur disqualifies team, 202

Sockertopp, Jossie (U.S.), 173

Socotra island, 336

Sola, Joe (U.S.), 27

solar-powered ovens, 283

soldiers frozen in Alps, 318

Sorensen, Lara (Canada), 68

soup from raw duck's blood, 293

southern gastric-brooding frog, 81

space, photograph left on the Moon, 27

spear gun shooting, 145

spiders
- bird-dung spider, 94
- Darwin's bark spider, 71
- makes fake spiders, 84
- raft spider, 71
- raining spiders, 107
- red-legged golden orb spider web, 73
- tarantulas as a snack, 285
- trapdoor spider, 106
- violin strings from spiderweb silk, 167
- young eat the mother, 81

spiderwort plant growing in bottle, 314

spine carved from newspapers, 247

sports
- 84-year-old NASCAR driver, 202
- 148-year-old baseball card, 202
- 266 marathons completed, 217
- athletes' autographs tattoos, 18
- barefoot soccer with fireball, 205
- baseball bat impales chest, 152
- batting for 24 hours straight, 225
- bicycle fire jumpers, 202
- black turf, 27
- blind pole vaulter, 212
- blind water skier, 196
- bloody sock sold, 207
- Cleveland Browns pallbearers, 30
- climber's chair, 45
- coma patient shoots baskets, 137
- diving, 27
- extreme mountain unicycling, 212
- fan catches two home-run balls, 217
- footgolf, 202
- guitar playing while playing basketball, 174
- Iditarod dog collapse, 39
- jockeys make weight with potatoes, 223
- kiteboarding, 205
- locker room toilet purchase, 217
- man killed by baseball to the head, 202
- marathon incorrect course, 225
- marathon runner around the world, 50
- martial arts displays, 205
- oldest pitcher, 217
- race car tire changes, 223
- scoreless baseball games, 207
- scuba diving, 213
- skateboarding mouse, 32–33
- skydiving, 36, 37
- soccer team masseur disqualifies team, 202
- sumo marathon, 34
- surf skiing, 40
- surfing pig, 82
- tejo, 212
- touchdown pass to self, 204
- wakeboarding in cranberry bog, 212
- wetsuit with wings, 33
- wingsuit skydiving, 53
- zip line wedding, 50

squid as liquor bottle, 292

squirrels
- damage lawn bowling club, 101
- escape zoo, 71
- knotted together, 24

INDEX

stainless steel ice cubes, 277

Stairway to Nothingness, 318

Standley, Eric (U.S.), 266

Star Trek

    Klingon Court and Romulan Court, 157

    Klingon wedding, 173

    living room as Federation Room, 172

Star Wars

    Darth Valley Challenge, 50

    Lars Homestead restoration, 56

    Navajo translation, 157

    Obi-Wan museum, 183

    walking in stormtrooper costume, 226

Starr, Robert H. (U.S.), 315

Steel, Jody (U.S.), 252–253

Stobaugh, Fred (U.S.), 158

stock market

    trading speed, 165

    typo cost millions, 175

Stoetter, Johannes (Italy), 268

Stoltenberg, Jens (Norway), 17

stowaways

    in cargo container, 52

    cat in luggage, 57

    in dashboard, 45

    inside car seat, 33

    in landing gear, 42

    in luggage compartment, 38

    in wheel arch of bus, 43

street artists

    Azooz, 262–263

    Deyaa, 262–263

    DS, 266

    Maryam, 262–263

    Maz, 262–263

    Nebay, 262

street sweeper made from brooms, 314

strength

    Greenstein, Joseph "The Mighty Atom," 208–211

    man cracks coconuts open, 196

man pulls items with teeth, 196

    Wild Men of Borneo, 138

    World's Strongest Man competition, 60

striped mountains, 324

stroke drug from vampire bat venom, 134

Stucki, Heinrich (Switzerland), 57

Styrofoam ship, 251

subway, retrieval of items, 63

Sudduth, Christopher (U.S.), 13

suitcase jail escape, 30

sumo marathon, 34

sun

    heat emission, 328

    Norwegian town, 339

    reflection melts metal, 312

Sunset Hills Cemetery and Funeral home, 42

superheroes, name changes, 19

superstitions, FDR traveling, 35

surf skiing, 40

surgery, items left, 119

Swain, Keshab (India), 196

Sweat Machine, 42

swimming

    around Isle of Wight, 205

    from Cuba to Florida, 212

    hauling bricks, 224

    while in bag, 216

Symonds, Laurence (U.K.), 267

tablecloth as truce flag, 322

talk show broadcast 62 hours, 161

Tambo, Tambo (Australia), 32

Tamu Massif volcano, 338

Tan, James Anthony (Malaysia), 309

TARDIS cake, 179

taste, restored after 40 years, 152

tattoos. *See also* body modification

    autographs, 18

    comic strip, 43

    doodles on woman's leg, 252–253

    entire body blue, 135

    eyeballs, 139

    Ford F-150 truck, 124

    hair loss replacement, 137

    leopard spots, 142–144

    most tattooed mayor, 127

    mother's eye on arm (Justin Bieber), 173

    Rapid Realty employees, 158

    of Robert Ripley, 13

    roulette gets Ryan Gosling tattoo, 165

    temporary advertising on bald head, 125

    tiger stripes over body, 54–55

    woman slices off, 32

taxidermy art, 259

Taylor, Russi (U.S.), 165

tea bag art, 249

teeth

    dolphin teeth as currency, 348

    dyed black, 332–333

    grown from urine stem cells, 145

    John Lennon's for DNA, 134

    man pulls heavy items, 196

    pulling cars with, 217

    vampire-like, 140

tejo, 212

Telli, Tarhan (Turkey), 342

Temperato, Mark (U.S.), 164

termites eat cash, 29

Tetris-like installations, 231

Texas SkyScreamer swing ride, 319

Thapa, Mukesh (India), 247

The Simpsons TV Show, 177

The Terror of Tiny Town movie, 187

theater

    ballet in car factory, 167

    floating, 157

    phantom train ride travelogues, 162–163

therapy for facing fears, 196

Thomas, Barbie (U.S.), 214–215

Thomas, Jake (Australia), 72

Thomas, Jane (Scotland), 266

thread portraits on skin, 60

three-dimensional paper dolls, 26

Thurmond, Tim (U.S.), 236

tie-dye cheesecake, 29

tiger stripes tattoo, 54–55

tiger with hairball, 11, 84

tigers

    attack simulation, 93

    hairball, 11, 84

tightlacing for waists, 148–151

tightrope walking, 196, 198–201

tinnitus, music type, 145

tire inflating with nose, 31

Titanic, mail on board, 61

Titanic model from ice cream sticks, 259

toad skins as fashion accessories, 170

Todd, Lewis (U.K.), 152

toenails

    extra long, 114–117

    man saves clippings, 124

toilet paper tube art, 241

toilet paper-finding app, 174

toilet with floor-to-ceiling windows, 329

Tolkien, J.R.R., 315

tongue with double taste buds, 145

Toppo, Nirmala (India), 82

tortoise, two-headed, 93

Toy Story live-action remake, 159

traffic jams, 342

trains

    phantom ride travelogues, 162–163

    rescue, 17

trampoline road, 308

Transformer, human, 183

Transformers art installation, 246

travel to 201 nations, 326–327

Tre, Ben (Vietnam), 267

treasure, sunken ships, 42

tree hole paintings, 232

trees

    with building around, 328

    replaced during WWI, 63

    transplant, 347

Treviño, Enrique (U.S.), 216

Troxel, Fred (U.S.), 102

Trugter, Kennedy (U.S.), 182

Tubal, Cain (Colombia), 118

Tufts, Bobby (U.S.), 30

tumbleweeds obscure house, 338

Turner Syndrome, 135

TV shows

    to choose most beautiful sheep, 158

    fireplace TV show, 157

    knitting show, 174

TV with 201-in screen, 174

twins

    24 sets in one grade, 32

    harpists, 190

Twitter wedding ceremony, 183

Tyler, Laura (U.S.), 192–193

Typaldos, Melanie (U.S.), 105

Uitto, Jeffro (U.S.), 257

umbilical cord art, 249

underwater landscape painting, 267

underwater photography, 16

Unger, Ivan (U.S.), 220

Uniface mask, 40

Upadhyaya, Dinesh Shivnath (India), 204

Uromastyx lizard, 281

U.S. most dangerous city, 332

Valentine, Veronica (U.S.), 152

vampires, 310

van Essen, Tamsin (U.K.), 257

van Gurp, Henk (Netherlands), 283

Vanatta, Nora (U.S.), 94

VanSant, Cal (U.S.), 342

vehicles

    1930 Packard still operational, 314

    Allied ambulance drivers, 315

    Aston Martin DBR1 replica, 224

    balanced on parking lot edge, 341

    Beetle shaped into sphere, 342–343

    car on balcony, 341

    Chevrolet Orlando, 315

    covered in coins, 342

    jet-powered coffin, 18

    leather covered, 342

    parking lot demolished around, 340

    sidewall surfing, 41

    in sinkhole, 340

    street sweeper, 314

    traffic jams, 342

    turkey roasted in exhaust, 342

    velvet-covered Porsche, 347

    wrought-iron, 310–311

venomous fish, 68

Verraes, Chris (U.K.), 275

Vickered, Brandon (Canada), 236

Vickers, Andrew (U.K.), 160

video games

    in cinema for birthday party, 189

    Grid 2: Mono Edition, 167

    memorabilia, 175

    seven-year-old creator, 189

    Tetris trains lazy eyes, 170

Vigmond, Jim (Canada), 217

Villafane, Ray (U.S.), 11, 286–291

vodka

    from cow's milk, 274

    from fermented hornets, 277

Voet, Raymond (U.S.), 189

volcano in Pacific Ocean, 338

Volpicelli, Michael (U.S.), 232

von Anhalt, Princess Tarinan (U.S.), 250

Von Muller, Omar (U.S.), 69

INDEX

von Singer, Leopold (Austria), 187

Wade, Ron (U.S.), 314
Waino, Wild Man of Borneo, 138
waist training, 148–151
Waite, Vanessa (U.K.), 82
wakeboarding in cranberry bog, 212
Waldner, Christian (Austria), 196
walnut sphinx caterpillars, 77
Walter, George (U.S.)
Wardley, Anna (U.K.), 205
Warner, Carl (U.K.), 11
Warrington, Amanda (U.K.), 223
Warther, David (U.S.), 253
wasp nest measuring 22 ft, 107
Watanabe, Masao (Japan), 161
watch returned 53 years later, 24
water
    converted from sweat, 42
    ocean water with caffeine, 308
    oldest free-flowing, 314
    spray freezes area, 316–317
    turns to ice when thrown, 323
water skiing blind, 196
waterfall rainbow, 325
Watkins, Lucy (U.K.), 104
Watson, Barry (U.K.), 347
Watson, Emma (U.K.), 183
Watson, Stephanie (Australia), 159
weather station in Siberia, 53
Webb, Isaiah and Angela (U.S.), 153
website as last name, 167
weddings. See also proposals
    blind couple's dogs introduced, 42
    bomb-disposal robot as
        ring bearer, 24
    cheap, 19
    date same as zip code, 37
    Doctor Who themed, 178
    dress from bread expiration tags, 159
    dress from divorce papers, 161

dress from soccer jerseys, 175
dresses from roadkill, 175
group ceremony on Fiji
    Airways plane, 56
Klingon, 173
marriage to bridge, 61
McDonald's reception, 281
owl as ring bearer, 83
severed head wedding cake, 282
trash the dress, 181
via Twitter, 183
zip line, 50
weight loss after hypnosis, 128
Weingarth, Meghan (U.S.), 72
West, Malcom (U.K.), 231
West Salem High School, 27
wheelchairs
    BASE jumper, 197
    for pig, 77
Whippet, Davey (Canada), 68
White, Vanna (U.S.), 159
Wigan, Willard (U.K.), 253
Wilcox, Dominic (U.K.), 165
Wild Men of Borneo, 138
Williams, Ayanna (U.S.), 114–117
Williams, Ralph Vaughan, 315
Williamson, Kieron (U.K.), 259
Willmott, Shane (Australia), 32–33
Wilson, Al (U.S.), 219, 221
Wilson, Scott (U.S.), 251
wine fight, 309
wing walking, 224
wingsuit skydiving, 53
Wirth, Josef Alexander (Germany), 312
wolf pack leader is a man, 78–79
woman recognizes one voice, 136
Wong, Laura (U.S.), 24
wooden building, 312
Woodhead, Sam (U.K.), 145
woodlice drink from either end, 101
Woodlief, Jonathan and Caitlin (U.S.), 136

World War I
    1914 Christmas celebration, 344
    Andorra, 338
    helmets, 338
    pigeons with cameras, 344
    truce flag, 322
worm grass parasite, 63
worms, flatworm head regrowth, 72
wrought-iron car, 310–311
Wu, Jiang (China), 39
Wyburn, Nathan (U.K.), 267
Wylie, Craig (Zimbabwe), 264
Wynkoop Brewing Company, 294

Xiaolian (China), 134
Xiugi, Sheng (China), 318

Yang, Fan (Canada), 216
Yonetani, Ken and Julia (Australia), 237
Yongbing, Nie (China), 31
Yorkshire Pudding Boat Race, 202
Yoshida, Masahito (Japan), 207
Youngkin, Ben (U.S.), 50
Youzhen, Yu (China), 38
Yue, Wang (China), 232
Yuhong, Yan (China), 152
Yuravliov, Yuri (Ukraine), 93
Yurick, Patrick (U.S.), 43

Zagami, Joseph and Joanne (U.S.), 37
Zarafa the giraffe, 98–99
Zhangye Danxia Landform
    Geological Park, 324
Zhizhenko, Ludmila (Belaruse), 235
Ziegler, Vivi (Austria), 136
Zigler, Charles (U.S.), 27
zip line wedding, 50
zombie cake, 278–279
Zuk, Michael (Canada), 134
ZZ Top line-up, 164

ACKNOWLEDGMENTS

COVER Laurentiu Garofeanu/Barcroft USA; **11** (tl) Ripley's Museum London, (tr) Ocean Park Hong Kong, (cr, br) Photo by James P. Judge; **12** Kelly Mill Elementary; **13** (tl) Christopher Z. Collier-Sudduth; **16–17** Yuri Ovchinnikov/Caters News; **18** Dennis Elliot; **19** Rui Vieira/PA Archive/Press Association Images; **20–23** (bkg) © Jeremy - Fotolia.com; **24** Animal Clinic of Regina; **26** Seattle Public Library; **27** NASA; **28** www.toursgallery.com; **29** Supplied by WENN.com; **30–31** Reuters/Stringer; **32** Tim Marsden/Newspix/Rex Features; **33** (tl, tr) Tim Marsden/ Newspix/Rex Features, (br) CBP/Rex Features; **34** Julian Makey/Rex; **36** (t) Newsflare/Caters News; **38** (b) Ross Parry Agency; **39** (t) WENN; **40** (b) Greg Huglin/Solent News/Rex Features; **41** Reuters/Mohamed Al Hwaity; **42** (t) James D. Morgan/Rex; **43** (cr) Patrick Yurick/Rex, (c) David Difuntorum Photography/Rex; **44** JoyLabz; **45** Caters News; **47** Maria Justamond; **50** Caters News; **51** REX/Austral Int.; **52** Brady Barr; **53** Caters News; **56** WENN; **57** Caters News; **58** Rex/James D. Morgan; **59** Keng Lye; **60** (bl) David Catá; **60–61** (t) Reuters/Aaron Harris; **62** (sp) © Viviane Moos/Corbis; **63** (tr) Gavin Maxwell/naturepl.com, (cl) Imagine China; **65** Cynthia Chambers; **66–67** Francois Savigny/naturepl.com; **68** Robert McLeod; **69** (br) Rex/ Timothy Clapin/Newspix; **70–71** (tl) Sell Your Photo; **71** (br) © Stephen Dalton/naturepl.com; **72** Elsie Mason of Ship to Shore Lobster Company, Owls Head Maine; **73** Isak Pretorius - theafricanphotographer.com; **74–75** Phil Lautner; **76** Patrick Castleberry/Caters News; **77** Rex/Steve Shinn; **78–79** Reuters/Lisi Niesner; **80** © Picture Alliance/Photoshot; **81** Sell Your Photo; **82–83** (t) Catalina Island Marine Institute; **84** Mauricio Handler/National Geographic Creative; **85** Jeff Cremer; **86–89** Michael Rougier/Time & Life Pictures/Getty Images; **90** Steven Downer/John Downer P/naturepl.com; **91** © Luiz Claudio Marigo/naturepl.com; **92** (sp) Ian Salisbury/Caters News; **93** Rex Features; **94** Nicky Bay; **95** Susheel Shrestha; **96** Myles S. Bratter; **97** (sp) Cynthia Chambers; **98** (c) Roger-Viollet/Topfoto; **98–99** (t) Anna Jurkovska - Shutterstock.com; **100** Getty Images; **101** © John Cancalosi/Alamy; **102** WENN; **103** Trond Larsen; **105** J.M. Storey, Carleton University; **106** Rex/Hans Christoph Kappel/Nature Picture Library; **107** EFE; **108–109** Gil Wizen; **110–111** www.skullsunlimited.com; **118** AFP/ Getty Images; **121** Library of Congress; **122** (tr) Getty Images, (bl) Library of Congress; **123** SSPL via Getty Images; **124** (l, br) Richard Gibson, (cr) © leisuretime70 - Fotolia.com; **125** (br) Windsor Star/Caters, (tr) QMI/Caters; **126–127** Reuters/Faisal Al Nasser; **129** VTC News; **134** Reuters/Stringer; **135** Sruli Recht; **136** Imagine China; **137** Amit Agrawal/Pavan Agrawal; **138** University of Syracuse; **139** (t) Jean Jabril Joesph, (bc) Keith Walters Photography, (br) Phillip Romano; **140** Rex/HAP/Quirky China News; **141** Laurentiu Garofeanu/Barcroft USA; **142** (sp) Laurentiu Garofeanu/Barcroft USA; **142–144** (bkg) © W.Scott; **143–144** Laurentiu Garofeanu/Barcroft USA; **146** Solent News; **147** Reuters/Marko Djurica; **148–149** John Robertson/Barcroft Media; **150** Mirrorpix; **151** (tl) Mary Evans Picture Library, (t) ©ullsteinbild/TopFoto; **153** Isaiah Webb; **154** Randy Hoff; **156–157** Laurentiu Garofeanu/ Barcroft USA; **158** Gabriel Chapman; **159** Double Vision Media; **160** Rex/Jonathan Pow; **161** Rex/Adam Duckworth/Geoffrey Robinson; **164** Kate Melton Photography; **165** Steven Lawton/ FilmMagic; **166** Courtesy of the Artist, Chrissy Conant © 2005; **168** (t) © Eye Ubiquitous/Photoshot, (cl) © Andrea Izzotti - Fotolia.com; **169** Rex/Quirky China News; **170** Francois Guillot/ AFP/Getty Images; **171** Studio Banana Things; **172** Steve Doman Nighteagle; **173** AFP/Getty Images; **174** Rex/Startraks Photo; **175** EatonNott/Barcroft Media; **176** Mikey Jones/Caters News; **177** Kayleigh O'Conner/Solent News/Rex; **178** (b) Tolga Akman/Rex; **178–179** (t) Bill Mudron/Caters News; **179** (cl) Caters News, (br) Getty Images; **180** Izzy Parnell and Ned, Eden Parnell and Ned, David Gaylord; **181** Rex/Imaginechina; **182** Randy Hoff; **183** Caters News; **184** (r) James G. Mundie; **185** (bl) Bob Blackmar; **186** (tr) Bob Blackmar, James G. Mundie; **187** (t) Library of Congress; **188–189** Noah Kalina; **190** Actual; **191** Juhana Nyrhinen and www.masauniverse.tumblr.com; **192–193** Nicole Wilder/Syfy/NBCU Photo Bank via Getty Images; **195** Mustang Wanted; **196** WENN.com; **197** Hotspot Media; **198** Courtesy of the Library of Congress; **199** (sp) © Pictorial Press Ltd/Alamy, (tr) Niagara Falls Public Library; **200** (bl) Niagara Falls Public Library; **201** (tr) Getty Images, (bc) Niagara Falls Public Library; **203** Rex/Naomi Jellicoe/Newspix; **204** Thomas Senf/Red Bull Content Pool; **205** Rex/ZUMA; **206** Simon de Trey White/Barcroft India; **207** Reuters/Darrin Zammit Lupi; **208** All Photos courtesy of Eastwind One Corp., Ed Spielman. Pres. All Materials in and to 'The Mighty Atom' - Copyright – Eastwind One Corp., Ed Spielman. Pres. *Content from the 'The Spirital Journey of Joseph L. Greenstein', 'The Mighty Atom', World's Strongest Man by Ed Spielman; **209** All Photos courtesy of Eastwind One Corp., Ed Spielman. Pres. All Materials in and to 'The Mighty Atom' - Copyright – Eastwind One Corp., Ed Spielman. Pres. *Content from the 'The Spirital Journey of Joseph L. Greenstein', 'The Mighty Atom', World's Strongest Man by Ed Spielman, (tl, r) Photos supplied by www.oldtimestrongman.com; **212** Ryan Taylor/Red Bull Content Pool; **213** Tim Sorenson/Red Bull Content Pool; **214–215** Barbara L. Thomas; **216** AFP/Getty Images; **218–219** © Underwood & Underwood/Underwood & Underwood/Corbis; **220** (l) Apic/Getty Images; **220–221** © Bettmann/Corbis; **221** (t, b) © Bettmann/Corbis; **222** Reuters/China Daily; **223** AFP/Getty Images; **224** Richard Pardon Photography; **225** AFP/Getty Images; **226–227** Mustang Wanted; **229** Johannes Stoetter; **230–231** Laura Benjamin; **232** Rex/HAP/Quirky China News; **233** Caters; **234–235** Ulf Lundin; **236** Charlie Layton; **237** Rex/Rob Prideaux; **238–239** Jelly Belly Candy Company; **240** (tr, br) Mariane Borgomani, (bl) AFP/Getty Images; **241** Anastassia Elias/Caters News; **242** Ariana Page Russell; **243** Ariana Page Russell; **246** Reuters/Ilya Naymushin; **247** Maskull Lasserre; **248–249** Edouard Martinet; **250** Edouard Martinet; **251** Caters/Museum of Bad Art; **252–253** Rex/Jody Steel; **254–255** Imagine China; **256** WENN.com; **258** Andrew Myers; **259** Isaac Salazar; **260** Rex/London News Pictures; **261** (tr, br) Rex/ISA HARSIN/SIPA, (bl) Rex/AGF s.r.l.; **262** (t) Rex/London News Pictures, (bl) Rex/ISA HARSIN/SIPA; **262–263** (bc) Rex/ISA HARSIN/SIPA; **263** (sp) Rex/ISA HARSIN/SIPA; **264–265** Irby Pace; **266** Supplied by WENN.com; **267** Chris Maynard; **268–269** Johannes Stoetter; **271** Ocean Park Hong Kong; **272–273** Julie Green/Toni Acock; **274–275** (t) Fantasy Fondant; **275** (br) Boy Eats Bug/Chris Verraes/Rex Features; **276** Reuters/Michael Dalder; **278–279** Elizabeth Marek/Artisan Cake Company; **280** The Frontier Chicago; **281** Reuters/Mohamed Al Hwaity; **282** Siderser Cake Studio; **283** Reuters/ Michael Kooren; **284** Rex/Sinopix Photo Agency Ltd; **285** George Nickels/Caters News; **286–291** Ocean Park Hong Kong; **292** © byjeng - Fotolia.com; **293** Rex/Kyle Bean; **294** Wynkoop Brewing Company; **295** Chocolate By Mueller; **296** Reuters/Yuriko Nakao; **297** Imagine China; **298** Reuters/Edgar Su; **299** Xinhua/Photoshot; **301** Boaz Rottem; **302–303** Andy Bardon/ National Geographic Creative; **304–305** © Palenque - Fotolia.com; **305** (br) Getty Images; **306–307** Utmost Adventure Treking; **307** (t) Zuma/Rex; **308** (t) Karli Luik/Caters News; **309** (t) Caters News, (b) Eduardo Blanco Mendizabal; **310–311** Vrbanus Workshop; **312** Reuters/Stringer; **313** Eric Lafforgue; **314** Reuters/Stringer; **315** Daniel Glover; **316–317** Reuters/John Gress; **318** Jason Shron; **319** Seabreacher; **320–321** Rex/Marc Henauer/Solent News; **321** (br) Mona and Chris Dienhart; **322** Getty Images; **323** François Gissy/Régis Rabineau; **324** ChinaFotoPress via Getty Images; **325** Justin Lee/Caters News; **326–327** Graham Hughes, Rocco Fasano, Grethe Børsum; **327** (tr) © mrtimmi - Fotolia.com, © i3alda - Fotolia.com, © AI - Fotolia.com; **328** Rex/HAP/Quirky China News; **329** Rex/Amos Chapple; **330–331** Simon Beck; **332–333** Boaz Rottem; **334** (tr) © Pictorial Press Ltd/Alamy, (b) © Royal Geographical Society/Alamy; **334–335** (bkg) © Sergey Kamshylin - Fotolia.com; **335** © Royal Geographical Society/Alamy, (br) © Pictorial Press Ltd/Alamy; **336** © Tony Waltham/Robert Harding World Imagery/Corbis; **337** Reuters/Stringer; **338** Bill Dixon; **339** Rex/Sipa Press; **340** (t) Lt. Matthew Hertzfeld/Toledo Fire & Rescue Department, (b) Reuters/Jon Woo; **340–341** (bkg) © Thomas Bethge/Shutterstock.com; **341** (t) © Imaginechina/Corbis, (b) Rex/East News; **343** See-ming Lee; **344** Rex/Warren Krupsaw/Solent News; **345** Mark Thiessen/ National Geographic Creative; **346** © Visions of America, LLC/Alamy; **347** Raccoon Vehicle Branding; **348** Reuters/Beawiharta; **349** Rex/KeystoneUSA-ZUMA; **351–353** Rex/Paul Koudounaris/Heavenly Bodies : Cult Treasures and Spectacular Saints/BNPS

Key: t = top, b = bottom, c = center, l = left, r = right, sp = single page, dp = double page, bkg = background

All other photos are from Ripley Entertainment Inc.

Every attempt has been made to acknowledge correctly and contact copyright holders and we apologize in advance for any unintentional errors or omissions, which will be corrected in future editions.